TRUST AND CONTRACTS

Other titles available from The Policy Press include:

Choosing staff: Involving people with learning difficulties in staff recruiting by Ruth Townsley and Margaret Macadam
ISBN 1 86134 042 7 £11.50 pbk

Theorising empowerment: Individual power and community care by Richard Servian
ISBN 1 86134 006 0 £11.95 pbk

Partnerships for progress: Good practice in the relationship between local government and voluntary organisations by Chris Bemrose and Joy MacKeith
ISBN 1 86134 009 5 £11.95 pbk

All the above titles are available from
Biblios Publishers' Distribution Services Ltd, Star Road,
Partridge Green, West Sussex RH13 8LD, UK
Telephone +44 (0)1403 710851, Fax +44 (0)1403 711143

TRUST AND CONTRACTS

Relationships in local government, health and public services

Edited by Andrew Coulson

The POLICY PRESS

First published in Great Britain in 1998 by

The Policy Press
University of Bristol
Rodney Lodge
Grange Road
Bristol BS8 4EA
Tel   +44 (0)117 973 8797
Fax   +44 (0) 117 973 7308
E-mail tpp@bristol.ac.uk
http://www.bristol.ac.uk/Publications/TPP

11824964

British Library Cataloguing in Publication Data

A catalogue record for this book is available from the British Library

ISBN 1 86134 086 9

Andrew Coulson is Senior Lecturer at the Institute of Local Government Studies, University of Birmingham.

Cover design by Qube Associates, Bristol. Original cover idea from Les Prince, Birmingham.

Printed in Great Britain by Hobbs the Printers, Southampton.

Contents

for Kieron Walsh

Preface

This is a book about trust – in local government, in the health service, in military leaders, between regulators and those they regulate, between citizens and the politicians they elect to govern them.

It was inspired by the work of Kieron Walsh, who died suddenly at the age of 46 in 1995, and who was both an academic expert on contracting and a trusted advisor to many local authorities and other agencies.

Its aim is to challenge every manager and every aspiring manager – as an incentive to examine their practice, and that of their organisations, to see how more trust, and a greater involvement of those who use their services, might lead to more efficiency.

It is also about how we make decisions, about citizen participation, and hence about the steps that might lead to greater trust in politicians and the political process of government.

Acknowledgements

This book develops some of the ideas of Kieron Walsh, who died unexpectedly at the height of his powers in 1995.

It was written largely without funding – a labour of love – although Chapters Two and Nine used time supported by the ESRC Research Grant R000236489, 'an Organisational Behaviour Approach to Client-Contractor Relations in British Local Authorities'. Simon Baddeley's video archive has been supported by the School of Public Policy at Birmingham University and the Department of Health Women's Unit.

Diego Gambetta gave permission for us to quote him in Chapter Two. We would like to acknowledge the influence of Oliver Williamson's explorations of transaction cost economics; also the social psychology of the book *Trust in organisations: Frontiers of theory and research* edited by R.M. Kramer and T.R. Tyler which reached us not long after we started work.

The Policy Press were encouraging from the time they first heard about the proposal, and were efficient throughout in bringing it forward into print. Beyond that I can only thank those many people, including the authors, who were convinced that there was something very significant here, and made sure that we kept going until the project was complete.

List of contributors

Simon Baddeley has taught at the Institute of Local Government Studies, the University of Birmingham, since 1973 and created an archive on video of interviews with leading politicians and chief officers in local government and the health service.

Marian Barnes is Director of Social Research in the Department of Social Policy and Social Work at the University of Birmingham. She is the author of the 1997 book *Care, communities and citizens*.

John Benington is Professor of Public Service Management and Director of the Local Government Centre at the Warwick Business School. He was previously a chief officer for Sheffield Council, head of a trade union funded resource centre in Coventry, and a leading figure in the British Government's Community Development Project in the 1970s.

Andrew Coulson has taught at the Institute of Local Government Studies since 1984. He worked previously for Sheffield Council and for the Government of Tanzania. He edited the book *Local government in Eastern Europe*.

Howard Davis is Senior Research Fellow and Project Coordinator for the Best Value Pilots Evaluation Study at the Local Government Centre, Warwick Business School. He worked previously for the Institute of Local Government Studies at the University of Birmingham and the Greater London Council. He has wide experience of local government contracting, in both Britain and Eastern Europe.

Nicholas Deakin is Professor of Social Policy and Administration at the University of Birmingham. Previously he worked for the Greater London Council and the Home Office. He has published widely on urban policy issues and on contracting. He is an authority on the role of the voluntary sector in the welfare state.

Lucy Gaster, of the Institute of Local Government Studies, has written extensively on quality, decentralisation and community involvement. She is the author of *Quality in public services: Managers' choices.*

Janet Newman is a specialist on patterns of change in public service management. She teaches at the Institute of Local Government Studies and coordinates the Public Services MBA. Her most recent book (written with John Clarke) is *The managerial state: Power, politics and ideology in the remaking of social welfare* (Sage, 1997).

Les Prince has a PhD in social psychology from Aston University and has taught at the Institute of Local Government Studies since 1990. His special interest is in leadership and small group dynamics, not least in the military.

David Prior works in the Policy Division of Birmingham City Council. He is an Honorary Lecturer at the Institute of Local Government Studies.

Ray Puffitt, a former local government officer, has taught at the Institute of Local Government Studies since 1970, specialising in management, planning systems, contracting and regulation.

Steward Ranson is Professor of Education in the School of Education at the University of Birmingham, and has written extensively on education, citizenship, and public sector management.

John Stewart is Professor of Local Government Studies at Birmingham University, and author of a series of texts on local government management.

Bruce Walker is Senior Lecturer at the Institute of Local Government Studies and undertakes research and consultancy on aspects of contracting in local government and on housing finance both in the UK and in Eastern Europe.

Andrew Wall is Visiting Senior Fellow at the Health Services Management Centre, and former Chief Executive of Bath Health District.

Peter Watt has taught at the Institute of Local Government Studies since 1978, and is author of a recent textbook, *Local Government: Principles and practice.* He specialises in local government finance and economics.

List of tables and figures

Tables

Figures

Part One

Concepts and ideas

ONE

Trust: the foundation of public sector management

Andrew Coulson

The public services depend fundamentally on successful relationships
– between individuals within organisations, between individual
consumers (or customers or citizens) and organisations, and between
more than one organisation. These include relationships in hierarchies
– between boss and worker, or senior and junior management.
Relationships at the top of organisations, between politicians or board
members on the one hand and senior managers or administrators on
the other, have special characteristics. Different situations arise in
relationships between the public and organisations, for example,
between patient and doctor, or a carer and a social services department.
Last but not least the public sector depends on relationships between
politicians and the people, whereby the politicians explain what the
public services are doing, justify the taxation to pay for them, and
defend them from criticisms in the press and in parliament. A successful
democracy is one where the people trust the politicians, and the
politicians speak for and unite the people.

The public sector is divided into many separate organisations. Many
activities, for example work with children, or to protect and enhance the
environment in which we live, depend on successful joint working
between more than one of these organisations, departments or agencies.
Often one part of the public sector contracts to provide services to another.
Thus 'direct labour organisations' compete with private companies to
win contracts to supply services. Whosoever wins, then there are
relationships between the 'client departments' which commission and
monitor the contracts, and (internal or external) 'contractors' which get
paid for carrying them out.

Another set of relationships arises when regulators, monitoring agents, auditors or inspectors are asked to ensure that activity is taking place as contracted and in accord with the law. The regulators are part of the public sector. Those who are regulated may be in the public or the private sectors, but as more activity is privatised much depends on public sector regulation of private sector activity. Inspectors, like the police and other 'street level bureaucrats', have some discretion as to whether to prosecute or to try and get changes by agreement. They often lack the information or evidence they need. They can often achieve more through constructive relationships than through the courts.

Achieving constructive relationships, sufficiently robust to manage the processes of institutional change, is the key to effective leadership. We explore these relationships through the concepts of 'trust' and 'contract', both of which are defined in more detail in the following two chapters. In broad terms, to trust means that you are prepared to make yourself vulnerable, to run a risk that the other partner will exploit you, and to build up credit by doing more than the minimum necessary in the hope that, if you have problems yourself, your partner will help you in return. If trust develops, then both parties feel justified and rewarded. This is true of trust between individuals and between organisations.

Many relationships break up. Trust is offered – but then one party or the other takes advantage of it. Expectations are not realised. Loyalty, or relevant information, is transferred to a third party. If trust is broken, the immediate response is anger and aggression (Hirschman's 'voice'). If the relationship is not quickly healed, then suspicion will cloud it into the future. One or other party may walk away (Hirschman's 'exit').

The costs of a broken relationship are usually high. A contractor may have to be replaced or have to repeat work already done. If staff do not trust their superiors, they will not work productively. If politicians fall out with senior executives then stalemate is the most likely outcome. The costs of recovering broken relationships or replacing them far exceed the normal costs of supervising a contract.

One party may seek redress. Here we enter the world of contract, for underlying almost every relationship is a network of rights and obligations. This is to take a broad view of contract. Contracts are not just between organisations, or with individuals who purchase goods and services from an organisation. They are also between an organisation and its employees, and between employees within an organisation. Thus a low level manager is contractually responsible to a more senior manager – and if the terms of that contract are broken the low level manager will suffer, perhaps only slightly (promotion may be delayed, or someone else may be given the most interesting tasks), but ultimately by the loss of employment. The threat of redundancy provides a powerful incentive to be loyal.

However, contracts are seldom easy to enforce. It takes time, and expensive lawyers, to force organisations or individuals to do what they do not wish to do – and someone forced to do something is unlikely to do it with conviction.

The costs of creating a contract, supervising it and, if need be, enforcing it are called 'transaction costs'. They are discussed at various points in this book. Where there is more rather than less trust, and it is not taken advantage of, transaction costs are minimised and the culture of trusting is reinforced. In that sense an organisation or society where trust is the norm is efficient. It is also likely to be a happy place to work. This is so at the individual level – you can walk around safely at night, buy a used car from a second-hand car dealer without first checking that the milometer has not been wound back, consult a doctor or lawyer and know that you will get good advice. You would not constantly get angry because work is not properly done, or threaten to go to law. Quality is taken for granted. No wonder trust is a part of every utopian vision.

The same arguments apply at a corporate level. Organisations can deal with each other on the basis of trust – minimising the costs of supervising and checking on each other, and not needing the expensive costs of lawyers and accountants.

These arguments are attractive to theorists such as Fukuyama who admire the trust they find in Japanese and Far Eastern societies, and which they feel is under threat in America and Britain. They provide an ideology for communitarian philosophers such as Etzioni who want to reconstruct societies on the basis of communities where people trust each other.

We must, however, be careful before we advocate utopias based on trust. A willingness to take advantage when the possibility presents itself is deeply embedded in our society. The social engineering required if we are to modify the culture and mores of western capitalism is breathtaking in its ambition. But at least we should be discussing how trust can be built. For if we can help both individuals and organisations to move in that direction, while remaining hard-headed over abuses of trust that inevitably will occur, then we will be moving in the direction of a society which is both more efficient and more rewarding for its citizens.

That is the ambition of this book. The foundation chapter which follows this shows how conceptions of trust are used by psychologists, sociologists and economists, defines terms such as transaction costs, and shows how game theory can assist in throwing light on some of the paradoxes of contract and trust. Janet Newman then writes about the difficulties and dangers of using an undifferentiated concept of trust across economics, politics and organisational studies. It is a slippery construction, "a highly promiscuous concept ... appropriated by both left and right". It easily reduces to meaningless claims – as when politicians who have lost the trust of the public claim that they should be trusted. The reality is that relationships are complicated, and embedded in the histories and cultures of different groups and organisations. It is unhelpful, if not downright misleading, to advocate trust without also considering the realities of power.

The next part of the book is about trust between individuals within an organisation. Simon Baddeley has studied successful relationships between political leaders and their chief executives at the top of British local authorities. He concludes that the two can only work effectively together when each concedes a specialisation to the other – the politician presents policy and gains the support needed to implement it, on the basis of options and opinions about what is possible provided by the professional. But then each party must also play part of the other's role – the professional must understand and sometimes play the political game of winning hearts and minds, the politician must be prepared to show appreciation of the technical and financial limits of what is possible. Andrew Wall and Simon Baddeley studied relationships between chief executives and chairs in the health service, which they identify as very personal, much like marriages, in which the two have to trust each other to succeed. Les Prince looks at a very different 'hidden' leadership that comes from below – not from the politicians and highly paid executives at the top of an organisation but from the workers and middle managers who are the supervisors and implementors of activity. He uses the most extreme situation in the public sector where management breaks down – the situation where soldiers refuse to obey orders — to show how a successful leader is one who earns trust from his or her followers.

Part Three examines the relationships of individual consumers or citizens with the welfare state. Marian Barnes and David Prior look at the potential contradictions of empowering 'consumers' of health services, who often lack the information or the power to stand up to doctors or other professionals. Some groups, such as mental patients or children at risk, probably cannot be trusted to make important decisions about their own lives. But where information could be shared, health service professionals are often reluctant to share it, fearing that patients with more information may make demands on the system that cannot be met, for expensive drugs or time-consuming treatments. Lucy Gaster and Nicholas Deakin suggest that the way forward is for trust to be built into the ethos of the service as a whole, and that this can be achieved if the standards of services are defined in terms of high quality and are carefully and sensitively monitored. This will not solve all the problems, but if the quality of a public service cannot be demonstrated, what democratic legitimacy does it have?

Part Four is concerned with trust between organisations, or parts of the same organisation, such as a 'client' and a 'contractor' which has won a contract in competition with the private sector. It includes two studies of compulsory tendering and contracting in British local government. In the first of these, concerned with blue-collar services contracted since 1980 and 1988, Howard Davis and Bruce Walker show how trust is needed when dealing with a contractor, but caution against too much reliance on trust. The second, by the economist Peter Watt, is an assessment of the issues raised by attempts to forcibly contract out white-collar services. This brings out the limitations both of compulsory tendering and of unrestricted in-house provision, and suggests that some relevant lessons have been learnt by the proponents of 'Best Value' as an alternative which tries to get the best of both. In a third chapter in this section, Ray Puffitt explores the ways in which a regulator or inspector can enforce compliance – and shows how this depends on creating a relationship between regulator and those being regulated, backed up by the fear of prosecution if trust is not sustained.

The last part of the book returns to the broad questions of how society can be ordered to encourage and reinforce trust. John Benington, following Ulrich Beck and Antony Giddens, describes the contemporary post-modern world as a 'risk society' where much of what happens cannot be predicted, calculated or controlled, and where individuals are frightened and respond by trying to protect their private spaces. The only way out of this 'Prisoner's Dilemma' is for leaders to promote not the state as a solution, certainly not the market, but a 'civil society' consisting of networks of voluntary and community organisations, underwritten in some cases by the state, and operating in a market economy, in which individuals can take responsibility for their own welfare and shape the world in which they want to live. Stewart Ranson and John Stewart believe that the way to this is by developing 'communicative rationality' and mutual learning – based on openness, discourse involving real communication and learning, shared conclusions and judgement, through which consensus is reached about what should be done. They conclude by advocating practical steps or approaches by which participation in decision making can be developed – citizens' juries or panels, deliberative opinion polls, consensus conferences. Through these, in their view, we can move towards a society where the people are more informed and involved, and hence have greater trust in their leaders.

TWO

Trust and contract in public sector management

Andrew Coulson

Social science research agrees that trusting behaviour is good and distrusting behaviour is bad. If everybody agrees with the generalisation, one wonders why it is necessary for so many people – theologians, politicians, psychotherapists, business executives – to continually urge their constituents to be more trusting. One would think that, by now, everybody would have learnt that nothing good can come from something so bad as not trusting. (Kipnis, 1996, pp 39-40)

Introduction

Civilisation is founded on trust. Without trust we would spend most of our time defining how we want to relate to our fellow human beings, and pursuing them through courts or other systems of arbitration when they did not behave as expected or agreed.

Here are some examples of trust in action, of increasing complexity:

- We trust that motorists will drive on the right-hand side of the road (except in a few aberrant countries such as the United Kingdom or Japan where we safely trust that they will continue to drive on the left).
- I hire an architect to design an extension to my house. I check this out as best I can, for example by looking at work that this architect has done elsewhere. But in the end I have to trust that the architect will do what I want, in the way that I want it.

- When I take my car to a garage for its regular service, I trust that the oil will in fact be changed, the pressure on the spare tyre checked, wear on the fan-belt spotted.
- A friend agrees to meet me at a certain time and place. I trust that (s)he will in fact be there – but if (s)he fails to show, then I know that person well enough to know that there is a good explanation.
- I play in a jazz band or football team, or work in a specialist team within my organisation. I know that the other members of the team will play their parts to the best of their abilities, so I play my part, supporting my colleagues, trusting that they will support me.
- A young child develops a trust in one person, usually its mother, which is derived from experience, and influences the way in which other relationships are formed.

Characteristics similar to those in these six illustrations demonstrate the diversity of relationships in which trust is found. In many situations trust is backed up by contracts, which specify what should happen if the trust breaks down. Behind these lies the law, with its civil or criminal penalties, though in practice these are only applied in a tiny proportion of the contract violations that occur. There are relationships which are informal, or one-off; trust is built up through experience (or reputation, or 'gossip'), and either party can walk away if the trust is abused. There are relationships which depend on membership of a team, or organisation, or group, or secret society. There are relationships which are essentially long term and where breakdown has a high cost, both psychological and in terms of shattered dreams and plans.

Psychologists have categorised trust relationships into three groups, illustrating how they can develop over time (Lewicki and Bunker, 1996). Of the six relationships summarised above, two can be placed in each of these three groups:

- The first two are 'calculation-based trust'.[1] This is where someone calculates that it is best to obey the law, or that it is likely to be better to use one architect rather than another.
- The second two illustrate 'experience-based trust'.[2] This occurs when you relate to another person or organisation repeatedly, until a situation arises when you can anticipate how the other person or organisation will behave. This is the trust you have in a person who has serviced your car many times, or the friend who promises to

meet you at a specific time and place (Lewicki and Bunker, 1996, p 122).

- The final two are examples of 'instinctive trust,'[3] where actions are almost instinctive, that is, without calculation.

Lewicki and Bunker explain how one of these types of trust can, with good experiences, grow into another. They can be seen as a continuum, where the trust has a gradually increasing intensity.

Any of them can fail, or be broken. The consequences may be minimal, or they may be dire. Thus if I drive on the wrong side of the road, I am likely to end up with expensive insurance claims and in court. If my architect does a bad job, I get a leaking roof – and may decide that it is worth suing the architect (or the builder, or the quantity surveyor, or all three) or the position may be so complicated that there is very little I can do except pay out more money to repair the roof. If my trusted small garage lets me down, then I will take my business elsewhere – and tell my neighbours, so that its reputation will suffer. If my friend *repeatedly* fails to show up as agreed, I shall choose other friends. If a team player does not pull his or her weight, or 'lets the side down', the sanctions are mainly internal and social, and if it continues that player will be dropped from the team. And if I lose a relationship with a parent or close friend or partner, the cost in emotion and psychological damage may be incalculable.

Transaction costs

If it works out – if trust turns out to be justified (or 'warranted') – then it minimises transaction costs. These are the costs before a decision is taken of calculating the odds on various outcomes, specifying the terms of a contract, and awarding it to one agent rather than another. After the decision is taken, transaction costs are the costs of monitoring the contract, and taking whatever action is necessary to ensure that it is carried out as agreed. Transaction costs are particularly associated with the work of Oliver Williamson, discussed later in this chapter. For the time being we simply note that trust has the potential to reduce the costs of setting up an activity. In the words of Kieron Walsh:

> **The more there is trust, then the easier it is to develop long-term relationships that are self-enforcing. It is valuable**

> to be trusted not for emotional but for purely practical
> reasons; ... the development of trust therefore works in the
> interest of those among whom it is developed by reducing
> costs which they face in managing their relationships with
> each other. (Walsh, 1995a, p 50)

Distrust and dishonesty

Trust is fundamental to daily living and to the organisation of production
and exchange. But distrust, dishonesty, fraud, deceit – what Oliver
Williamson (1996a, p 253 and elsewhere) calls 'opportunism' or 'self-
interest seeking with guile' – is also a feature of society today, as it was for
Machiavelli.

Again we can use examples to illustrate this:

- I get used to catching the 9.03 train which arrives in town at 9.20
  for meetings which start at 9.30. But if the train fails to come on
  time once or twice, I quickly lose my trust, because I cannot afford
  to be late.
- I buy pears from a greengrocer. They are cheap, but every so often
  they are bad; I take my trade elsewhere.
- I am not happy with a doctor's diagnosis. So I pay for a second, or
  third, opinion.
- I begin to fear that I have been sold a less than wonderful personal
  pension. I complain, first to the pension company, then to an
  ombudsman. Finally I go to the press.
- I collaborate with another researcher on the basis of give and take.
  But if I get nothing back, I start complaining. My colleague's
  reputation suffers.
- I begin to suspect my business partner of lining his own nest. There
  are tell-tale signs, but nothing conclusive. So I set up a situation
  that will produce one piece of definitive evidence. If untrustworthy
  behaviour is proved, I end the relationship.

In the first two cases, the trust is based on experience, and invalidated by
experience. Once broken, it will take hard work to put it together again.
In the second two situations, you cannot be certain; you can pay good
money to get a second opinion, or take a chance. In the final two cases,
my trust is undermined, and the relationship will never be the same again.

So we note that trust has to be earned. The move from trust based on calculation to trust based on experience is slow. But trust can be broken very quickly, and then to recover it is also slow, if not impossible. We also note two types of sanction that can be brought into effect. I can complain (what Hirschman calls 'voice'), or I can take my trade elsewhere ('exit').

We can also see some of the extra costs of breaking trust, as disillusion sets in and we thrash around testing the contractual position and looking for alternatives. In the future I will be less trusting, anticipate problems, be instinctively suspicious, get second opinions to support my case where possible, and insist on putting as much as possible in the form of a binding contract. The deeper the trust – the less based on calculation, the more on instinct – the worse the likely disillusion or despair.

Towards a definition of trust

Up to this point we have used the word trust without clarifying what exactly we mean. It is not easy to find a definition which covers all the various angles: trust is one of those concepts where the general idea seems straightforward, but turning it into a precise definition reveals subtle distinctions. A recent American collection of articles on trust (Kramer and Tyler, 1996) includes at least 16 definitions of trust, all slightly different from each other.

Psychologists such as Bowlby (1973; 1982) or Marris (1996) define trust in terms of personality traits, many associated with early years – notably the attachment of a child to its mother and then the ability of children at play in a group to develop trust in each other. This affects how individuals develop (or fail to develop) relationships in later life. It may be based on experience, such as the mother being the source of food and love, but it becomes instinctive. The ability to trust blindly is thereby deeply rooted in an individual's personality. It can lead to what Dunn (1988, p 76) calls 'human passion', sometimes completely against rational odds. When this sort of trust is broken, a person's life is changed, sometimes destroyed.

Sociologists and social anthropologists stress that trust is culturally determined. Thus people in some societies are more likely to trust other people than are those in others. People's willingness to trust may also vary over time: in Britain people were more willing to trust the welfare state in the 1960s than they are now. The willingness to trust authoritarian political leaders is extremely variable. And the willingness to trust competitor businesses with sensitive information seems to be greater in so-called middle Italy than in most parts of Britain (Powell, 1996).

Fukuyama (1995) is one of a number of contemporary writers who applaud elements of Asian, especially Japanese, culture, where trust, perceived as a social responsibility, gives that type of society a competitive advantage over the aggressive individualism of the West. Granovetter (1988) writes about trust being 'embedded' in close relationships. You are more likely to trust members of your immediate family than people that you only deal with from time to time. This is obviously so – as is the broader point that trust is related to culture, and that degrees of trust in a given culture can vary over time.

In contrast, many scholars (Deutsch quoted in Lewicki and Bunker, 1996, p 116; most of the writers, but not Dunn, in the 1988 collection edited by Gambetta; and Williamson up to but not after 1993) specify trust in terms of risk. Thus one is supposed to calculate the odds and 'trust' if the benefits from collaborating are sufficiently good and the disbenefits, if your collaborator lets you down, are not too severe. But is something as calculating as this really trust? And what happens if there is no reliable way of calculating the odds?

The definition which follows is that of Aneil Mishra (in Kramer and Tyler, 1996, p 265):

Trust is one party's willingness to be vulnerable to another party based on the belief that the latter party is:
(a) competent,
(b) open,
(c) concerned, and
(d) reliable.

This allows the term to be used both for trust based on calculation or experience, and trust based on instinct. But either way it must involve an element of risk: you are vulnerable, so the party being trusted may exploit you, or let you down. It also includes an element of belief, which may be based on calculation, research or instinct. It is voluntary: it involves willingness, not compulsion. And it includes a view of the other party: ultimately that they are 'trustworthy' – you believe that they will not let you down. Mishra was able to use his definition in interviews with workers in motor assembly factories which set out to understand why they did or did not trust certain managers. In Chapter Six in this collection

Les Prince shows how trust in appointed leaders, even military leaders, is not automatic, but has to be earned. In Chapter Thirteen Stewart Ranson and John Stewart use a similar conception to explore how a society might be created where more individuals have confidence in the institutions of the state and are able to influence the way it behaves towards them.

The definition also covers the decision of one organisation to trust another. As Janet Newman points out in the next chapter, this will be easier in some cultures than others, and will be influenced by the history of the relationships between the two parties.

The paradoxes of contract and trust

So far we have tried to understand trust, but made only slight mention of contract. Contract, 'specifying the details of a relationship in a form that can be enforced', is often presented as an alternative to trust. Certainly those who have trusted and been disappointed often turn to the law, or to the provisions in the contract, to recover their position. They will take care to consider all conceivable outcomes and where they would stand before continuing the relationship.

But contract and trust are not alternatives. A fundamental paradox is that the more one tries to specify every detail in a contract, the harder it becomes to enforce, and the more compromise and judgement come into play. This is partly because even the longest and most perfect contract will not anticipate every possibility; partly because, if they have to be applied, some of the provisions and penalties will seem to be unreasonable, or would have unhelpful consequences (such as putting the other party out of business); and especially because, with a very detailed contract, there are likely to be so many violations or failures that the system of arbitration gets bogged down sorting out interminable disputes.

Something similar occurs in management within an organisation. Thus even in relatively predictable situations, such as running a railway, the attempt to specify every possibility or contingency leads to a 'rule book' which in practice is unworkable. Then if the workforce have a dispute with the management, and want a form of industrial action which avoids the legal and financial consequences of a strike, all they have to do is to 'work-to-rule' – that is, to follow every rule in the book – and this will take so long that the system will grind to a halt.

Similar dilemmas face inspectors, such as factory inspectors or environmental health officers, and those who prescribe the rules under which they operate. Thus if everything is written in detail there will be such a complicated set of rules, with so many inevitable violations, that discretion is actually increased, since the regulators have to decide which rules to enforce. Regulators prefer to take enforcement action only occasionally, and instead to negotiate with offenders, that is, give them opportunities to improve, rather than to prosecute. If this works, it saves time, hassle, legal costs, and enables the violating firm to stay in business. This sociology of regulation is explored by Ray Puffitt in Chapter Eleven.

Going one stage further, we can note that a contract actually assumes an underlying relationship of trust: because if you expected to have to take your contractor to court you would not have chosen that contractor in the first place. In terms of our definition above, you are vulnerable, willing, but believe the contractor is reasonably competent and reliable, and is not going to use the contract to exploit you.

This type of underlying trust is taken to extremes when banks lend money on the basis of someone's word without any documentation. (See the chapter by Timothy Green, a banker, in Baker, 1996, for how this is changing with the coming of computers and the opening up of banking to more than a few individuals; and Williamson, 1996a, pp 258 and 262 for a discussion which suggests that this may still be on the basis of calculation rather than trust.) Something similar occurs in some illegal business where contracts cannot easily be written down (such as illegal street betting – see Webb, 1996, pp 288-9). If this kind of trust is broken, the reputation of the misbehaving individual suffers. This is an effective sanction where the deals are with a small group of people, and where both parties expect to go on dealing with each other in the future.

Oliver Williamson points out that there is an asymmetry before and after the award of a contract. Thus before the contract is awarded, it could go to a number of possible competitors. But after it is awarded, there are only two parties involved in the contract, the 'client' and the 'contractor'. There are high costs in breaking it, or taking it away from the winner, so both parties have an incentive to get together and make it work. If there are unexpected variations, then they need to compromise in deciding how these should be handled. If something goes badly wrong (a major piece of machinery fails perhaps) it probably does not pay the client simply to enforce all available sanctions: much better to be understanding to the contractor until the machine is mended (and then perhaps if something goes wrong on the client side, the contractor will be reasonable in turn). There are also obvious benefits in sharing information although, short of a full-blown merger, there will be limits to this on both sides.

So contract and trust are not alternatives – we can benefit from trust with or without contract. And without trust there are many situations in which a contractor can make life extremely difficult for the client.

Towards a deeper theoretical understanding: four contributions

The next sections of this introduction are summaries of the argument and conclusions of four contrasting pieces of research. Taken together they allow us to delve more deeply into the dynamics of trust, and how it can develop.

- A study of the game Prisoner's Dilemma by the political scientist turned mathematician and computer buff Robin Axelrod.
- The collection *Trust: Making and breaking cooperative relations*, with contributions by political philosophers, psychologists, economists, anthropologists, sociologists and historians, edited by Diego Gambetta and published in 1988.
- The economist Oliver Williamson, who has conceptualised the situations where it makes economic sense for an organisation to undertake an activity in-house, and where to contract that work out to another organisation. The key to this decision, as we shall see, is the study of transaction costs.
- The work of Kieron Walsh who took some of Williamson's ideas and applied them to contracting in the public sector. He was working towards using trust as a unifying theme in his work when he died suddenly of heart failure in 1995.

The evolution of cooperation

Prisoner's Dilemma is a game played between two individuals who have no contact with each other. It is defined as follows. Good results occur if both parties separately decide to cooperate. Poor results are the outcome if neither party decides to cooperate. But if one decides to cooperate, while the other does not, then the 'sucker' who cooperates loses out, while the individual who breaks trust (the 'opportunist') gets the highest pay-off.[4]

There are many situations which approximate to Prisoner's Dilemma. One of these is where two businesses are competing in the same market. If they share their information they get the best possible result. If they refuse to share information each gets something. But if one shares and the other uses the information without giving anything in return, then the one who shares gets very little (the sucker pay-off) while the other has access to the whole market and does very well.

The world described by theorists such as Fukuyama is a kind of cosmic Prisoner's Dilemma. Here, the worst outcomes arise when nobody trusts anybody else (his interpretation of the state of much of British and American industry) and the best outcomes arise where trust is endemic (in middle Italian industrial districts, or the relationships between Japanese sub-contractors and a large-scale assembler). But if there are one or two players who are opportunistic and use the information available without sharing, then they can do unduly well at everybody else's expense.

In most real-life situations, Prisoner's Dilemma is not just played once but over and over again. So the decision as to whether to trust the other player is influenced by whether they trusted you last time round. And conversely, if you want the other player to trust you, and thus, over repeated plays, for the two of you to get the best results, then it may pay to trust him even if initially he does not trust you.[5]

In 1984 Robert Axelrod published a book, *The evolution of cooperation,* which reported on two competitions which he had run. In the first, experienced game theorists were invited to submit programmes that would provide strategies for a player playing repeated games of Prisoner's Dilemma. There were 14 entries, and each of these programmes were set up to play the game repeatedly against each other. Each received scores for each outcome (3 each if both parties cooperated; 1 each if neither cooperated; and 5 for the opportunist, zero for the sucker if one cooperated and the other did not).

When the scores over all the games were added up – with a discount rate to recognise that results in future periods are worth slightly less than the same results obtained earlier – the remarkable result was that a very simple programme won. It involved a strategy called 'tit-for-tat'. This starts by cooperating; and thereafter does whatever the other player did the previous time. Thus if the other player cooperated, it cooperates. If the other player played dirty, it punishes by refusing to cooperate next time round.

Axelrod wrote a paper describing the results and why tit-for-tat was successful, and then repeated the exercise. This time he called for entries in computer magazines, so that amateur programmers with access to micro-computers could enter. They were given Axelrod's explanation of how tit-for-tat had done well in the previous competition, so the challenge was to improve on that strategy. This time there were 62 entries (the youngest aged 10), and similarly all were made to play against each other, and their scores totalled. And again tit-for-tat won, enabling Axelrod to develop his theories of why it was successful into the argument of his book.

Axelrod shows (with mathematics where appropriate) the secret of tit-for-tat's success. First of all it is clear and simple, which means that other players quickly come to understand the strategy being adopted by their opponent. Secondly it is nice: it starts by trusting, and never tries to take advantage of the other player unless they first take advantage of it. In the competition, the best of the 'nice' rules did well playing against each other, as one would expect, but tit-for-tat did especially well against rules that included attempts to take advantage, because it always retaliated. But, fourthly, tit-for-tat is forgiving: it only retaliates once. Thereafter it has an open mind about how its opponent will play. Finally, it is robust: Axelrod was able to show that it would do well in a wide variety of environments. If the gain from opportunism is too high, the game does not work; if the gain from cooperation is very high, then it becomes self-evidently the best strategy. He even managed to show that, if everybody was playing tit-for-tat and an 'intruder' arrived playing dirty, this intruder would not survive in competition with the others. And that in a dirty world, where no one was cooperating, if a small group started playing tit-for-tat that is, cooperating with each other and retaliating against those who did not cooperate with them, this small group would survive and prosper. The implications are explored for widely differing situations – including evolutionary biology (where a group of insects, cells or monkeys that decide to cooperate instead of competing will have an evolutionary advantage), and international peacekeeping endeavours, where again it can pay to be a peacemaker provided others do so too.[6]

For our concerns here the conclusions are equally optimistic: trusting can be a paying, competitive strategy in the long run. It is not naive strategy. Retaliation against those who take advantage of you is necessary, but in a clear unambiguous manner, and not for ever. More profoundly this work shows that trust can develop, to beneficial advantage, among those who have only relatively rare contact with each other, provided only that they remember the results of previous encounters. This is in contrast to the views of psychologists or political theorists who see trust as embedded in national ties or family upbringing and hence not an option for individuals who do not have such ties.

The world we live in is inevitably more complex than any computer simulation. There are great inequalities of power, so that very strong companies or agencies have less need to trust others than those who are weaker, even when the benefits of trust can be demonstrated (Marris, 1996, pp 148-52). Trust inevitably means a loss of independence, or sovereignty. It is not easy to trust in situations of tension or war. The strength of Axelrod's approach is that it shows the potential gains from trusting, and how a small group of people or organisations who trust each other can exert and extend their influence.

Can we trust trust?

Our second source of theoretical insight is a book edited by Diego Gambetta called *Trust: Making and breaking cooperative relations*. This was the outcome of a seminar run in Cambridge in 1985-86 which Gambetta set up to help him understand why the southern part of Italy remained backward compared with the north – and why the Mafia had arisen and continued. The participants in the seminar, leading figures from a wide range of disciplines, were as much concerned with the continuation of distrust (as in southern Italy) as with the creation of trust.

The first article in the collection, by the philosopher Bernard Williams, starts by suggesting that Prisoner's Dilemma is not the only possible scenario. You can have situations where the best outcome for both parties is to cooperate, but the decision whether to cooperate or not is cost sensitive. Williams looks at possible types of motivation to cooperate, and concludes that no single type of motivation can be relied on to promote a culture of trust. If it is imposed from above, there will be incentives to break the trust; if based on immediate incentives, such as money reward, then these will not always be sufficient.

Less negative conclusions are found in the third article in the collection by David Good, which uses a different model, the Trucking Game, illustrated in Figure 1. This involves two transport companies who can send lorries by different routes. The shortest route is very narrow, so that lorries cannot pass; if both companies choose this route, then neither gets through quickly. So each must choose between *either* a long, but reliable route, or a short one which will be much quicker *provided the other company does not choose it as well!* As a further complication, in order to protect the short route there are gates, one controlled by each of the companies, which can be used to prevent the other company's vehicles passing.

This game was developed by Deutsch and Kraus in the 1960s and used in trials with students and others. They discovered that if the gates were absent, then trust developed rapidly – for example, each company might permit the other to use the fast route on alternate days. But if the gates were there, then both parties tended to use them aggressively. Another conclusion was that if the rewards from the game started at low levels, and subsequently rose, then cooperation was more likely: it worked better if there was a learning process which started slowly. This supports the psychological perspective which we have already used, of trust

Figure 1: Map for the Trucking Game

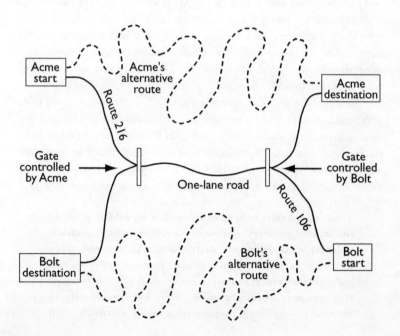

developing from calculation, through experience, to a point where it becomes almost instinctive.

Another model is presented in the fourth chapter, by the economist Partha Dasgupta. This considers the question whether or not to buy a car from a suspect second-hand car dealer (Gambetta himself, in his article on the Mafia, finds the same problem posed in 1863 of whether it was sensible to buy a used horse from a suspect horse dealer!) Dasgupta models this as a decision-tree. First, will you buy a car from this showroom? Secondly, from the point of view of the dealer, will you sell honestly or dishonestly?

Dasgupta explores the problems of reputation: it may pay the dealer to sell a good car, because while sale of a bad one makes a quick profit, it could easily be the last he sells. To go on selling cars, he needs to protect his reputation. So you may be able to trade successfully with a dishonest dealer if he is likely to want to continue in the market and to sell to you again or to other people later.

Space does not allow us to summarise the remaining articles, some theoretical, others historical or case studies, but in his concluding chapter Gambetta asks fundamental questions about why we sometimes trust and sometimes do not. It may be that we want the apparent freedom of competition. Or that we lack sufficient sanctions to use against those who do not trust us. But Gambetta points out that competition and cooperation are not necessarily mutually exclusive: indeed competition depends on a great deal of cooperation, or at least restraint in taking advantage of others.

One possibility is to "economise on trust" – not to risk more than you need. Another is to understand that trust needs to build slowly, over time, starting with smaller risks. But even then it is important to note that 'cooperation' is not the same as trust – you may decide to cooperate with someone you do not trust, such as the suspect second-hand car dealer discussed above. So the existence of trust cannot be proved:

> **Trust is a peculiar belief predicated not on evidence but on the lack of contrary evidence – a feature which makes it vulnerable to deliberate destruction. In contrast, deep distrust is very difficult to invalidate through experience ... once distrust has set in it soon becomes impossible to know if it was ever in fact justified, for it has the capacity to become self-fulfilling, to generate a reality consistent with**

itself. It then becomes individually 'rational' to behave accordingly.... Only accident or a third party may set up the right kind of 'experiment' to prove distrust unfounded.... (Gambetta, 1988, p 234)

He continues:

These properties indicate two general reasons why ... it may be rational to trust trust and distrust distrust.... The first is that if we do not we may never find out: trust begins with keeping oneself open to evidence, acting as if one trusted, at least until more stable beliefs can be established on the basis of further information. The second is that trust is not a resource that is depleted through use; on the contrary, the more there is the more there is likely to be.... Trust is depleted through not being used.

And he concludes:

But the point is that if we are not prepared to bank on trust, then the alternatives will be so drastic, painful, and possibly immoral that they can never be lightly entertained. Being wrong is an inevitable part of the wager, of the learning process strung between success and disappointment, where only if we are prepared to endure the latter can we hope to enjoy the former. Asking too little of trust is just as ill advised as asking too much. (Gambetta, 1988, p 235)

It is strange that a book that starts so sceptically should end on such an optimistic note.

Transaction costs

The American economist Oliver Williamson has devoted much of his academic life to developing what has become a new branch of economics, on the borderlines with organisational behaviour, concerned with the economics of large and complex organisations. The key concept is that of 'transaction costs'. Williamson has written more than 40 articles, republished in three large books (Williamson, 1975; 1985; 1996a).

Williamson is not an easy read. His work is repetitive, even within the same publication, as he works out his logic in subtly differing directions. Many of the arguments are directed at other economists, especially the neo-classic free-marketeers of the University of Chicago. He is often seen as unduly pessimistic because, while claiming to be value-free, he builds in assumptions about opportunism, or devious behaviour, assuming that those who have the opportunity to be devious and make a quick buck will in fact do so.

His writing asks a series of related questions:

- What stops a large corporation expanding indefinitely, by taking over its competitors?
- Or by buying out those who supply it? Or those to whom it sells? How is it that we all do not end up working for just one giant firm?
- When is it likely to be competitively economic for a firm to contract out part of its business to another firm? And conversely when should it not do this, but retain the activity in-house?
- How is it that many small businesses can compete with large ones? In what circumstances is this likely to be possible?
- What is likely to be an appropriate management structure for a large conglomerate firm, and how much discretion should be given to its branch managers?
- How much risk is there of a large firm exploiting its dominant position in a market? And what action, in terms of 'anti-trust' (American) or 'anti-monopoly' (British) legislation should a government take to regulate the activities of very large firms that dominate particular segments of economic activity?
- What can be said in favour of collective bargaining and trade unions?

Williamson uses a set of building blocks to create what he calls 'institutional economics':

Bounded rationality: it is not possible for a firm or manager to consider every possibility. So when making a decision they bring together as much information as they can that appears to be relevant. But they are limited, partly by knowledge, partly by communications difficulties (other people may have the knowledge but the decision makers may not be successful in drawing on it), and partly by uncertainty, that is things in the future which cannot be predicted in a way that can be included in a calculation, including some of the frailties of human nature. As Herbert Simon understood (quoted in Williamson, 1985, p 45), it is a situation where decision makers intend to be rational, but in reality this rationality is limited.

Opportunism: this is what Frank Knight called 'moral hazard'; others have called it deviousness, or deceitfulness. It means that people take advantage of situations where they can benefit by so doing. It includes "blatant forms such as lying, stealing, and cheating", and more subtle forms such as "the incomplete or distorted disclosure of information, ... calculated efforts to mislead, distort, disguise, obfuscate, or otherwise confuse" (Williamson, 1985, p 47). It can happen before or after a contract is awarded or a decision made.

Specialised assets: Williamson calls this 'asset specificity'. This describes a situation where some parties bidding for a contract or involved in a decision have advantages over others. This may be because they alone control some specific assets – specialised machinery, or the site on which a project will take place. Or they may control intellectual property – for example, the experience already gained by doing the job. Anyone new coming in must pay 'start-up costs', which may be substantial. In some cases no one else could do the job, and so one party has virtually a monopoly.

Williamson put these together in a table (Table 1).[7] In Situation 1, there is perfect knowledge, but operators have the opportunity to act deviously, and possess specialised attributes. In this situation every possibility can be specified in a contract, with a remedy for every possible abuse. Williamson calls this 'planning'.

Table 1: Institutional economics and the contracting process

	Behavioural assumptions ...			Implied contracting process
	Bounded rationality	Opportunism	Specialised assets	
Situation 1	No	Yes	Yes	Planning
Situation 2	Yes	No	Yes	Promise
Situation 3	Yes	Yes	No	Competition
Situation 4	Yes	Yes	Yes	Governance

In situation 2, individuals do not act deviously: they trust each other. So formal contracts are not needed. Details can be worked out as the (not fully predicted) future unfolds, and be settled on the basis of goodwill. Williamson calls this situation 'promise'.

In situation 3, no one has any advantage over anyone else. There is then no advantage to a client continuing long term with a particular contractor or supplier. In this situation, with imperfect knowledge and the possibility of devious behaviour, it is appropriate to go out to competition in the market.

But most of the time the real world approximates to Situation 4, when all these attributes apply. Here we can let Williamson speak for himself:

> **Each of the three devices fails when bounded rationality, opportunism and asset specificity are joined. Planning is necessarily incomplete (because of bounded rationality), promise predictably breaks down (because of opportunism), and the ... identity of the parties now matters (because of asset specificity). This is the world of governance.... This is the world with which transaction cost economics is concerned. The organizational imperative which emerges in such situations is this: Organize transactions so as to economize on bounded rationality while simultaneously safeguarding them against the hazards of opportunism. (Williamson, 1985, p 32)**

Transaction costs arise before an agreement is signed: they are the costs of "drafting, negotiating and safeguarding an agreement" (Williamson, 1985, p 20). They also arise when an agreement is being implemented, as the costs of adapting the agreement to new situations. (Anyone familiar with 'variations' in the construction industry when a small change has to be made to a design under construction knows how difficult this can be. Indeed, some contractors make most of their profits out of such variations.) They also include the costs of settling disputes, through informal arrangements, or through arbitration or the courts. Ex-post transaction costs include the costs of 'bonding' with the contractor – the initial process of client and contractor getting to know one another and setting up the relationships of give and take which are necessary to make a contract function effectively (Williamson, 1985, p 21).

With this apparatus "any problem that can be posed directly or indirectly as a contracting problem is usefully investigated in transaction cost terms" (Williamson, 1985, p 41). And his basic conclusion, which we shall pick up below in the discussion of the work of Kieron Walsh, is that "transaction cost economics maintains that there are rational economic reasons for organising some transactions one way and other transactions another" (Williamson, 1985, p 52).

We can also get a feel of the type of answers that Williamson suggests. The limits to the size of a conglomerate firm are related to the problems of handling information. In theory, it might be possible to give the managers of branches, or cost centres, the same discretion that they would have if they managed their own businesses; but in practice the way they will act will not be the same, and top management will be brought in to rescue branches from situations of crisis, to resolve disputes between branches, and to second-guess major investment decisions. Managers of branches may also act opportunistically, feathering their own nests at the expense of the company as a whole. So it is the ability of the centre of a conglomerate firm to handle information and to monitor devolved activity which dictates the number of cost centres and activities that can be managed by a single organisation.

So what determines whether an activity should be contracted out or handled in-house? Here the crucial element is the degree of uncertainty in the activity. If it can easily be prescribed in contractual terms, and monitored on an on-going basis without ambiguity (for example, has an order for paper met the prescribed specification?), there is little advantage in taking the supply activity in-house – and one is advised to tender and contract externally. But if there is real difficulty in monitoring, such as in the case of medical treatment, or research and development, or production of a key component which you do not want to be available to your competitors, then you are well advised to undertake the activity internally. Then the contract with an outside agent is replaced by contracts of employment with your staff: you may pay more for this, but it avoids the hassle of negotiating and supervising contracts for detailed, hard-to-measure work, and you gain the loyalty that comes with working inside an organisation.

Small businesses compete successfully with large ones by cutting down transaction costs and overheads such as marketing. They depend on loyalty, goodwill and repeat orders, often in situations where it is hard to monitor whether work has been done or done well – for example, servicing a car, or building an extension to a house. They may of course also have lower costs through paying lower wage rates, or poorer pensions, and so on for their staff – but this is not an aspect on which Williamson dwells.

Williamson is less antagonistic to monopoly than many other economists. He can see the advantages of large conglomerate businesses and stresses the difficulties of using monopoly power over long periods. He sees a role for trade unions and collective bargaining in maintaining reasonably high basic levels of remuneration in situations where otherwise dominant large firms might pay very low wages to some of their staff.

Overall, "incentives for trading weaken as transactions become progressively more idiosyncratic ..." (Williamson, 1985, p 78). Much depends on whether a contractor expects to deal with you again, in which case there is less incentive for opportunistic behaviour, but also greater likelihood of building up specialised assets or knowledge which will give the contractor an extra competitive advantage second time round. And once a process has been learnt, that is, the industry becomes mature on an in-house basis, it may be possible to contract out more parts of the process.

It was not until 1993 that Williamson clarified his position on trust. Most of what we call trust, Williamson believes is based on calculation, and can therefore be handled as a form of risk analysis. Thus if a bank lends money without a contract, that is, on the basis of experience and reputation, there is a strong probability that the money will be repaid as agreed, and if it is not the receiver will lose his reputation and not be able to borrow from any source. On that basis trust:

> **... is redundant at best and it can be misleading to use the term 'trust' to describe commercial exchange for which cost-effective safeguards have been devised in support of more efficient exchange. Calculative trust is a contradiction in terms. (Williamson, 1996a, p 256)**

This may be so. But it does not stop Williamson comparing cultures with different levels of trust (1975, pp 106-8), or using institutional analysis to make observations about the success of countries in East Asia with high growth rates (1996a, p 322ff). Williamson is clear that warranted trust reduces transaction costs and that whether trust is warranted is at least partly culturally determined. However, he is very reluctant to prescribe how a government might increase levels of trust, choosing instead to take refuge in the analysis of risk, with the cultural position as given.

Public services, market mechanisms and trust

So to consider those questions, and to see how the ideas of transactions cost can be applied to the public sector, we turn to the work of Kieron Walsh.

Before his death in 1995, Walsh was the leading specialist on contracting in British local government. In 1980 the Local Government Planning and Land Act – the first legislation affecting local government passed by the newly elected Thatcher administration – included 'compulsory competitive tendering' for a large part of housing repairs. Councils were required to define the work required, and to offer it to private contractors in competition with their own workforces. At the time it was bitterly resisted by many politicians (of all parties) but it came to be welcomed by many managers, not so much as a means of reducing costs but because it gave them a means of asserting their authority, and of confronting vested interests in their workforces which had resisted productivity improvements. In 1988 the principle was extended to other areas of local government activity – refuse collection from households, street cleaning, building cleaning, vehicle maintenance, and the up-keep of parks and grounds – and in 1995 it was extended to a range of professional services.

Walsh spent much of the 1980s touring the country teaching managers how to adapt to the new system, how to define specifications for contracts, how to engage in constructive dialogues with their workforces and how to exploit the many and varied loopholes in the legislation. He was contracted to conduct evaluative studies of this process for the government, in the course of which he made it clear that he was reluctant to put clear money figures to the financial savings derived from compulsory contracting, arguing instead that it was primarily a device for enabling managers to bring about changes which they could (but perhaps would not) have done without the legislation. His book *Public services and market mechanisms,* published in 1995, is an academic reflection on this research and consultancy.

Walsh was fascinated by the nature of the contracts used in compulsory competitive tendering – huge 'schedules of rates' which included prices for every possible kind of job, area of land or building. He contrasted these with the much shorter documentation of many commercial contracts, or the almost absence of documentation in similar contracts in France, or if work was carried out in-house.

He was influenced by the work of Oliver Williamson, and realised that transaction costs depended on the transparency of the services offered. So, for example, contracts work well when they involve emptying dustbins or cleaning buildings, where there is little ambiguity – the work is either done or not done. They work less well when they involve maintaining gardens or running sections of the health service, which are constantly open to disputes as to whether the services are being delivered precisely as specified. On that basis it is likely to be even more difficult with services provided by professionals such as doctors, lawyers or social workers, where concepts relating to quality have to be measured and incorporated into a contract.

Walsh realised that contracts are not independent of culture, nor of trust:

> **Contracts involve more than promise, and are essentially a means of sharing risks, benefits and responsibilities, or, more abstractly, a means of 'making the future present'. The contract is a means of making the future more tractable, without knowing what the detailed nature of those decisions will be. It involves the creation of institutions that allow the postponement of choice. The different forms of contract will depend on what can be observed, and how much the observation of performance will cost. For example if it is difficult to assess objectively whether or not the contractor has performed, then it may be necessary to build contract forms that incorporate trust and reputation. (Walsh, 1995a, p 41)**

He drew on the work of the lawyer Ian Macneil who pointed out that the complexity of modern organisations often meant that the framework for the contract, the way it would handle disputes, and ultimately the way it would be ended, was often more important than the precise provisions in the legal document. There were important differences between contracts that were one-off, such as simple purchases of a good or service, and contracts that were expected to continue, in one form or another, for many years.

And so the discussion of contract brought Walsh to consideration of trust:

> The development of trust, therefore, works in the interest of those amongst whom it is developed by reducing the costs which they face in managing their relationships with each other. This will be particularly important in the public service because it will often be difficult to measure effectively the levels of quality of performance. It will be necessary for the purchasers of service to have some means of knowing that they can trust providers, through, for example, third party audit systems or processes of quality assurance, and, perhaps, at a deeper level, commitment to appropriate sets of values. (Walsh, 1995a, pp 50-1)

And conversely:

> The development of trust is central to the maintenance of social systems, and the danger of contract is that it undermines trust, through basing contracts on punishment for failure. If we undermine trust then we may find that the making of agreements, and ensuring that they are kept, will become very costly. (Walsh, 1995a, p 255)

The means by which trust might be developed was the subject of another book, *Citizenship: Rights, community and participation*, written by Walsh shortly before his death, jointly with David Prior and John Stewart. This is a study of the relationships between individuals and the state. It argues for a local dimension to these relationships, and especially for a role for local democratic institutions, reformed to make them more accessible, and more responsive to the needs, aspirations and fears of ordinary people.

Trust and contract – key themes

In this final section, we summarise our argument, and restate a number of themes which are central to a mature understanding of management in the public sector.

Trust describes a relationship which can be between two or more individuals, between individuals and an organisation (such as a company or social services department), or between several organisations. As society becomes more fragmented (with large corporations dividing up, or decentralising, and increasingly contracting out parts of their activities) relationships become more complex. In order to succeed, an individual, or an organisation, has to be able to build and maintain relationships, and without trust this is almost impossible.

The way we trust or distrust is part of our culture – which means both that it is difficult to change, and that it can be changed. We are more likely to trust those we know well, or members of our families, than people we may never meet again. It is easier to trust if you are powerful, and can afford to risk some of your wealth, or to move your sources of supply from one firm to another until you find one you can trust. It may be especially difficult if you are weak and have no obvious alternative source of supply (such as a claimant forced to use the local social services department and benefits office). Those who cannot trust – or who are not trusted – often find themselves in a weak position vis-à-vis those with power. There are therefore special concerns which relate to trust and inequality in the public services.

Trust is a process of learning. It grows through use, starting with calculation, developing with experience, and eventually it may reach a point where it is as much a matter of intuition and instinct as of calculation. But distrust can easily set in. Distrust is a natural reaction for anyone faced with risk, especially risk where the consequences could be significant. It is far easier to create a milieu of distrust that one of trust, and after that it is a slow and often painful process to rediscover that it is worth trusting. Distrust of public services, and the politicians who are seemingly responsible for them, is a common situation. It is not remedied easily, or in most cases quickly; but openness, accountability and clear measures of efficiency are probably essential if trust is to be recreated and enhanced.

The natural reaction to a breakdown of trust is contract – to specify all likely eventualities, and the consequences that would follow from each. But contracts are expensive to prepare and monitor, and are seldom complete. Trust, provided that it is not abused, reduces transaction costs: the costs of creating contracts, monitoring them, going to arbitration or court, enforcing the outcome, and so on. However, contract and trust are not alternatives; the existence of a contract implies trust in the first place, and a commitment to work together. The supervision or monitoring of a contractual relationship is a form of regulation, and regulators can adopt a variety of tactics, depending on how much trust and respect they command, and how much discretion they have.

Despite the risks of opportunist or dishonest behaviour, more rather than less trust can often be a rational strategy, provided groups of actors who are trusting also take clear and severe action against those who take advantage of them. It is possible for trusting communities to develop even in a world of opportunists. But trusting is not a 'soft', or easy, or 'other-worldly' strategy. It must always be backed by a willingness to take tough action against those who do not conform.

Attitudes to trust are today under formidable cultural attack, from the social changes brought about by TV and the motor car (which make for individualism, and break the links in which a family lives, works, plays and shops in one place, one community), from changes in social structure (more people living on their own, with fewer family links), and from aggressive media. If we want to live in a more trusting society, a stakeholder economy, a community of communities, then it will not happen these days without conscious action. In the words of the political commentator Anna Coote:

> ... the only [strategy] I regard as a runner is to build a high-trust democracy. Trust has broken down because politics is characterised by secrecy, spin-doctoring and special pleading. A high-trust democracy is built on understanding and consensus, not on instruction and obedience. It involves an adult-to-adult relationship between citizens and their representatives. It implies mutual trust; not blind faith, but the kind of measured confidence that comes from informed understanding. (New Statesman, 9 August 1996, pp 32-3)

Creation of such a 'high-trust democracy' is the task to which we are committed (for explicit developments of this see the final two chapters of this collection). Because trust links so many parts of social science, it provides a framework concept for the study of how this might, or might not, be done. The fact that it can, and often is, broken does not detract from this. Nor that it is culturally 'embedded'. Nor that to develop trust requires imagination, leadership, decision making – the whole range of skills that together we call management.

Author's acknowledgements

The author would like to acknowledge constructive comments and suggestions from Simon Baddeley, John Benington, Lucy Gaster, Janet Newman, John Stewart and Peter Watt.

Notes

[1] Shapiro, Sheppard and Cheraskin (1992) call this 'deterrence-based trust', but this is too negative; the calculation may be of positive gains that can result from trusting. Lewicki and Bunker (1996) prefer 'calculus-based trust', but this is an unnecessary use of a complicated word.

[2] Lewicki and Bunker call this 'knowledge-based trust', but this does not distinguish it clearly from the first category, which is also based on knowledge and the research that is involved if calculations are to be made.

[3] Psychologists such as Lewicki and Bunker use the term 'identification-based trust', as does Janet Newman in Chapter Three, but for our purposes it is needlessly abstract. The key is that it is not calculated, either directly, or on the basis of experience. For Williamson (1993) this is the essence of trust: anything that can be calculated is better conceived as risk.

[4] The name arises from the situation in which "two people are arrested for a crime for which the police do not have the evidence to convict. But they do have enough evidence to convict on a lesser charge. Each criminal is offered the chance to confess to the bigger crime, and receive leniency for himself while his partner goes to jail. If both confess, both go to jail, though with reduced sentences; if both keep quiet, then both get convicted on the lesser charge only" (Dowding, 1996, p 15). Thus if you confess, the worst that can happen is that you go to jail with a light sentence. But it you could be sure that the other prisoner would not confess, you would be best not to confess either.

[5] Axelrod gives many other examples of situations which have been modelled using Prisoner's Dilemma. "In the last 15 years there have been hundreds of articles on the Prisoner's Dilemma cited in Psychological Abstracts. The iterated Prisoner's Dilemma has become the E. coli of social psychology." (p 28).

[6] There have been many differing uses of game theory to examine the problems of cooperation since publication of Axelrod's book in 1984. There are other games than Prisoner's Dilemma, including those with more than two players at a time. For a more recent assessment see Udehn, 1996, Chapter 5.

[7] This is Table 1.1 from Williamson (1985, p 31), slightly adapted.

THREE

The dynamics of trust

Janet Newman

> Truth, trust, restraint and obligation – these are among the
> social virtues grounded in religious belief which are now
> seen to play a central role in the functioning of an
> individualistic, contractual economy. (Hirsch, 1977, p 141)

This quotation captures some of the tensions around the concept of
trust. It symbolises values whose loss resonates across a range of responses
to social, economic and management changes. It is a deeply conservative
concept, evoking nostalgia for a lost world of order and predictability, in
which the social relations were built on the foundations of hierarchy and
deference. At the same time it lies at the heart of New Labour's discourses
on economy and society. In the economy, notions of 'stakeholding' and
trust between employers and employees underpin the desired
transformations of the firm, while models of economic activity from
Japan and the so-called 'Asian Tigers', based on cultures of reciprocity
and trust, are used to encourage the UK to compete successfully in the
global marketplace. In civil society, the virtues of community, mutuality
and responsibility are evoked as solutions to the perceived crisis of the
welfare state, and as responses to social problems from juvenile crime to
the so-called breakdown of the traditional family.

Trust is an affective concept, concerned with the world of personal
relationships, emotions and intuitions. At the same time, it is emerging
as one of the key concepts in the search for the secrets of competitive
success, and in discussions of the changing political relationships between
citizen and state. It appears to flow easily across the boundaries of public
and private, commerce and politics, psychology and economics. The
multiplicity of domains in which an interest in trust is developing suggests

that it has become a highly promiscuous concept. As has been the case with other such concepts in public management (notably 'quality', 'community', 'empowerment'), this promiscuity means that the notion of trust can be and has been coopted to a range of different purposes and contexts. It has been appropriated by both left and right, and has become central to debates on a wide range of issues from the operation of markets and contracting to those of social exclusion and local community regeneration.

However, the very promiscuity of trust brings problems. It is often treated as something which is either present or absent, rather than something which is rooted in dynamic sets of social, political and cultural forces. This chapter offers a critical perspective on notions of trust emerging in the discourses of governance, management and contract by attempting to sketch some of the dynamics of trust, drawing on a set of key concepts: those of culture, power, legitimacy and diversity.

Trust and public management: mapping the domains

The shift towards the use of contracts in the delivery of public services – and a concern with the subsequent identification of the problems of developing, specifying and monitoring complex services – has been one of the driving forces for the new interest in trust in public management. However, this contract relationship cannot be analysed in isolation from a set of broader relationships, each themselves undergoing profound change (see Figure 2). One concerns the changing relationships between users and producers in the delivery of services: for example, the issues arising from the changing power and role of professionals. A second focuses on the relations between management and workforce: for example, changes in the 'psychological contract' arising from changing career patterns and new organisational forms. A third concerns the changing dynamics of interorganisational relationships, characterised by emerging models of 'partnership' and the mixed economy of service provision. Each of these is framed within the changing political context of public services. Here the sharpening of concern around issues of probity and accountability raises questions about the legitimacy of social action in public policy and management.

Each of these changing sets of relationships is considered in turn. The aim is two-fold: first to distinguish the different meanings and usages of 'trust', not all of which are transferable from one domain to another (for example, 'trust the leader' means something rather different from 'trust the contract'). The second aim is to explore the dynamics of change within each domain. Here I suggest that there is no wholesale shift from 'old' to 'new' forms of trust. The focus on the dynamic nature of social relationships means that we are not witnessing any generalised shift from hierarchy to contract to trust in economic exchange, from Fordism to post-Fordism in organisational design, nor from traditional to post-modern patterns of identity. We are witnessing a set of complex and overlaid articulations between calculus-based and identification-based forms of trust.[1] Sometimes the shift appears to be in one direction, sometimes another, sometimes there is movement in both directions at once. Rather than looking for general shifts, it seems more important to explore changes in the type of calculative trust, or in the mode of identification, as public service relationships undergo change.

Figure 2: Public service change and the dynamics of trust

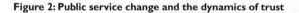

Litigation or legitimacy? The dynamics of the service relationship

Different forms of trust are potentially involved here: the trust by the user in the judgement and knowledge of the professional (for example, trusting the medical profession), and in the equity and fairness of the allocation of scarce public goods and services (for example, trusting the old 'points' system for the allocation of council housing). Both forms of trust were institutionalised in the organisational form on which the delivery of social welfare was based: the professional bureaucracy (Mintzberg, 1983). However, both were challenged as the regime became subject to New Right critiques through the 1970s and 1980s. Professional activity was flawed by the paternalism with which professional judgements were often made, and many professions – notably teachers and social workers – have been represented by politicians and the media as not to be trusted. At the same time trust in the 'fairness' of bureaucratic rules and allocation procedures has become eroded as resources have been squeezed, necessitating the increasing targeting of these resources and the subordination of bureaucratic systems to managerial judgements and priorities. Whatever the constraints and rationales, from the user's point of view the loss of services brings with it a sense of unfairness and an erosion of trust, the latter leading to an increase in litigation in many sectors.

But trust is a two-way process. The dynamics of public service also raise questions about how far those delivering services trust the service user. The twin institutions of professional judgement and bureaucratic administration were partly built on assumptions of the untrustworthiness of those in receipt of services. The history of the postwar welfare state has been characterised by a long list of demons: 'scroungers', 'single parents', 'promiscuous teenagers', 'inadequate mothers' and so on. This dimension of trust has received scant attention in the literature on trust because it is concerned with the realm of symbolic constructions. These constructions both fill in the 'knowledge' basis of trust (our knowledge of the world is partly formed through such stereotypic constructions) and form the basis of our 'calculations' about who is and is not to be trusted. These constructions change over time, and a quick scan of the tabloids will provide an indication of current social demons and moral outcasts who are seen as not to be trusted to make proper use of the services provided.

There are two structural changes taking place which potentially alter these relationships. The first is that of consumerism, in which service users are constituted not as grateful recipients but as customers with entitlements and choices. However elusive these are in practice, the shift in discourse brings with it a shift in the balance and relations of power within which relationships of trust are formed. In the business world the building of trust is based on the need to develop customer loyalty. This in turn means viewing economic exchange not as a series of one-off impersonal transactions in the marketplace, but as the development of long-term relationships with customers. There are of course many differences between the customer–provider relationship in the public and private sectors. Even though customers in the public sector may have little choice about providers, for instance, the latter nevertheless have to establish their legitimacy as public services both in the eyes of their users and of the wider community of stakeholders and citizens. That is, they have to be concerned not just with the commercial dimensions of trust but with its political dimensions too.

The second, but related, structural change is that of the 'quality' movement, which can be viewed in part as the attempted formalisation and codification of trust through quality standards, customer charters, service entitlements and so on. Whatever their flaws, these have the potential for reducing some of the disbenefits of professional judgement and the power imbalances between professional and client. At the same time, however, they may serve to standardise norms of performance which are unresponsive to different sets of interests, needs or requirements on the part of service users: that is, to issues of social diversity (for further discussion see Chapter Eight by Lucy Gaster and Nicholas Deakin). Alongside such formalised systems a new raft of informal processes is developing, in which users are to be consulted, involved, empowered, and invited to become 'partners' or 'co-producers' in the delivery of services (see Benington, Chapter Twelve, and Stewart Ranson and John Stewart, Chapter Thirteen). What is at stake here is how far these are genuine attempts to change the balance of power between service users and providers, or whether they remain little more than a symbolic gloss on a reality which is not much different from the days of bureaucratic paternalism.

Trust the vision? The social relations of management

Both consumerism and quality imply significant shifts in the relationships between providers and users, which in turn require changes within provider organisations. The shift towards greater devolution and decentralisation marks a significant shift in management–workforce relations, and to the social relations of trust within organisations.

Patterns of management change have led to an increasing interest in the idea of trust in management–workforce relations. For example, Handy (1995) sets out the need for new forms of trust-based relationship in the context of the emergence of 'virtual' organisations, characterised by more complex, fragmented and arms-length relationships. In this context, it is argued, it is necessary to develop a common vision and sense of purpose – that is, a unifying set of identifications. This is not an easy project. Any organisation will be cross cut by different patterns of identity, based on historical attachments, gender, ethnicity, occupation, department, social or community affiliations, informal allegiancies and so on. Such multiple identifications invoke different – and sometimes contradictory – pressures. Trust is easy where commitments involve simple choices or identifications, where knowledge is based on common cultural identity (even perhaps common membership of a form of 'club culture' in which trust is the mirror image of collusion). It is more problematic when multiple commitments and identifications are invoked.

Change is not only concerned with a process of displacement of hierarchical modes of control by attempts to develop identification-based trust. New patterns of control based on performance and contract are displacing the collegial, professional and corporate forms of trust which characterised the 'old' public sector. One of the strands of this new articulation is the erosion of institutionalised forms of management–workforce negotiation in which, even if managers and workforce did not trust each other, they each conformed to the rituals and machinery of collective bargaining, joint consultation committees and so on. Many factors have played a part in the demise of these institutions. They have been eroded by successive pieces of anti-trades union legislation and the parallel development of 'human resource management' and its anti-collectivist focus. They have also, however, lost legitimacy in the face of challenges by groups within the workforce – part-time staff, women, black and minority ethnic employees, staff on temporary contracts – whose interests could not be encompassed in a single set of claims.

The shift to 'human resource management' has been based on attempts to build common identifications between managers and workforce. The development of symbolic leadership, corporate culture and mission, communication and training programmes is intended to create common loyalties and identifications across workforce–management divisions. But this is not the only story. The picture of organisational dynamics is overlaid with wider social and economic trends which have fundamentally altered the patterns of 'career' and the nature of the psychological contract between employer and employee. The old psychological contract has been broken as a result of externalisation and the search for workforce flexibility. Public service organisations increasingly claim that they can no longer afford to be 'good employers', and staff are being asked to trust the contract rather than the employer. The ways in which change has been managed has often succeeded in further eroding trust between manager and workforce, especially where there have been significant gaps between the language of change (empowerment, trust, consultation, commitment) and the reality of its practice.

These shifts in both the employment and the psychological contracts bring with them a much sharper emphasis on work as a temporary process of exchange: the exchange of labour for the rewards of a salary or wage for the employee, or the exchange of the benefits of training and development for the rewards of loyalty to the employer. New practices are developing to attempt to fill the resulting 'trust vacuums'. Sickness absence management, time recording and individual target setting can be viewed as attempts to formalise and codify norms which might otherwise be held in place through cultural mores and informal sanctions. That is, they replace identification-based trust (will it be unfair to my colleagues if I'm off sick for too long?) with calculative judgements (how many days sickness am I entitled to?). This may lead to the development of a vicious circle in which the lack of trust results in people behaving in less trustworthy ways.

The analysis of shifts in management-workforce relations reveals a contradictory process in which the rhetoric is of identity-based trust (developing commitment and attachment) while the practice is one of increasing emphasis on contract. Some traces of this can also be identified when we turn to the domain of interorganisational relations.

The paradoxes of partnership: interorganisational relations

Contracts and partnership arrangements require organisations to develop trust across organisational boundaries. The majority of the literature here has focused on the need to establish trust in order to minimise the transaction costs of specifying and monitoring detailed contracts for complex services. However, the dynamics of partnership involve much wider questions about the changing relationships between the voluntary and statutory sectors, between public and private sector organisations in joint development projects, between statutory bodies engaged in activities such as joint commissioning, between formal organisations and informal community networks and so on.

Transaction cost theory assumes that organisational choices are rational, even if the information on which they are based is imperfect ('bounded rationality'). But such choices are framed within patterns of relationships both in the marketplace and within organisations. In the marketplace, the type of contract – transactional or relational – may depend partly on the relative power of client and contractor organisations (as well as the type of service involved). In situations with many providers, the market may be shaped by purchasing organisations seeking to drive down prices or secure other benefits. Contracts tend to be short term where switching between different provider organisations is likely to deliver benefits to the client. In situations with few, powerful providers, the market is more likely to be shaped by providers themselves, who may seek to secure the benefits of longer-term, relational contracts.

Transaction cost theory also concludes that choices about what services should be contracted out are based on the characteristics of different services, with those which are easy to specify and monitor being more 'rational' choices for outsourcing than those which are complex or difficult to specify. However, choices about what service should be subjected to market testing or outsourcing decisions are also the subject of the interplay of power and interests. Rational choice theory suggests that such decisions will be based on a rational assessment of the likely transaction costs for different forms of service. But they may also be shaped by the pattern of interests within organisations, as suggested by Dunleavy's 'bureau-shaping' theory (Dunleavy, 1991). The dynamics of decision making about what services to contract, and what forms of contract to develop, may not be solely based on economic considerations.

A third common assumption of transaction cost theory is that the costs of contract are considered in relation to the client organisation alone; that is, that the client need not take account of the potential costs of contracting to the provider. The problem here is that many public sector organisations have social goals as well as efficiency goals, and may seek to retain a diversity of providers. The effects of the contracting process on voluntary and community organisations may be to reduce diversity in at least two ways. The first is that some may be driven out of business by reliance on contracts rather than direct grants. The second, more subtle, effect may be to force voluntary and community organisations into a straitjacket of uniform business procedures, management arrangements and organisational forms as the precondition for being awarded contracts. This 'isomorphic' tendency has the effect of reducing the diversity (if not the number) of providers, thus limiting their capacity both to challenge the norms and assumptions of the purchasing organisation, and to retain the trust of their members and communities.

The shift from hierarchies to contracts as modes of coordination in public services has changed the social relations of trust. It is not that trust develops as a new form of coordination (as is sometimes suggested in sequential images such as 'from hierarchy to contract to trust'). Rather, old forms of relationship, and the trust on which these were based, are being displaced, while new forms of trust have to be forged around different sets of processes and conditions. In other words, the old forms of trust – based, for example, on respect, authority and expertise – are being dismantled before new forms of trust can be established. And we are not yet very sure what the basis for these should be. It is here that the work of Kieron Walsh and others who have begun to explore the social and economic institutions of markets and contracts is of critical importance (Walsh, 1995a; Mackintosh, 1995).

I want to suggest, however, that there is much to be gained by adding a cultural dimension to the analysis of contracts and partnership arrangements. Working across boundaries means working with and through cultural differences, where trust is made difficult by differences of values, language, norms and goals. The symbolic dimensions of the social relations of trust may be both help and hindrance. Relationships may be as much based on myths and stereotypes of partner organisations – what public sector bodies assume about the private sector, what health authorities assume about social services, what white managers assume about black community groups, and vice versa – each of which may make trust hard to establish. Equally dangerous, however, is the premature establishment of trust based on assumptions about common values and goals which have not been properly explored. Here the myth of trust may be a barrier to negotiating the reality of its practice in a rigorous way.

Legitimacy and accountability: the political dynamics of trust

Each of these sets of relationships is framed within a broader set of concerns arising from the political context in which public services are delivered. For example, many working within public services welcome warmly the development of relational contracting, seeing it perhaps as offering a counter to the harsh realities of the marketplace, or as a new axis around which common public service values can be developed across organisational boundaries. Relational contracting, or indeed the Labour Party's proposals for 'Best Value', seems to offer a 'third way' to those who recognise the limitations of hierarchy but are not content with the idea of market mechanisms as the arbiter of decisions on the allocation of public goods. It is highly attractive to those steeped in the values and ethos of public service culture and brings potential benefits of reduced transaction costs and mutual investment in innovation and development. However, lines of accountability may be weakened as a result of a reduction in detailed monitoring, inspection and other formalised processes of control. The boundaries between trust and collusion (for example, in public–private initiatives) or trust and risk (for example, in local authority relationships with residential establishments for children) are difficult to draw with any precision. These tensions are expressed in the potential contradictions between 'accountability' and 'trust' as explored further by Howard Davis and Bruce Walker (Chapter Nine) and Peter Watt (Chapter Ten).

There are also tensions between different political objectives: those of efficiency (in the interests of the taxpayer) and of accountability (in the interests of the citizen). There may be significant efficiency gains to be made through establishing public–private partnerships or long-term relational contracting. However, these may need to be balanced against the need to protect the mechanisms through which the trust of politicians and citizens is secured – those of accountability, probity, scrutiny and stewardship. The traditional characteristic of the public sector – that of balancing multiple goals and stakeholder requirements – is transformed into the need to manage multiple and conflicting legitimation processes. This may not be as cheap as those who advocate trust as a mechanism of reducing transaction costs assume.

These processes are framed by broader concerns about trust in the political process itself. Much of the political agenda in recent years has been shaped round the decline of trust in politicians and government.[2]

Trust has emerged as a central concept in the work of the Scott and Nolan enquiries into standards in public life in Britain, and in the analysis of quangos and the privatisation of public utilities. The legitimacy of actions taken by ministers and others has been challenged and the accountability of public bodies and privatised utilities has been questioned. Trust also emerged as a key feature of the party political 'battle for hearts and minds' which took place around the 1997 general election. The Conservative Party cast 'New Labour' as untrustworthy, while the Labour Party deployed the language of mutuality and reciprocity in its new communitarian and stakeholder visions. It is the very slipperiness of the concept that makes trust so potent as a political concept. But there is a paradox here; it is precisely the decline of trust in public life that both gives the concept its extra resonance in political discourse, and hinders politicians' ability to lay claim to it. It is the dynamic links between trust, legitimacy and accountability that signal deeper processes of change in the relationships between citizen and government, the state and the market, public and private actions.

The forms of legitimacy which underpinned the foundation of the postwar welfare state were based on a particular conception of the relationship between state and citizen. This has undergone a major transformation as the social and economic fabric on which it was based has changed, and Britain is now a more complex and culturally diverse society. The establishment of trust across social and cultural boundaries in an increasingly differentiated society is challenging, and its failure evident in emerging patterns of disaffection and social exclusion.

The search for the re-establishment of trust in public institutions will continue (see, not least, Chapter Twelve by John Benington and Chapter Thirteen by Stewart Ranson and John Stewart). Public managers have a part to play in this: as the political dynamics of trust become more problematic, the struggle for legitimacy in service design and delivery seems to be growing in importance. However, this can only be a part of the story. Public management will continue to be framed within a wider set of political processes involving the reforging of relationships between the state, the economy and civil society (Clarke and Newman, 1997).

Trust and social theory

The analysis of the previous sections has drawn on a set of key concepts: those of culture, power, legitimacy and diversity. These are important to the project of developing a critical perspective on the analysis of trust in public management and beyond and on the broader political context in which it is framed.

Culture and the politics of diversity

Culture has been a core concept in the emerging literature on trust. Fukuyama (1995) sees trust as a form of social capital embedded in social institutions and national cultures. Cultures based on strong kinship patterns and dense networks of association generate the forms of trust which underpin economic growth and political stability. His work has been greeted with a mixed response, with some seeing it as a welcome challenge to the free market individualism of the West, and a reminder of the importance of investment in a nation's human and social capital. Others, however, have pointed to its superficiality, its basis in unfounded generalisations and its unrigorous mix of economic and cultural theory. Fukuyama's analysis of the cultural foundations of trust carries important insights. It identifies the importance of values, symbols, traditions and patterns of relationships. But the analysis ignores important questions about the potential role of culture in economic and political life. The first is about how to balance the benefits of tight-knit, solidaristic cultures with their potential social disbenefits: those of exclusivity and lack of tolerance for outsiders and for those who do not conform to strong social norms. The restoration of universalist notions of citizenship, cultural homogeneity, tight-knit family structures and the moral authoritarianism which tends to accompany these is hopefully not an option for the UK.

The second, and related, problem concerns how far it is possible to translate cultural features from one context to another: that is, for the West to mimic the cultures of China or Japan, or the so-called 'Asia Tigers', with their very different histories, traditions, kinship patterns and economic and political trajectories of change. I am not suggesting that there are not things to be learned from other nations – the arrogance of the West remains deeply entrenched. Rather I want to suggest that there are dangers in attempting to transpose cultural norms and values across nations. In much cross-cultural analysis (Fukuyama, 1995; Hofstede, 1991; Trompenaars, 1993), culture is treated as a static variable: something that a nation or group has which distinguishes it from other nations or groups. This ignores issues of cultural diversity *within* nations or societies. Britain encompasses a plurality of cultures, embracing different notions of reciprocity, different foundations of solidarity, different 'rules of the game' for social and economic transactions. Trust can be built across such differences, but only where the differences – and the patterns of inequality which may be linked to them – are recognised, acknowledged and understood.

The analysis of culture and diversity is not just a question of defining neatly circumscribed subcultures (as found in flawed notions such as 'the black community', 'Asian entrepreneurs' or 'working-class culture'). Any rapidly changing society will produce cross-cutting and shifting patterns of identification based on notions of race, ethnicity, locality, generation, gender and other social groupings. In building the legitimacy on which trust is founded, these patterns of identification are crucial. This raises important questions about how those involved in governance and management define the 'public' to whom they wish to lay claim in seeking to ensure accountability, consultation or involvement (Newman, 1996)

When linked to the politics of diversity, culture becomes not a static descriptive category but an analytical tool which can help to illuminate the processes through which trust is formed (or eroded) across different cultural norms, expectations or identities.

Power and the politics of equity

Power tends to be a missing component of the economic models which underpin much of the analysis of trust. It tends to appear only in the form of 'opportunistic' power – the power of one party to take advantage of another. Yet power occurs in many forms, including the ways in which decisions are framed and agendas shaped. It may be formal (based on the legitimacy of role or office) or informal (often based on the personal power to influence or persuade). It may be coercive, based on sanctions and punishment; remunerative, based on incentives; or normative, based on symbolic rewards – for example, a sense of belonging and identification (Etzioni, 1961). The contracting process involves both formal and informal power in the processes of negotiation and problem solving. Contracts embody coercive powers (the power of redress), remunerative power (the power to reward), and symbolic power (the power to enhance the reputation of one party by linking them symbolically to the other).

Power, in all its forms, is of critical importance to an analysis of trust for several reasons. First, naive views of trust tend to ignore differences of power. There is a tendency to focus on what the parties might have in common – values, goals and so on – and to ignore differences since these are harder to deal with. The potential problems here are that the assumption of common values or goals may have been framed by the parties with the stronger agenda-setting power while other parties may not truly subscribe to them. A second area of difficulty arises where an ethos of equality within, say, a team of co-workers or a partnership between organisations masks fundamental differences of power and resources. This may produce premature trust on the part of those with little power. It may also result in a lack of attention to issues of partnership working on the part of those with more power. The history of relations between the voluntary and statutory sector is littered with such examples.

Symbols, myths and the struggle for legitimacy

Trust is grounded in the relationships in which it is formed and developed. Such relationships may be personal (for example, those between members of a team), impersonal (for example, market relationships), or symbolic (most forms of relationship between state and citizen). But each involves issues of equality and inequality: of resources, of information, of status, of access to the use of coercive power, of social inclusion and exclusion. It is possible for trust to be sustained across inequalities of power, but only when the use of power is viewed as legitimate.

Information power enables social actors to make rational calculations about the trustworthiness or otherwise of others. However, the social relations of trust are only partly based on such calculative logics. Where direct information is not available, and often even where it is, trust may be based on myths, images, reputations and other symbolic constructions. An awareness of these symbolic elements of trust is important in exploring the claims for legitimacy on which trust is founded. Much of the struggle for legitimacy is concerned with constructing, appropriating or rewriting appropriate myths, images, language and history. The claims and counter-claims of political parties to be the legitimate inheritors to power depend on the manipulation of historical associations and images (as in the 'New Labour – New Danger' media campaign in the run-up to the 1997 election). In this sense, trust is manufactured through the construction or manipulation of images. Significant gaps between image and reality are hard to sustain, but images and myths are powerful constituents of reputation as the cornerstone of trust.

Here public institutions face major challenges. Trust between citizen and government declined through the 1980s and much of the 1990s, and this has framed concerns about the legitimacy and accountability of public bodies. A report by the Henley Centre Consultancy in 1997 suggested that far more people now have faith in famous brands such as Marks and Spencers or Kelloggs than in many British public institutions, including the church, the palace and the police as well as parliament and the press (*The Guardian*, 23 November 1997, p 19). The increased use of marketing techniques – by political parties, by public bodies and provider organisations – all indicate a desire to rebuild trust in public institutions. But it is evident that marketing techniques alone will not succeed unless they are accompanied by a transformation of the institutions themselves.

Conclusion

This chapter has drawn on the concepts of culture, diversity, power, inequality and legitimacy in tracing some of the dynamics of trust in different aspects of public management. If we map these concepts on to the analysis of the dynamics of change in each domain, some key focal points emerge (see Table 2). These focal points indicate critical junctures in the development of models of public management appropriate to the mixed economy of service provision. They also indicate important political agendas concerned with rebuilding or restoring the legitimacy of public institutions and public bodies.

Producing such maps with columns and boxes does of course give an illusion of neat, distinguishable categories. However, the social relations of trust are becoming more complex as different sets of relationships become overlaid on each other. Sometimes the desire to restore trust is based on a struggle to establish new patterns of identification and loyalty (within nations, within communities, within organisations), though the increasing fluidity of economic and social relations do not make this an easy task. Sometimes the desire to build trust results in an explosion of formalised mechanisms – specifications, contracts, charters, standards, inspection, audit and monitoring – though the cost of these is only just beginning to be fully recognised. These different forms – identification-based trust and contract-based trust – often interact in rather uncomfortable and mutually contradictory ways.

Concerns about the loss of trust lie at the core of changing relations between citizen and government, the interaction between civil service, ministers and parliament, and probity in public life. In each, the issue of legitimacy is central to the establishment of trust. The challenge of securing or re-establishing legitimacy following a period of uncertainty and mistrust is enormous. It cannot be accomplished through the manipulation of symbols alone, however powerful: it must involve realignments of the relationships of power – between citizen and state, between users and providers, between managers and workforce, between private forms of provision and public accountability. In each of the domains of action I have discussed, there are emerging questions of the

Table 2: Focal points for the dynamics of trust

	Diversity	Power	Legitimacy
Political dynamics	Changing patterns of identification and questions of 'representation'	Issues of inequality and social exclusion	Accountability, stewardship and probity Managing political risk
Service dynamics	Responding to the diversity of user needs and interests	Changing the balance of power between user and producers	Balancing multiple legitimations: customers, stakeholders and citizens
	Balancing market responses to diversity (niche markets) with planned responses to equality agendas	Building trust in users	
Management dynamics	Managing diverse workforce loyalties and allegiancies	Balancing empowerment and control Overcoming vicious circles of declining workforce–management trust	Balancing managerial leadership and political direction
Inter-organisational dynamics	Working with and through cultural differences	Developing responses to inequalities of power and information	Balancing vertical accountability (stewardship) with horizontal trust (efficiency) Managing financial risk

appropriate *balance* between multiple demands and interests in securing the legitimacy for action. What may be seen as legitimate by one set of stakeholders – such as funders – may be seen as deeply flawed by others.

All of this means that the development and analysis of trust are both challenging and important. The potency of trust derives from its role as a symbolic carrier of lost values, acting as a counter to economic individualism in the marketplace, to hierarchy within organisations, and to the effects of fragmentation across contractualised relationships. The idea of trust offers to restore value to an increasingly impoverished and calculative set of relationships between individuals and groups within the new managerial cultures of public institutions. Trust is at the same time a means of pursuing economic and efficiency goals, and a symbolic counter to business values and the power of economic rationality. But it is this polyvalence that leads to the problems of talking about trust in a coherent and consistent way. Its promiscuous use within widely different sets of discourses and institutions may lead to its potential impoverishment. The idea of trust may come to mean little more than a nostalgic gloss on representations of the past, or anticipatory excitement about an imagined future of harmonious communities in which cultural differences are transcended, and in which differences of power are are resolved. Short of this dream, the task of analysis must be developed in ways which address some of the very real issues arising in the dynamics of political and economic change.

Notes

[1]   I am drawing here on Lewicki and Bunker's (1996) identification of three types of trust which Andrew Coulson discussed and adapted in Chapter Two. In their classification, the three forms are calculus-based trust, knowledge-based trust and identification-based trust. These, the authors argue, form part of a continuum: relations of trust tend to begin with rational calculation, become stronger as personal knowledge is built up, and become embedded with the establishment of patterns of common identification. While this may indeed characterise many relationships, it is based on a model of interpersonal relationships – those of courtship and marriage – which cannot necessarily be applied to other forms of relationship.

[2]   I have deliberately focused on politics in terms of citizen–state relationships, rather than considering the relations of trust between politicians and civil servants, or members and officers, which are analysed extensively elsewhere.

Part Two

Trust within organisations

FOUR

Constructing trust at the top of local government

Simon Baddeley

The relationship between policy and administration is as nebulous in a way as the distinction between officer and member at that level. Whilst the definitions and the roles are very clear – Brian is a politician and I am an officer – we inhabit each other's worlds. Brian helps me to make the administrative systems work better – to be more accountable – and I can help the political wheels to go more smoothly. (School of Public Policy Video Archive, Clements and Brooks, 1995)

"The great benefit of trust is that it is efficient" (Walsh, 1995a, p 50). More significant in its application to the relationships described in this chapter is Walsh's point that the disruption of "traditional conventions underlying trust", especially the increasing unavailability of hierarchical authority creates the need to "build new bases for trust"(1995a, pp 130, 51). One of these is the public relationship of politicians and officers in local government. In private associations such as friendship, trust is expected to evolve. In government, electoral contingency and professional mobility bring different people together at short notice and require them to develop robust working partnerships. Furthermore, as local government adapts to new functions and different ways of working, a relationship confined to senior members and officers needs to be understood and diffused. Where Walsh has referred to 'building' new bases for trust I use the phrase 'constructing trust' and will show, in the words of practitioners, something of what it entails.

Politics, professionalism and management

John Stewart has suggested that between officers and members in local government "the formal rules and the real roles necessarily differ" and that:

> ... problems are built into the system because councillors and officers are cast for different roles and because they are drawn from different backgrounds. The councillor is to a degree the outsider drawn from outside the organisation, but yet in charge of it, directing it and at times changing it. The officer is to a degree the insider, a part of the organisation, appointed to it, carrying out its main business. (Stewart, 1994)

As well as role differences, there are differences in the *spirit* of political, professional and managerial activities. We have designed constitutional forms and adopted and evolved certain governmental principles which require politicians and officers to be scrupulous about observing their separation. When the Conservative statesman Rab Butler defined politics as "the art of the possible" – the title of his 1971 autobiography – it seems that he was really seeking to describe the art of *governing* which, as this chapter suggests, emerges in the mingling of political, professional and managerial activity exemplified by Butler's distinguished career. This is not to say that individuals are not able to play a variety of roles but that they work with others across the overlapping boundaries of distinct areas of value and practice – political, professional and managerial.

Thus, politics treated as a separate activity focuses on mobilising power to make or resist choices about how 'we' shall live, about how people with opposing values can share the same space without resorting to violence and, notwithstanding Churchill's preference for 'jaw-jaw' over 'war-war', about the legitimation of force to defend a polity. It is about the authoritative establishment of value, engaging people in debate about, for instance, the meaning of 'freedom', of 'health' and the definition of a 'good society'. It is also, notoriously, about the process of determining who gets what, when and where. Politics may also entail such things as defining community and maintaining public discourse. Unlike professionalism and management, politics can entertain dreams and acknowledge the role of happenstance in human affairs – Machiavelli's *fortunae* – as well as the paradox of unintended consequences observed by Weber.

Professionalism, while being no less able to elicit passion and enthusiasm, is altogether quieter than politics. It is associated with respect for scientific method, the eschewal of subjectivity and, in government, respect for the principle of political neutrality and the relative stability of a salaried career based on specialised training and accreditation, supervised by regulatory bodies which guarantee professional probity and expertise. Professionalism implies a disciplined competence based on qualification and, even within accountancy, moral inhibition about factoring cost into matters of value to the profession.

In contrast, management in government emphasises the belief that state administration must be audited, analysed and made accountable. While its focus is on efficiency and effectiveness in the spending, monitoring and saving of public money, it is not embarrassed by the process of *making* money for government. Claiming to be outside politics, management theory encompasses ideas about leadership, motivation, organisation, personality and government itself. It is an ideology pretending not to be, valuing pragmatism as an end as well as a means. It offers tools appropriate to purposes and values formulated elsewhere, its practitioners being "able to move across disciplines unencumbered by any baggage of substantive commitments to a service or a policy" (Laffin and Young, 1990, p 110). Nonetheless the especial value of managerialism lies in its relentless optimism – some would say faith – that anything and everything *can* be managed.

Local government, often referred to as a 'political–management system', can also be observed as a political–managerial–professional complex in which individuals interact across boundaries created by our understanding of good government. Against a background of relationships between agencies, this chapter focuses on a foreground in which individual politicians and officers have developed ways of working with one another across these artificial boundaries.

Methodology for exploring trust

To assist in gaining a deeper understanding of the qualities and skills exercised within these interactions, I have, since the 1970s, used video interviews to immerse students in conversations that go on between politicians and officers. My teaching has focused on understanding skills and values exercised at the point where officers and politicians interact (Baddeley and James, 1987a; 1987b; 1991; Baddeley, 1989; 1992; 1997).

Video is well suited to showing both the verbal and non-verbal dimensions of these interactions. While it has no privileged capacity to elicit candour, it does provide practitioners, willing to talk to me and with one another about how they work, with a richer descriptive brush. For the sake of my reputation and that of the University of Birmingham, I have been assiduous about ensuring that my video material is made and used with interviewees' approval and then solely for research and teaching. Interviews lasting about an hour explore the following questions:

- In what circumstances did you begin to work together? How did you each approach the relationship and what expectations did each of you have of it?
- What are the practicalities of the relationship? How do you keep in touch with each other?
- What is the purpose of your relationship? How do you each involve the other in a developing initiative?
- How does your relationship fit in with the other relationships you each have with your own colleagues and with one another's? Are there tensions and how do you deal with them?
- What do you each regard as your greatest joint successes? Have there been any occasions when the relationship didn't work so well?
- What qualities in the other has contributed to the success of the relationship?

The nature of the largely unwritten contract and the guarantees it contains of good faith between me as a representative of the University and the interviewees is vital. They are entrusting their performance, at a moment in time, to a medium where it can be submitted to interrogation over years. A form of trust is sought between researcher, interviewee and student which extends to the transcripts used in this chapter.* Prior to interviews I remind people that I am not seeking to discover anything they do not want to tell me and that the purpose of the video is to record the understandings and explanations that they *want* to share.

The preferred setting for learning from these videos is one where students sit in front of the television and video recorder making use of forward, review and stop-frame and where, on occasion, they may be joined in their discussions by the individuals they have been watching on video. Time codes on each tape allow reference to different parts of the interview.

A continuing debate about interview method and the representation and analysis of conversational interaction influences my enquiries (Chamberlayne and King, 1996; Dunbar, 1996; Reason and Rowan, 1981; Tannen, 1984). As text rather than video, some aspects of conversation – especially the non-verbal dimension – are inevitably filtered out, but the transcripts which follow still have much to tell about officer–member working relations.

Trust, intimacy and friendship

Where, as in local government, there is an elected political leadership served by salaried managers and professionals, the concept of the separation of the political and the executive and the ideal of the politically neutral officer are engrained in Book One of Civics. What this seems to mean is that relationships in government between politicians and officers should be formal and strictly functional. Speaking of Italian local government one observer writes that:

> ... a personal relationship of trust with the political leadership is not possible; if it existed, it would be in contrast with the articles of the constitution relating to administrative impartiality. (Rolla, in Batley and Campbell, 1992, p 67)

This is a view entrenched in much casual understanding of local government and it is sustained by the formal recommendations of the many UK codes of practice on member–officer relations.[1] On the other hand the Chief Executive of Birmingham suggested to me that:

> ML: Where authorities work well very often one of the important factors is that there is a good close relationship between the Leader and Chief Executive. An actual change in Leader can actually be more profound than changes in political groups.... (Video Archive, Stewart and Lyons, 1995)

My informants constantly describe trust between members and officers as fundamental:

> RB: I'd like to start with one word and that's called 'trust'. I think a place like Birmingham exists – in terms of its financial advice and its acceptance of advice on trust.... (Video Archive, Burton and Baddeley, 1994)

TS: I trust Michael completely otherwise it wouldn't work.
(Video Archive, Stewart and Lyons, 1995)

SP: It is absolutely fundamental to the success of the
organisation – because if you don't trust each other and if
you don't build up that trust fairly quickly – you have to
earn his trust. (Video Archive, Orton and Pierce, 1994)

DR: It comes back to some of the things that we said before.
Things like trust, confidence, loyalty, respect. (Video Archive,
Robson and Smith, 1993)

BH: And it comes down to personal credibility I suppose
and the degree of trust that exists between an officer and a
member. (Video Archive, Baguley and Hewlett, 1992)

JB: I am answerable for the organisation but if you want to
make an organisation work well it has to trust you as well
as be trusted by you and Brian has to carry the trust of ...
political colleagues. (Video Archive, Clements and Brooks,
1995)

Interviewees speak of being driven "closer and closer together" (DT), to
knowing "each other warts and all" (PK), to having "this very very regular
and intimate and informal contact" (RT), supporting such observations with
supplementary tone and gesture. Here a chair of social services says:

What I absolutely know about the relationship between a
chief officer and a chair – or certainly me and any chief
officer I might have – is if I didn't like them personally I
would have a great deal of trouble working with them. I
would find it almost impossible. (Video Archive, Brook
and Evans, 1997)

'Liking' and 'friendship' are terms used openly and frequently to describe
public governmental relationships. Yet no text or code on the conduct
of member–officer relationship *recommends* the presence of such conditions
– rather the opposite. Sociologists studying friendship in contrast to
more formal and functional relationships (Duck, 1977; 1994; Eisenstadt
and Roniger, 1984, p 5; Leyton, 1974) have picked up a widespread
distinction between 'kin' relations – which can include friendship, love

and liking – and 'anti-kinship' relations which reflects "the horror of nepotism that once held together a part of the British flag of empire" and is held by some "to distinguish between 'developed' and 'underdeveloped' countries" (Wallman, in Leyton, 1974, pp 111, 112). In much of the rest of Europe it appears more acceptable to mingle political, managerial and professional skills at the point where legal executive powers exist (Batley and Campbell, 1992). Until and unless we innovate, the nearest Britain comes to this is in "the non-statutory partnership between the council leader and the chief executive" (Norton, 1992, p 37). Norton's interviews with chief executives led him to observe that:

> **The most intimate responsibility of a chief executive in decision formation is that to the council leader. (Norton, 1992, p 37)**

Roger Taylor, when Chief Executive of Birmingham, described his relationship with the Council Leader, Sir Richard Knowles:

> **RT: ... it's so important to have this very very regular and intimate and informal contact. You can't pick that up if you just have a series of formal meetings about particular issues. So it's very very important for me – with all the political parties on the city council – to have a very very comprehensive understanding of what's happening within them, where their policies are taking them, particularly with the controlling group, what ever party that is, that understanding their policies, the nuances, the shifts, the way in which the shifts in power are influencing the development of that policy is very important and that's what I pick up from being able to have this easy relationship with Dick all the time. (Video Archive, Knowles and Taylor, 1994)**

Jim Brooks' phrase "we inhabit each other's worlds" – which introduced the chapter exemplifies such intimacy, as do his remarks about discussing policy with his Leader:

> **... we just put something in between us and talk round it, and provided it seems to hold up then we proceed, and I think sometimes we need to give each other cover or a sense of comfort on it. (Video Archive, Clements and Brooks, 1995)**

Something similar is being suggested by Patricia Kirwan, Westminster's Chairman of Housing who, not long after telling me this, was among those who gave up the local party whip and made a formal complaint about the conduct of her Leader, Lady Shirley Porter:

> **You have something written. You've got to talk to somebody. You've got to have a drink with somebody. You've got to sit down and discuss things with them. You've got to know each other warts and all.** (Video Archive, Kirwan and Baddeley, 1987)

Sylvie Pierce described her first lesson from the Leader, Mike Orton, when she was appointed Chief Executive at Reading, as:

> **... indelibly imprinted on my heart really ... you might not have said it, but I think you did – which was Mike saying to me that – em – we had to work very very closely together and that I would need to know what he was thinking before he thought it and – er – which left me in a state of kind of – oh – I don't think I've been like that with anybody.** (Video Archive, Orton and Pierce, 1994)

Observing this sample of many similar observations spoken for public consumption and, in most cases, when both parties to the relationship were in conversation, I am aware of how they parallel observations made by Andrew Wall in the next chapter about chair–chief executive relations in the NHS. There he refers to people talking like partners to a marriage. In similar mode, the Leader of Durham County Council speaks of his relationship with his Chief Executive, Kingsley Smith:

> **DR: ... throughout the 28 years I have been a councillor I have never crossed the rubicon in the sense that I ever became personally friendly with anyone, because I felt that there were times, and there are times, when I have to be very strong and very hard in relation to misperformance or misdirection ... I never wanted ever to be friendly with a person in that sense, and I've done that right the way through. But as the project developed and the relationship with Kingsley has developed I've found that that has gone in the one instance of all the people I've met, and I see**

Kingsley not as an officer working for me or working to the direction of the political party, but someone who really believes in the same things that I want to achieve for the people I represent, and therefore I say now that he is a friend, but he knows as well as I do that because of the relationship it could only have become that because we speak very frankly to each other and very openly and therefore we do disagree and when we disagree there has to be someone who makes the decision and – that's worked out. (Video Archive, Robson and Smith, 1993)

There is a pause before the last phrase – "that's worked out". Kingsley joins in:

KS: No pet lips afterwards I think –

DR: No that's it.

KS: We frankly talk and we may disagree, the decision's taken. You get on with the business. You know? I mean the partnership is too important. What we're trying to achieve is far too important to let little things like that in the way, but the personal relationships wouldn't allow it anyway. How you build it up over a period of time –

This prompts Don Robson to point out, as an example of their relationship, that:

DR: ... he's a Sunderland supporter; I'm a Newcastle supporter. Can you believe it – and we're friends? I mean that – that more or less explains everything and every Monday morning if Newcastle's won he gets some stick. If – if Sunderland have won – well I don't go in till 11 o'clock. But I mean that's the sort of relationship –

KS: Fortunately we see eye to eye on the cricket. (Video Archive, Robson and Smith, 1993)

The leadership of Durham County Council by Councillor Don Robson and his Chief Executive, Kingsley Smith, has never been impugned on grounds of probity, yet these extracts can raise eyebrows. They would be challenged by observers seeking a clearer separation of the roles of officers and members, conscious that one person's idea of collaboration might be another's idea of impropriety. Yet over and over again, though each relationship is unique – itself a circumstance which opposes the idea of a formal codifiable arrangement – interviewees refer to elements which draw on the energies of friendship and the vitality of interpersonal trust. Yet Don Robson doesn't mince words in describing the conditionality of his friendship with Kingsley. Closeness does not preclude a grasp of the need for boundaries. It is just that they are hardly the coded ones.

Public relationships with private features

In an introduction to a collection of essays on Foucault called *Studies in governmentality* Burchell et al argue that "The sense and object of governmental acts do not fall from the sky or emerge ready formed from social practice. They are things which have had to be ... invented." (Burchell et al, 1991, p x). The relationship between a politician and an officer is a focus for the invention of government. Churchill said "the English never draw a line without blurring it" and what has struck me when demonstrating these dialogues to students is that the individuals in these relationships have successfully overcome the misunderstanding and possible tensions associated with their required role separation. They appear to have done it by being open to friendship, to the enjoyment of the relationship, while being able to avoid the imputation of cosiness or, more serious, impropriety. These are not private relationships being discussed in public – where the main accountabilities are to the parties within the relationship – but public relationships being discussed in public where public responsibilities attach both to the individuals and to the relationship. Nor is this a question of peeking at the private space of public figures. We are observing people involved in making government work. Though we can surmise that we are seeing that aspect of the relationship which the parties to it wish to show an interviewer they trust, they are content to have others observe at some length – hardly a brief public relations photo-call – the closeness of their relationship. This in itself seems an act of trust.

These are not friendships enjoyed for their own sake but relationships of government in which salaried officers responsible for leading large staffs are working with elected politicians accountable to the public for their policies and the budgets attached to them. If boundaries are crossed there is an implication that an idea of good government is at risk – that politicians and officers must maintain differentiated roles and different spheres of activity – yet the individuals in these relationships constantly refer to the overlapping of activities, indeed to repeat Jim Brooks' (1995) phrase, they seek to "inhabit each other's worlds".

Ken Newton, in his study of member–officer relationships in Birmingham, quoted a practitioner saying that "a good officer should be like a good politician and a good politician should be like a good officer" (Newton, 1976, p 160). I suggest that trust provides the medium within which this contradiction is resolved and that trust between a politician and an officer – meeting each other from different subjective worlds separated by invented boundaries – is where government is being invented.

Such relationships are close yet open, intimate but distanced, public and private. They observe constitutional proprieties yet benefit from the energies of friendship. They balance inclusivity and exclusivity. And it is for this reason that people may be alert to the associated dangers. If this is a relationship which makes government, it is also one which can unmake it. Pervasive mistrust of government prompted the work of Lord Nolan. Within a trusting relationship, as opposed to a tightly specified contract between parties, it is by definition easy to betray that trust. It is possible to betray it within the relationship and it is possible for the parties to the relationship to betray those the relationship serves. This is why the Prisoner's Dilemma is so intriguing and useful to game theorists seeking a pure logic of trust. Trust has a morally dæmonic quality in that it is also vital to a relationship that involves improper conduct. You are seldom so intimate with another person as when you collude with them in an agreed dishonesty, being bonded by your share in the consequences of having your wrong-doing uncovered. Theologians know that evil resides closest to virtue. The hazard of these relationships is that probity and corruption are proximate rather than polar.

Trust in the work of government: "the growing grey area"

Trust is important in government because it impossible to do the work of government without mingling politics, professionalism and management. It literally demands intimate working relationships between politicians and officers. David Blunkett, when Leader of Sheffield, spoke over 18 years ago of "a growing grey area" where it is difficult to have:

... any clear-cut idea that there are two separate groups, the politicians who get on with formulation and direction of policy and officers who are aloof from this, who have nothing to do with the political arena and actually get on with implementation. Both officers and members know that isn't true and that officers are inherently involved in the formulation of policy because of the nature of information-giving that they are very deeply involved in. (Video Archive, Blunkett, 1980)

Michael Lyons, Chief Executive of Birmingham, and the Leader of Birmingham, Councillor Theresa Stewart, expand on this:

ML: ... the truth is that it's very difficult to actually map out where the boundaries lie ... I'm quite clear that the process for making decisions on behalf of the council lies with the elected members and the leader manages that process. I'm equally clear that officers who are worth their salt do try to help the controlling group of the day – to give shape to their policy aspirations and to deliver.... If you get officers standing back from that then you get bad policy, so there is a dialogue not only at an early stage but at a continuing stage, because you're always reviewing what you're doing. It's not just that once you've got the policy – its set up and off we go. So I think my job here is to be a resource at all stages in the policy process – I do think there is some challenge there as well which is –

TS: Very important.

ML: – is a bit of a tension in the relationship. Perhaps in a minute we might come on to talk about the party politics of this because I do see that as being a delicate matter but actually an area in which we have some fairly clear idea of where officers stop and members – and that's wholly the territory of members, but again it's not easy to define the boundaries.

TS: It *is* very difficult. Policy and management. Sometimes I talk to the chief executive about management – a bit apologetically sometimes. Well yes it impinges on the role of the councillor and the direction of the council and council services delivery. It isn't straightforward. It isn't clear cut. It isn't that I have this pile of policies that are at my side of the table and he's at his side either receiving them or saying well we'll take this this way or that way. Because it is an exchange.... (Video Archive, Stewart and Lyons, 1995)

The reiterated point here is that things are not clear cut. The codes of conduct require a strict observance of constitutional propriety, but the actual working of government means this cannot be guaranteed by the strict observance of separate roles nor is it likely to be a process whose probity could easily be audited. In these circumstances it is not surprising that the gap between the sounding of alarm bells about conduct in Westminster City Council and the announcement of improper conduct was over five years. There are still those – who are not partisan for or against the accused individuals – who would say the auditor's announcement about gerrymandering was premature, so difficult is it to separate close and acceptable relationships from close and unacceptable ones. Thus although, as Alan Norton observes, neither the leader–chief executive nor the chair–chief officer relationship are executive relationships in British local government, there are, following "broad committee decisions":

ML: ... matters of detail which need to be sorted out which in practice – whether or not they are formally delegated to officers – are in any authority tested out and that's where the Leader in particular has a very important part in actually giving a steer on issues even if they're delegated – even if the framework's been set up by committee, so there is actually an executive element to it. I don't want to overstress that and – it isn't fully recognised by the legislation – but that's the only way the place is working and indeed in an increasingly complex fast moving society it is the only way that you're not constantly having to go back and revise the frameworks.... (Video Archive, Stewart and Lyons, 1995)

What is invaluable to the politician is to be able to clarify instantly the truth of what resources are or are not available. No time is spent verifying the truth of what the chief executive is saying. The politician trusts the officer. The officer need waste no time producing evidence. That now and then they may expect to go through the ordeal of committee interrogation may be valued as an opportunity to compile accountable material and have that basic trust tested more publicly. These exchanges are all about linking the expertise contained within the professions to public purposes and audiences. Thus a treasurer deals with one of the most complex areas of knowledge relating to an authority's freedom to make policy. It is through the treasurer that professional knowledge, continually topped up with more understanding about what public finance is about, feeds via that treasurer's exchanges with a leader or chair of policy and resources or finance into political space. What makes trust so vital is the potential for confusion, obfuscation and deception in an exchange which requires such economy in the flow of information between expert and non-expert:

> **RB: a place like Birmingham exists – in terms of its financial advice and its acceptance of advice on *trust* which means as chief financial officer I've got to build up that trust – and that means that members are prepared to accept that what I say to them is actually how it is. There's a lot of questioning goes on – but I think if members didn't have the trust in the advice and information that I'm providing them with we would fall apart financially. We would not be able to cope with the complexities. (Video Archive, Burton and Baddeley, 1994)**

Trust, though it is not, as we shall see later, as unconditional as may appear from these words alone, is the 'royal highway' to information flow between politician and officer. Expert knowledge is transferred and applied to the world through regular conversation. Derek Thomas, Chief Executive of Surrey County Council, talks about the way he worked with his Leader, Douglas Robertson:

> **DT: Douglas clearly wanted to understand finance without becoming the treasurer and I think I had to try and understand the political nuances without becoming a politician and these were the things that I think drove us closer and closer together ... one of the things I used to admire particularly about Douglas was his absolute mastery of the issues ... he could go into the group and he could describe the issues with the same degree of clarity that I would have expected of the County Treasurer, and ... that was a tribute to the way we were worked together. So he**

was thirsting for knowledge and wanting to understand
issues, not because he wanted to actually make the decisions
in a financial sense but in order to convert those into a
political dimension.

DR: It was an interesting discussion once I remember very
clearly where I told Derek that I had no wish to become an
apprentice County Treasurer and that my job was a different
one from his. That didn't stop me wanting all the briefing
he could sling at me and it had to be translated in a way
that I could translate it to a committee, or to the public for
that matter. (Video Archive, Robertson and Thomas, 1993)

The highest craft in the working of member–officer relationships is
exercised in hung or balanced authorities. Being hung or balanced is
difficult for everyone. It is a situation where the officer can take advantage
of the control they have over the flow of information between political
leaders and, almost equally problematic, where they can be suspected of
doing that. The officer rightly has a separate relationship of confidence
with the leaders of all the parties on the council which, of course, enables
the officer to frame the information they have in confidence from one
politician in discussing it with another. The members trust the officers
not to use this situation as a screen to sustain an officer agenda. Officers
hope members will, despite the tricky electoral mathematics, provide
them with the information about their intentions that officers need to
steer a politically determined course. In its absence they can be forced
into the exigency of having to risk the reproach of having made officer
policy – because there was no member policy. Trust is a critical lubricant
of this potentially tangled web. Jim Brooks observes that in Poole where
a Liberal Democrat administration has no overall majority:

JB: ... the decision about the actual strategic objective or
the vision that you're heading for isn't an officer's – but it
isn't the preserve of a single councillor or a single councillor
group. Generally speaking it's about some sort of shared
consensus, and so I think the role of a good management
team is to tease that out – is to help members to come to
that consensus view and then somehow express it in a way
that's accessible – that you can share. (Video Archive,
Clements and Brooks, 1995)

This idea of teasing out is repeated by John Metcalf, the majority group leader of Hertfordshire. He speaks of the problem in a hung council of getting predictability into the decision-making process rather than:

> **JM:** ... leaving it to an alliance at the last minute in the Council because not only does that make it difficult for us, it also, I think, makes it difficult for the officers and the structure of the Council, that they don't know early on what – which – decision is going to come out, which way to bend things, and so on. OK, on the whole, we've found them helpful and co-operative in trying to give an early indication of where – which – way we are going. (Video Archive, Briscoe, Gordon, Metcalf and White, 1994)

In what seems like a slip of the tongue we hear the politician praising the officers for trying to give an idea of where "we are going". In fact it is an accurate observation of the way the officers, having listened to the different leaders separately, can feed back an impression of the decisions on which all three parties are likely to agree prior to committee or full council. The craft of this brokerage role is described in an exchange between the Chief Executive and the Leader of Three Rivers, also a balanced council:

> **AR:** You will tell me some very confidential things at times. The problem ... is that I've got other leaders of political groups who do the same thing and part of the skill is to see where there are lines that can be drawn to together there – perhaps by me, either overtly or by subtly suggesting things, at the same time that as leaders you're each – you've got relationships and you may be picking up those cues anyway and you may not – to some extent I have to try and judge whether I think you are or not or whether there's a slight prod. The big danger is that a prod in certain directions – if it reveals that some of the confidences are in effect being betrayed. If it looks as though they are – then the whole pack of cards can come tumbling down....
>
> **AS:** But it was interesting because people always assume – or have heretofore always assumed – that a balanced council is a weak council and I've never felt that was necessarily the case and I think the last few years have convinced me that it isn't the case. It can give you a quite different range of strengths.

AR: If you pull together....

AS: Yes

AR: ... it can be very strong indeed....

AS: He'll only have to make one serious mistake and the
pack of cards comes tumbling down. (Video Archive, Shaw
and Robertson, 1995)

Being trusted by the leadership and everyone else

This process of making government involves another delicate balance
between the need to be seen as serving the whole council and the reality
of being expected, as an officer, to give special attention to the needs of
the majority party and within that majority the needs of a smaller ruling
group or even simply the leader. In the following conversation, member
and officer appear to be struggling over a difference created by a senior
officer's desire to communicate as widely as possible with members,
including the opposition, and a senior and ruling member's claim to
special attention:

> BH: – I've got to make sure that there's an opportunity for
> that [members' political views] to influence the shape and
> direction of the model that we come up with [for providing
> social services at Borough level].

> SBG: So your role would actually be facilitating and allowing
> that input to go in. Do you not think you put in some of it
> as well?

> BH: Yeah I do. Inevitably. Is anybody apolitical? The idea
> of an officer being totally professional and – I think it's
> hard. I think at the end of the day what I've got to recognise
> is that I've got to take account of your own wishes but also
> the wishes of the minority party –

> SBG: Hm

> BH: – em – who I think as – as you've said in previous

times could well be my future employers – em – but it also recognises from my point of view that no one group or one person has a monopoly of the ideas and as so often is the case if you can actually involve others in testing out your hypothesis – whatever – you can actually improve the model – em – and doing it by testing it out with other – other members from other political parties – em – may point towards areas where your particular model – your particular desires could be frustrated. [pause] Now the question I have then what do I share with you and what do I share with – with the other political party. And it comes down to personal credibility I suppose and the degree of trust that exists between an officer and a member –

SBG: hm

BH: And – em – it can be a little blurred but at the end of the day I think it does – it – you and I – our relationship is – is one of – two people recognising they're coming from different directions. And – and we know that we won't meet in *all* parts –

SBG: yuh

BH: but there – there's a lot of common ground. There will be a lot of common ground if I was to speak to the minority party spokesman on that issue as well and – but there would be differences and I suppose what – what I would be aiming to do is to highlight some of those differences – which I could bring out in discussions with you and with them –

SBG: Yes. I mean – I think it is right that – that oppositions have a chance to comment on things – and they do occasionally come up with good ideas. Not often, but I mean occasionally – you see I can make a joke about it and you laugh but you don't – no – yes all right – yes, but I think – I think there is – there are times when there would be something said and I think this –

BH: yeah

> SBG: – is what we would need to work on, when I would
> need to say to you "This has got to be kept within a certain
> framework."

> BH: Yup

> SBG: And that means the majority party, maybe even the
> leader and myself and perhaps one other committee
> chairman, and – and to keep it tight for those very reasons
> I would need you to accept that without – almost without
> questioning in a way. (Video Archive, Baguley and Hewlett,
> 1992)

The codes of conduct do not mention, or at best gloss over, this aspect of
member–officer working. Yet it can put a special burden on the officer
trying to maintain a trust based on a reputation for delivering objective
professional knowledge to councillors – as required by the 'rules' – while
maintaining a special loyalty to the political leader. Roger Burton, a
Birmingham Treasurer, was quoted earlier saying that "a place like
Birmingham exists in terms of its financial advice and its acceptance of
advice on trust" (Video Archive, Burton and Baddeley, 1994). If he says
something is true he *must* be believed or the whole system falters. Yet
during the same interview he talks about his relationship with the Leader
of the Council:

> RB: ... you also sometimes have to protect the leader....
> Because of the enormous pressure the leader is under
> occasionally they may say something they regret, or give a
> promise they regret, and you have to try and help them get
> out of it. And sometimes, just sometimes, to go a little bit
> back on what I said, you have to be slightly economical
> with the truth and not actually talk about some of the issues
> ... within the wider group or even the group executive.
> And there are one or two things that are done just, if you
> like, with the leader which are all done for ... good sound
> reasons and that's where you're back to political sensitivity.
> Within that group executive there are a number of individuals
> who've actually got their own agendas. And again I'm not
> saying I've got the utmost political skill but it is important
> for me to know some of those agendas and some of the
> areas where it's very difficult to be able to discuss in what I

**would say is an honest and up-front manner where you
actually have to do one or two things with the leader a little
bit behind the scenes. (Video Archive, Burton and Baddeley,
1994)**

This need to have a differential level of trust with different people around
you is not unusual but it seems to contradict the definition of trust. In
fact, similar dilemmas occur in families where trust between spouses or
between parent and child can be compromised if one or other family
member asks for a confidence to be preserved from any of the others. To
agree to such confidence is to collude in excluding the other member or
members of the family from what has been revealed in confidence to
one of them. To reveal to those excluded what was proffered in confidence
in the hope of maintaining trust with *them* is to breach trust with the
confidante. The constant negotiation of this moral minefield is part of
life and certainly part of government. An additional layer of complexity
is added to these circumstances by the fact that in families, as indeed in
government, many people recognise the presence of these dynamics and
may actually impart 'in confidence', as in the Three Rivers example,
something intended to be passed on. A process of negotiation is occurring
where one person appears to be trusting another to risk being
untrustworthy. The novelist Iain McEwan describes public figures who
move around in this moral maze by navigating the complicated channels
that run between truth and lying:

> **... with sure instincts while retaining a large measure of
> dignity. Only occasionally, as a consequence of tactical error,
> was it necessary to lie significantly, or tell an important
> truth. Mostly it was sure-footed scampering between the
> two extremes. Wasn't the interior life much the same?
> (McEwan, 1988, p 182)**

McEwan captures the moral nimbleness that accompanies grown-up
behaviour – public and private – where corruption and probity are
proximate rather than polar and the process of retaining integrity requires
wit[2] and where rules at best are casuistical. The persistence of the
presumption that politically neutral officers implement policies
determined by elected members suggests it has moral importance in the
way government should be conducted. It is over 150 years since the
Northcote–Trevelyan Report marked a determination to use appointment

by competitive exam to create a cadre of civil expertise not dependent on the patronage of the latest elected leadership. The preservation of officers' political neutrality was a concern of the Widdicombe Committee on the Conduct of Local Authority Business (1986) and a decade later the Nolan Committee on Standards in Public Life has been exploring the effectiveness of codes of practice as these protect the separate roles of councillors and officers. Yet within government, even as the value of the ideal is affirmed, a different reality is acknowledged and approved. Though it was caricatured as such in the relationship of Jim Hacker and Sir Humphrey Appleby in the BBC comedy *Yes Minister,* the imputation that any relationship which does not preserve strict boundaries therefore harbours duplicity is simplistic.

Conclusion

At the core of the political–management relationship is a dilemma of government. What are the interpersonal dimensions of these moments at Weber's "profound source of tension" between politics and bureaucracy (Giddens, 1972) when a priori aspirations from political space meet or cross a posteriori data unearthed in professional space? How does the impartial serve the partial? How do professed values serve a process that *makes* values? If politics is the authoritative establishment of value, this might be one of the places where this *establishing* occurs. I am certainly aware that when I sit with students, looking at how two people talk with each other, my tutorial work is immersive, imparting nous about government by osmosis rather than via the political cribs criticised by Oakeshott (1962, p 129).

The conversations studied add to understanding of how the personal and the constitutional interact – how, for instance, conversations between individuals may extrapolate a relationship of trust between individuals to an organisation and even a government.[3] Each relationship, like a marriage, has unique *and* universal features. Foucault's (1978) term 'governmentality' referred to the possibility of *inventing* government in ourselves, in our families and other associations as well as in the nation or internationally. This chapter has explored how government is being made in conversations between politicians and officers and the part of trust in that process. These are public relationships involving the actual exercise and symbolic representation of authority and they contain, observably and reportedly, such private features as friendship, conviviality, calculative and emotional trust – in Coulson's phrase 'instinctive trust' (see Chapter Two, p 11) – which spill into the public sphere. They are interpersonal relationships but they occur in the context of relationships between supposedly discrete activity – political, managerial and professional. The existence of codes of practice is evidence of a widespread sense that it is important to define and regulate them. On the other hand, as with other relationships, each is unique – in terms of the personalities involved and the chemistry of their association.

> **JH: You can't have a standard model for a relationship between a chief executive and a leader. It's really about two personalities and the driving forces.... (Video Archive, Ball and Hehir, 1994)**

Dr Johnson suggested it was impossible to "tell the precise moment when friendship is formed. As in filling a vessel drop by drop, there is at last a drop which makes it run over ..." (Boswell, 1976, p 849). As with friendship, so with making government, there is a moment in a conversation between a politician and an officer when something crystallises. What was hitherto absent, impractical or bizarre is conjured into reality. I am not talking about the moment when an idea becomes formally recognised as policy but of the interpersonal events prior to that, when understandings were arrived at in the juncture of politics, professionalism and management. Such principles as 'habeas corpus' or 'ultra vires' or the 'age of consent' had such moments – as would their dissolution. The emergence or submergence of such principles, perhaps via intense resistance, into conditional support and then 'common sense', occurs in intimate conversation between people occupying different spaces. By constructing trust across the boundaries between them, these relationships, as various and as conventional as marriage, make government possible.

Notes

[1] For example, Birmingham City Council (1995) *A protocol for member/officer relations*; City of Westminster (1995) *Charter for partnership between members and officers*; Local Government Management Board (1995) *Code of conduct for local government employees*; Northampton Borough Council (1993) *Guideline for member –employee relations*. On behalf of the Nolan Committee, Sir William Utting wanted to be sure that adherence to these codes was a "living reality", *Local Government Chronicle* 'Nolan to probe conduct codes', 10 November 1995.

[2] In 1966, in *A man for all seasons*, Robert Bolt put these words in the mouth of Sir Thomas More as he tried to explain to his daughter, Margaret, why he would try to sign an opportunistic legal document to save himself: "Listen Meg. God made the angels to show him splendour as he made animals for innocence and plants for their simplicity, but man he made to serve him wittily in the tangle of his mind. If he suffers us to come to such a case that there is no escaping, then we may stand to our tackle as best we can.... But it's God's part, not our own, to bring ourselves to such a pass. Our natural business lies in escaping. If I can take this oath I will."

[3] On the other hand, Stewart (in Batley and Campbell, 1992, p 8) sees current political–management arrangements in the UK clouding "the reality of political control", blocking public learning about how government works.

[*] Transcripts in this chapter should not be copied or quoted without respect for the contract between interviewer and interviewees that this material was made for teaching and research. Except where another name is given, video interviews were by Simon Baddeley. Enquiries should be made to him at 0121 414 4999 or s.j.baddeley@bham.ac.uk

School of Public Policy Video Archive

Councillor Sheila Baguley, Chair Leisure Services, Ipswich Borough Council and Bill Hewlett, Group Manager, Housing/Social Need 1992.

Councillor David Ball, Leader of Ipswich Borough Council and James Hehir, Chief Executive 1994.

Councillor David Blunkett, Leader of Sheffield City Council 1980.

Brian Briscoe, Chief Executive of Hertfordshire County Council, Councillors Robert Gordon, John Metcalf and Chris White 1994.

Councillor Eve Brook, Chair of Social Services, Birmingham City Council and Richard Evans, Director 1997.

Roger Burton, Director of Finance, Birmingham City Council 1994.

Councillor Brian Clements, Leader of Poole Borough Council and Jim Brooks, Chief Executive 1995.

Councillor Patricia Kirwan, Chairman of Housing, Westminster City Council 1987.

Councillor Sir Richard Knowles, Leader of Birmingham City Council and Roger Taylor, Chief Executive 1994.

Councillor Mike Orton, Leader of Reading Borough Council and Sylvie Pierce, Chief Executive 1994.

Councillor Douglas Robertson, Leader of Surrey County Council and Derek Thomas, Chief Executive 1993.

Councillor Don Robson, Leader of Durham County Council and Kingsley Smith, Chief Executive, interviewed by Chris Game 1993.

Councillor Anne Shaw, Leader of Three Rivers District Council and Alistair Robertson, Chief Executive 1995.

Councillor Theresa Stewart, Leader of Birmingham City Council and Michael Lyons, Chief Executive 1995.

FIVE

Chair–chief executive relationships in the National Health Service

Andrew Wall and Simon Baddeley

Introduction

Following the legislative changes of 1990, the management of the National Health Service at local level is in the hands of two types of organisation: health authorities responsible for commissioning and purchasing health services for given populations, and the providers, NHS trusts, whose size and budgets vary widely. Both types of organisation are managed in a similar manner, with boards comprising executive and non-executive members, headed by a chairman and a chief executive.

In contrast to local government, the chairman is not elected and in no formal way has constituents. He or she is in effect appointed by the Secretary of State for Health and serves for a limited period. The chief executive may already be in post when a new chairman arrives. The chairman will only be involved in choosing a chief executive if the incumbent moves on for career reasons or if the relationship between the two of them breaks down.

The genesis of the chair–chief executive relationship is therefore somewhat arbitrary. How do they then achieve a good working relationship? Functional analysis of the roles only goes a little way in exploring the relationship particularly as it appears that there is a considerable overlap of duties.

We were interested in exploring those elements of the relationship which were less explicit and those that described the experience in the relationships as much as the duties attached to the roles. Using video, in a similar manner as the local authority interviews described by Baddeley in the previous chapter, ten couples discussed their relationships. Subsequent analysis has been undertaken in class by the couples themselves, others in similar positions, and more generally by health service managers and MBA students.

This chapter explores the issues which have arisen and attempts to offer insights into what makes for successful and trusting relationships in a public service which requires rigorous and resourceful management without the constraints of local political accountability.

Trust – the vital component

Ask a chairman or a chief executive in the NHS what they expect of each other and they will often say there should be no surprises: "We established very early on a no surprise rule," says Maureen,[1] a chief executive. It is clear that neither wishes to be caught out: the chair would suffer considerable loss of face and authority if he or she appeared not to be aware of some key issue in the running of the health authority or trust. The chief executive would feel cornered or embarrassed if the chair had, without checking first, given an undertaking which could not be honoured. The relationship is, it appears, finely balanced. And yet its genesis is almost wantonly arbitrary. Sometimes the two come together as in some arranged marriage but more often it is even less designed. Given this, can it ever work and, where it does, what is the vital component?

'Trust' is a word often used in our interviews with NHS chair–chief executive pairs; "Shared values enable a level of trust," (Alison and Kathy), "I was looking for someone I could trust"(Stuart). But its use may betray an underlying anxiety that, after all, this pair may not be able to trust each other. Given the history of this relationship in the NHS since 1991, when the new managerial arrangements came into force, it is not surprising that the couples should feel a little worried. An unprecedented number of chief executives have moved jobs, sometimes as a result of career advancement but often in an all too public breakdown of the relationship with their chair. And it is almost always the chief executive who goes rather than the chair.

The effect on the individuals concerned may be devastating as they face an early end to what was intended to be a life-time career, or at the very least they suffer the opprobrium which is always attached to such sudden departures. For the NHS the loss of these experienced senior people may well be debilitating in the example that it sets to all others in that organisation. Where anxiety spreads so does caution. Enterprise, imagination and courage wither in the face of this uncertainty. In a service under pressure from politics, from professional expectations and from shortage of resources, the last thing that is needed is constant change at the top leading to insecurity further down the managerial chain.

So how can this destructive scenario be avoided? What are the causes? It might be assumed that a breakdown in relationships at the highest level is due to dysfunctionality which could easily be corrected by a little more attention being paid to who does what. But functional analysis, even at a rudimentary level, shows that one of the principal characteristics of the NHS chair–chief executive relationship, is the large amount of overlap between them. Statements such as "The chair manages the board, the chief executive manages the organisation" are somewhat glib. Equally "The chair manages external relationships and the chief executive the internal" quickly comes to grief when it is revealed that the chief executive is far more likely to handle the press than the chair. Appearing in the media is, for most of the population, the manifestation of being in charge, and most chief executives are only too willing to make the most of their opportunities in this respect. Whether this is right is more debatable, especially as one of the few unique elements of the chair's role could be said to be handling political issues.[2]

Traditional analysis of roles in organisations only goes so far ("this post has these duties attached to it"). What is not so clear is what behaviours are attached to the roles and how these influence events. Are certain behaviours requisite for relationships to be successful and if so how do we discover what they are?

The interviews

Ten NHS chair–chief executive couples were chosen for interview. It must be stressed that they did not represent a random sample for the simple reason that their cooperation was only likely if they themselves saw their relationship as being successful and therefore appropriate to be viewed by strangers. The ensuing analysis suggested that there were elements of their relationship which were not as successful – whatever is meant by this term – as the participants believed; but at least they were not embarrassed sufficiently to refuse to take part. Nor did any of the ten ask for retakes or editing of any part of the video interview. It was part of the contract with the authors that the participants had an absolute right of approval as nothing would be gained by showing an unauthorised interview.

Of course, such selectivity had its own limitations. Surely we would learn more about the nature of the relationship by studying casualties rather than successes? Divorces must always be more interesting than happy marriages. Pathology is intriguing, being well is just boring. This may be true to a point, but the very sensationalism attached to ruptured relationships can also obscure other interesting aspects. Claims of unreasonable behaviour do not define what is reasonable and that, in this case, seemed worthy of discovery.

Despite the biased nature of the selection, the sample was not unrepresentative. The couples were examples of the following:

- three health authorities, seven trusts;
- acute, community, specialist trusts;
- male/male; male/female; female/male; female/female couples;
- new and established couples;
- chairs with explicit political affiliations and those without;
- chairs with business, managerial, professional and voluntary service backgrounds;
- chief executive backgrounds were predominately NHS managers but one came from a local authority and one was originally a nurse.

The process of the interviews was similar to that used with the local authority leaders and chief executives. Each couple was sounded out by Andrew Wall, after which those who had agreed were interviewed by one of us at the University television studio. Before arriving they were sent the broad questions they would be asked. These were:

- When did you two first meet?
- When did you start working together in this capacity?
- How do you organise your work together?
- How does your relationship fit in with the rest of the board and more widely with the organisation?
- How do you deal with differences between you?
- What do you regard as your greatest success?
- What is the most important thing that has contributed to the success of your relationship?

Several of the couples reported that the discussion in the car on the way to the studio had been a valuable and, for some of them, a new opportunity to look at how they worked together. They had, it seemed, taken their relationship for granted. Once in the studio they were interviewed in as open a manner as possible, that is, the interviewer did not attempt to put them under pressure, although follow-up questions were used to explore interesting points. The use of camera shots from the three cameras was determined entirely by the studio director on his own judgement. The interviews lasted between 45 and 50 minutes, and there was no subsequent editing of the tapes.

The methodology has drawbacks. The very setting could be said to be constraining, with the couples on their best behaviour in an alien environment. One of the interviewers, Andrew Wall, was known by the couples and this might have influenced their responses. But the nature of the set-up could be said in some ways to reflect the sort of world these couples appear in; they are often performing as a duo on a public stage. It is also clear in looking at the tapes that the non-verbal relationships between the two are interesting and not necessarily contrived for the occasion – something which is difficult to do unless the subjects are professional actors used to representing a consistent persona.

The origins of the relationship

Since the inception of the NHS there has been an appointed chair at the head of the organisation responsible for running the component parts of the NHS. In the early days there were hospital management committees, with subsidiary house committees, regional hospital boards and executive councils. In 1974 these were superseded by area health authorities, family practitioner committees and regional health authorities. 1982 saw the demise of the area health authorities in favour of district health authorities but still with up to 19 members and served by an executive team headed, from 1984, by a district general manager. Such arrangements served some of the processes of democracy as the non-executive members were selected as representatives of various interests in the communities they served. Although one representative doctor and one nurse were full members of the authority board, the other managerial executives were officers to their boards.

This changed fundamentally in 1991 with the 1990 National Health Service and Community Care Act. Unitary boards were introduced with a balanced membership of executive and non-executive members usually 11 strong. The roles of the chair and chief executive altered. Whereas with a large district health authority, it had been relatively easy – and indeed sometimes absolutely necessary – to operate a divide-and-rule regime in order for any decisions to be made at board level, the new arrangements required a much more shared approach from each member of the board. Studies of board behaviour showed that some chairs and chief executives were more successful in handling this change of style than others. Some non-executives still complain that they see little of the action. Some executives still act as officers.

But however the boards work in practice, formally they are a more corporate body than before. This is clear, but what is much less so is the formal relationship between the chair and the chief executive. Descriptions of the chair's role exist, but they are generalised and excite rather more questions than they answer. So, for instance, when it is said that the chair leads the organisation, what does this mean? Leadership studies have shown that models of leadership are highly various. In this case there is a complication in that this very component is shared with the chief executive. So if inspiring the organisation with a set of values is part of leadership, whose values here predominate, the chair's or the chief executive's?

Negotiation is used to resolve such issues. But as we know by observation of any social exchange, negotiation takes place at various levels: explicitly through the exchange of words and ideas, more subtly through manipulation of those ideas by metaphor and emotion and additionally through physical demeanour, what we call body language.

The video interviews have proved a rich quarry for observing the relationships between chairs and chief executives at all these levels and it is this ability to reveal what is often felt but not so often discussed which has proved particularly valuable.

The explicit relationship

One of the fascinations of this study is its exploration of both public and private behaviours that are often interwoven in a manner which make unpicking them difficult. The public or explicit relationship relies heavily on convention. This puts the chair at the top of the organisational tree, with roles as set out in the DoH document mentioned above. They include:

- provides leadership to the board;
- enables all board members to make a full contribution to the board's affairs and ensure that board acts as a team;
- ensures that key and appropriate issues are discussed by the board in a timely manner.

The next paragraph says that "a complementary relationship between the chairman and the chief executive is important."

There is an assumption here that it is an easy matter to allocate functions to role. This sort of formality is endorsed by language and deference. In the interviews the chief executives in several instances referred to the chair by title rather than by their name. Interestingly one chief executive, Matthew, elaborated this formality by never referring to his chair except as "Chairman" or "Mr Hastings". Andrew Wall queried this with the chair, Paul Hastings, after the interview was over and Paul responded with a dry laugh saying he had been unable to change Matthew's custom in this respect and he added "He even does it when we are playing golf together!" What is going on here? It seems to us that Matthew is using formality to keep a distance between him and Paul, not because he believes in the sacrosanct nature of the convention that you do not address your boss intimately – a convention which might have been universal 40 or 50 years ago – but rather to protect himself. This is a common enough managerial dilemma: if you allow too much intimacy, you become vulnerable.

This example shows how a rational discussion on the roles of the two people quite fails to reveal what is going on. Our interpretation is that Matthew wished to hold himself at a distance from Paul so that he could keep his amour propre intact. He may require this at a later date, and to become too intimate with Paul could, if times got hard and disagreements arose, lead to a sense of personal loss and feelings of betrayal. Indeed subsequent events validated this view when both he and Paul were required to "fall upon their swords" when their Trust had severe financial problems. But Stuart, who subsequently faced prolonged press exposure on a rationing issue, made the point that the chief executive may need the chair for 'protection' against critics. We see here the delicacy of a relationship where the chair is seen both as the ultimate critic and also the protector against other critics. We also see the tension between the loyalty which is a characteristic of friendship and a formal accountability of the chief executive to the chair which is not.

Some may feel that such analysis is overblown and that there is little significance in these minor nuances of social interaction; we cannot agree. Everywhere apparent in these interviews is the significance of the subtext.

It is true, however, that some couples seemed to thrive more on an explicit relationship than others. Annabelle and Tony started their relationship with explicit expectations on both sides. A new health commission was being set up (subsequently this became a health authority) and Annabelle as chair had a list of attributes she wished to see in a chief executive:

> **... an open, participative style, not embodying the old command and control style ... very into talking to people, listening as well as delivering, and who had good process skills.**

All such lists tend to be utopian. But similarly Tony, a local authority chief officer looking for "more managerial space and discretion" than he had had in local government, also had other criteria: "continue to be in a change situation, not a maintenance job", a job that "would broaden me". He wanted a chair who would "respect and value me". The real turning point when he decided to go for the job was when he met Annabelle and found what he calls "an extra bonus", that her values were very similar to his. Here appeared to be the ideal conditions for an arranged marriage; Tony even brought a dowry with him, his knowledge of local government.

What was the longer-term effect of this designed attempt to match expectations? Were they disappointed in each other? Was it too rational, too contrived? Apparently not: they are still together four years later. The obvious advantage of this sort of care in matching each other's expectations is that it engenders a sense of mutual obligation, a sense of a contract between the two. But in case the coming together of these two seems too calculated, it is worth recording that when the veil was removed and they actually met, there was something extra: they also *liked* each other. Another chief executive, Kathy, agrees when she says simply of Alison, her chair "we like each other.... I bless the good fortune which brought us together".

Juliet and Sheila were much more instinctive in their coming together. Significant was that they were both women: "... it helped being women". Sheila describes their initial meetings as "... the business of chemistry ...

the chemistry was good almost immediately." Edwin also uses this word in describing why he was attracted to Jake rather than other candidates: "It's all about chemistry." Here there is not so much the matching of intellects as the uniting of common spirits.

Can we learn anything from these examples? Is the gradual and careful preparation displayed by Annabelle and Tony or the inspirational éclat described by Juliet and Sheila more likely to lead to success? The former seems more respectable in that there is a sense of seriousness and formality which, it might be said, should attach itself to these major jobs in the public sector. Surely the haphazard and more instinctive response displayed by Juliet and Sheila is rather wayward? Is it not more appropriate to have appointing procedures which seek to reduce personal preferences and prejudices to a minimum? Annabelle even went as far as using a head hunter and Tony explored several options before deciding on this one.

The counter argument is that if the organisation is to have any personality which separates it from other similar organisations it stems from the personal chemistry of these two top people. They set the values, they gather the enterprise, they motivate, they inspire and of course they also carry the can. Personality, energy, enthusiasm and excitement are what make an organisation a place where people want to work. Such characteristics give savour to life. It is noticeable that although several couples use this sort of language, the way they express it varies widely. Alison and Kathy are idealistic but their manner describing their enthusiasm is unenthusiastic and low key. In contrast Juliet and Sheila almost boil over with their eagerness. It is a truism that messages require the right medium.

What happens, however, when the volatility gets almost too much to handle and the rest of the organisation has to pick up the loose ends as the chair and chief executive run headlong after their current crazes? Roger and Elspeth could be said to represent this situation. Their responsibility was for services for people with learning disabilities (the trust has now been merged). Such institutions have been notorious for uninspired management and poor professional standards. But in the last 20 years, managers have often been able to make major changes in the way these services are provided without being encumbered, as they see it, with professional constraints. For Roger and Elspeth the situation was irresistible. As chair he saw the chance to inspire an organisation to a vision of giving rights to patients who had been denied common liberties for so many years. Elspeth was no less enthusiastic. But picking through the interstices of their narrative, we were left with uneasy feelings about how the rest of the organisation adapted to this charismatic approach. Consider the following from the perspective of another member of the board or the managerial team:

> **Roger: Because all management requires a metaphor ... the metaphor we have decided on is the litter principle 'whoever gets there first picks it up.' I was quite a culture shock in the organisation and I was taking on an executive role ... sometimes Elspeth was the chairman and I was the chief executive....**

One of the explicit purposes of the chair is to keep the chief executive in order, to ensure that he or she does not get too absorbed in internal and off-centre enthusiasms. Don, a chief executive of a large general hospital, had ambitions to make his hospital even bigger by absorbing another one in the city. But he acknowledged that it was only when Bill became the chair that he was able to make progress. From their interview we might assume this is because Bill tugs on Don's reins. Observe the following interchange:

> **Don: Bill and I achieved what I hadn't been able to achieve on my own ... er ... and also supporting me through what was a very difficult process because I had double the number of managers, double the number of executives I ...**
>
> **[Bill interrupts]: and the public consultation [reminding Don what he had given insufficient attention to.]**

But what happens if the chair does not, in the chief executive's eyes, keep the non-executives in order? Colin offered some mild criticism that Ewan had been unable to keep non-executives to consideration of strategic items particularly as the executives had worked hard at the preparation of the issues:

> **Colin: I was quite surprised that there was not more challenge of the fundamental direction of the strategy than the wording of it.**

But interestingly as soon as Colin says this he leans over backwards to find justification for the non-executive's interest in detail. This is an example of the way a chief executive tests the boundaries of his relationship with the chair. Ewan, for his part, caps Colin's remarks by pointing out that he and another non-executive had experience in the matter under discussion and were quite right to draw the detail out. Their relationship does not appear to suffer from this delicately poised spat.

Deeper into the relationship

At one level the interviews can be examined as straightforward accounts of what the two people say. But there is more going on than this when we consider the significance of the metaphors they use, their tone of voice, their body language. Metaphors say two things at once, what we say and what we mean. So when Don says Bill was " a dog with a bone" the image is both descriptive of Bill's tenacity and of Don's rather rueful response to Bill's tenacity. But metaphors can become tired and clichéd. Almost every discussion about these interviews likens the relationship to a marriage. Is this revealing or misleading? In that it suggests commitment, a contract, intimacy, it is useful. Furthermore it gives some sense of a framework for behaviour. Within a marriage, a wide range of behaviour can be tolerated without the marriage necessarily breaking down. This is a useful analogy and is broader than metaphors based on contract or consistent behaviour.

But the marriage metaphor also has its limitations in the area of intimacy. One of the fascinations of examining these interviews has been to explore potential gender differences: for instance, do women behave differently to men in these jobs? Without pursuing this question further it is worth at least asking whether sexual attraction has any place in the relationships. Here we are in some difficulty as it may be considered improper to expose our subjects to this sort of analysis; even if they were attracted to each other, this is not a matter for consideration by third parties. But this is an overscrupulous objection. All interpersonal relationships have some element of attraction and repulsion. What we are interested in is how this influences the relationship between the chairs and chief executives we interviewed.

In those cases where the two people are of the same sex we might assume that the enquiry is irrelevant unless either person was gay. But even in same sex relationships there may be gender-related behaviours. Tannen (1992) has pointed out that habitually men compete and women affiliate. Juliet and Sheila had been described to Andrew Wall before he met them as so well attuned that they were almost indistinguishable, "almost twin sisters". But the very closeness of this relationship, at least as perceived by others, might have a down-side in that it was too mutually dependent and self-contained. Without asking questions of their colleagues we can make no judgement on this, but it is worth emphasising that an obviously successful pairing may, because of its exclusivity, contain seeds of failure.

In Annabelle and Tony's case, although the genders are different, no gender-related remarks have been made by people who have analysed the interviews. Simply, we are looking at two people; their gender is immaterial. But in Roger and Elspeth's case that is not so. Roger's joie de vivre and Tigger-like enthusiasms affect viewers differently; some find him irresistible while others view him with a degree of horror. What is apparent is that a chief executive working with such a chair must find ways of putting some boundaries around his enthusiasm if she wants to have any sort of control. Kanter, in her seminal study *Men and women of the corporation* (1977), explored the issue of gender particularly in the context of a boss (male) and personal secretary (female). The behaviours that women use, she suggested, were derived from three female roles: mother, wife and mistress. Attached to these roles are strategies for control of the man. What we may be seeing in the interview is Elspeth operating a sort of push–pull strategy. It is noted by viewers that she is well made-up, and wears a split skirt revealing her thigh. Some viewers say that her dress is inappropriate for work. Others (including Elspeth herself when Andrew Wall asked if she minded this sort of analysis) have said that she has a right to dress to please herself. Either way how she looks is seen as significant. And so is how she handles the interview. For instance, although Roger constantly looks to her for affirmation – son to mother – she in turn is very parsimonious with her gaze and in her replies often appears to reinterpret what Roger has said, almost as though she was explaining in adult language the somewhat riotous ideas of a child. And yet they got on and reported that they enjoyed working together.

So is the metaphor of marriage, or of parent–child transaction, useful? Or is it an impediment leading to invalid interpretations or, even more disturbing, to behaviours from the subjects which enact the metaphor rather than what they might feel easier doing. Here we enter the difficult area of the significance of metaphor in shaping or interpreting behaviour. But we have already noted that nearly every couple used the metaphor of 'marriage' to describe their relationship. At one level this is inappropriate in that the couple are not equal, organisationally, the chair being senior to the chief executive. However, it is also appropriate in that it describes a personal contract. Indeed, it may be that that some of the observed behaviour demonstrated this very ambiguity that they were equal, but not really.

One way of handling this ambiguity is by nuance, inflection and innuendo. Don, a chief executive, deals with Bill's implied criticism that he may not have taken public opinion sufficiently into account, by a repertoire of irony, inflection and verbal timing. When he says: "... but we actually have got a better organisation, but I think some of that was down to Bill – the dog with the bone – wouldn't let go of me and made me carry on and get right down to sector general managers and that's it. I didn't believe it was possible ... [pause] I may not be convinced now but there you go", [both laugh] we are seeing the process clearly. First a degree of flattery of Bill, then a metaphor which helps Don to live with the degree of pressure put upon him by Bill, then irony to show Bill that Don is still his own man, and the pause to emphasise that point, which is acknowledged when they both laugh.

Concluding analysis

There is a possibility in this micro-analysis that in treading dangerously near other methods such as structuralism or discourse analysis our points will be lost. So what does this piece of research demonstrate and what can be learnt from it?

First, that the formal description of the relationship of chair and chief executive in the NHS only goes a little way in describing the real nature of that relationship. While a job description may be necessary as a starting point for the sake of public accountability at least, it does not explain what goes on and what it is like to be in such a relationship. Nor does it register the ambiguity involved. It therefore follows that the relationship may be built on an insubstantial foundation of shallow assumptions. That this is dangerous can be seen by the number of chief executive casualties and by boards where members feel undervalued and underachieving. Our attempt to sensitise holders of these jobs and others to the real nature of the relationship is on the assumption that a greater sensitivity will lead to more constructive relationships which do not end with a "clear-your-desk-by-lunchtime" scenario.

Second, and this is scarcely original, we believe that the quality of the relationship between the chair and the chief executive has an effect on the rest of the organisation. Not only is this a matter of values but of process. So their visible relationship – how they feel about each other – gives messages to the rest of the organisation. If the chief executive says, sighing slightly "The chairman wants to do this and you know what he's like...", everyone listening will get the message that "the chairman is wrong but he is the boss so there we are". Small wonder if cynicism follows fast upon the heels of such a remark.

Several of the interviewees maintain that they share the same values and consider it to be prerequisite. But might not some degree of difference be considered healthy? Interestingly Cadbury in his report on the financial aspects of corporate governance (1992) recommended that boards are best served by two people at the top because he feels that some degree of separation of duties is more likely to ensure probity. Another reason for having two people is more obvious: the chair and chief executive benefit by being able to check out each other's ideas and to have what Maureen calls "a good knockabout session".

It would be naive to assume, however, that their relationship is conducted entirely at an explicit level. Indeed we maintain that there is always an element of less explicit negotiation which uses a repertoire of verbal and non-verbal behaviours.

But is any of this analysis really useful or is it merely a protracted statement of what we all know? The point we are making is that at the centre of the relationship are several paradoxes:

- *It is a formal relationship which works best when its informality is most acknowledged.* Few people work well if constrained within a rigid role specification. All of the couples studied reported considerable flexibility in their contacts with each other.
- *It is an intimate relationship, with boundaries which are constantly tested but seldom transgressed.* The chair and chief executive spend a great deal of time together and often alone. Given this mutual exposure the relationship will take on many of the qualities of friendship. Where that friendship is across gender there may be an added element of attraction. But successful relationships cannot transgress certain limits and therefore the friendship is bounded. Finding these limits can be difficult and is constantly being tested, often by means of joking exchanges. The rules of friendship – "She's my friend. I'll always stand by her especially when she's in trouble," clearly cannot

apply invariably. Indeed when the chief executive is in trouble that is usually when the seeming friendship suddenly ceases.

• *When the relationship breaks down it is usually for personal reasons.* This is not a study of failed relationships, even though such breakdowns have been a characteristic of the NHS during the years since 1990 and a significant number of chief executives have left their jobs precipitately. Chairs have considerable power to dismiss on the spot but chief executives who wish to continue their careers elsewhere are thereby constrained from making too much complaint as to how they have been dealt with. If the dismissal was due to dereliction of duty or incompetence it presumably could have been more fairly dealt with in a more formal manner, involving other non-executive members of the board. The fact that this has so seldom happened suggests that, despite its constant invocation, trust is frail. The final dislocation is because the relationship has failed at a personal level.

• *Successful relationships are characterised as trusting but that trust has to be constructed.* Trust implies faith and faith cannot be measured – you either have it or you don't. Yet here we have relationships whose success requires an act of faith – trust – to be constructed. To be able to do this requires much that is personal, private and sensitive and yet it has to be done in the glare of public accountability.

Notes

[1] Names have been changed.

[2] In the press reporting of the case of Child B denied treatment by the Cambridge and Huntingdon Health Authority, the chair was scarcely mentioned but the chief executive was continually in the public eye. Such a case highlighted the question as to whether political issues should more appropriately be handled by the chair on the grounds that he or she is more obviously the agent of the government of the day than the career manager. See Wall, 1995.

SIX

The neglected rules: on leadership and dissent

Les Prince

Trust, like the soul, once gone is gone forever. (Catullus)

Introduction

This chapter considers the concept of 'leadership' in relation to its apparent antithesis: dissent. Two main arguments are advanced as part of this examination. First, that dominant 'structurist' models of leadership are deficient because they ignore fundamental aspects of context and process, specifically the part that so-called 'followers' have to play. Second, it is argued that there are fundamental rules applying to situations of leadership, based in trust, which are formulated not by 'leaders', but by 'followers'.

In elaborating these arguments, the 'structurist' models of leadership are contrasted with models from a relational perspective. It is argued that the bulk of the traditional literature is actually about 'leaders' (people in charge) rather than 'leadership' (processes by which people are persuaded to cooperate), set within an entitative model of organisation – that is, a model emphasising an alleged unity of purpose, goals and values within an organisation. Such an approach ignores important considerations of process – specifically cognitive, social and political process – within a complex social context, portraying an unwarranted and unhelpful image of 'followers' as fully dependent on 'leaders'. Issues such as trust cannot properly be comprehended within such a formulation.

By contrast the relational approach highlights process issues. Leadership from this point of view is understood as a negotiated social order in which influence is achieved through trust, reduction of uncertainty, and the achievement of frameworks for action which are largely acceptable to followers. This perspective emphasises interdependencies between 'leaders' and 'followers', and sometimes even highlights situations where 'leaders' may be wholly dependent on 'followers'. Furthermore, while traditional models of leadership imply, or frankly describe, followers as if they were passively reactive to circumstances and in particular the behaviour of 'leaders', 'followership' in this perspective is an active consequence of choice.

To illustrate these claims, examples are taken from accounts of dissent in a military setting during wartime. The extreme context can help make apparent the critical role played by so-called followers in setting the parameters of acceptability and, more important, unacceptability, in the relations between leaders and followers, and therefore shed light on the more mundane relations of everyday life.

Finally, a note of caution. There are three key terms used throughout this chapter: leader, leadership, and follower. Each presents its own difficulties. Those surrounding 'leader' and 'leadership' are considered separately below, but something must be said at this point about the problems associated with 'follower'. Use of this word in the leadership literatures generally has unfortunate and negative connotations in that it implies, as noted earlier, an unwarranted assumption of docility or passivity, particularly when taken in relation to the implied heroism of leaders. Nevertheless, alternative constructions are seldom satisfactory; one is either forced into using neologisms or unwieldy constructions such as 'those who are subject to influence attempts'. Throughout the discussion, therefore, non-leaders *will* be referred to by the standard term 'follower', but this is for want of a better term. To highlight the problematic nature of the word, however, it is placed within inverted commas throughout (what philosophers often refer to as 'scream quotes').

On dissent

Conceptualising dissent is both straightforward and difficult. It is straightforward in the sense that everyone understands the underlying absence or distance from wholehearted commitment that dissent implies; the sense of contradicting or disagreeing with someone. Most people would also readily accept that dissent, like inclinations toward cooperation, in this straightforward sense also involves both cognitive and behavioural aspects. For example, that one might disagree with someone, but choose not to express it. The concept becomes complex when considering such disagreements within a context of power relations, especially institutional power, between people.

For the purposes of this chapter, dissent is *any* example where people in a subordinate position withhold active cooperation, or exhibit a marked reluctance to obey orders. This may conjure up all sorts of lurid images of bloodletting, but violent rebellion is not really the subject matter here.

There *are* some examples of outright rebellion, such as organised strike action (Dallas and Gill, 1985; James, 1987; Rothstein, 1985), or mutiny (Guttridge, 1992), but for the most part these are not discussed here because they introduce factors that tend to complicate the main arguments. Thus well known mutinies such as that at Etaples during the First World War (Dallas and Gill, 1985), the Nore and Spithead Mutinies (Guttridge, 1992; Mainwaring and Dobrée, 1935), the mutiny at Invergordon (Ereira, 1981; Guttridge, 1992) and, of course, the Mutiny of the Bounty (Barrow, 1989), have elements of organisation about them which may suggest, to some, that they are simply the work of congenital malcontents.

More relevant are the 'small' and spontaneous acts of rebellion, particularly those carried out by people who do not really want to confront or subvert the established order. These highlight, more than any large-scale bloody uprising, the rules underlying 'leadership' and underline the *active* nature of 'followership'. The problem, however, is that these tend not to receive much attention in their own right and must be teased out line by line from accounts of larger activities. Nevertheless, they are the real focus of the chapter and, wherever possible, the arguments will be illustrated with accounts of these small 'rebellions'.

Dissent in a wartime military context

There are two reasons for using military examples – one trivial, the other fundamental to the arguments in the chapter.

The first, and least important, reason is that, whether some people like it or not, the military is an important strand of public service, albeit one that is often neglected in favour of more obvious candidates such as the health service or local government. As such it falls squarely within the remit of this book, and is a useful reminder of the scope of public service.

Second, and far more important, *any* dissent in a military context is *dangerous*, especially during wartime, and therefore has much to teach us about everyday life. It has not been chosen as a subject gratuitously, nor has it been selected simply to be controversial. Indeed, although the term 'mutiny', which is applied to military dissent, is controversial – and often avoided altogether by military authorities because of its connotations of mayhem and murder – most historical mutinies were rather mundane affairs:

> **They were protests by servicemen who felt that their sufferings had become so unbearable that only the last resort of collective action could achieve relief. Such mutineers believed that they were justified by natural justice and that this, coupled with the seriousness of their complaints, outweighed all the forms of naval and military law which they were breaking. (James, 1987, p 13)**

The importance of such protests lies not in the form they took, which in any case often mirrored forms of protest in civilian life, but in the context in which they took place. During peacetime it is easy to dismiss cases of dissent – strikes and the like – simply as the work of 'troublemakers', 'agitators', 'extremists' and so on. In some cases they may well be, but as the single explanation for all cases of resistance it has an obvious and self-serving ideological basis, often masking important issues and lessons. In blaming 'professional malcontents' for resistance, such 'explanations' do two things. First they contrast a largely mythological 'docile' workforce with malign and ill-intentioned extremists bent on the destruction of 'civilisation as we know it'. Second, and far more important for the arguments here, they divert attention away from the relationship between those in charge and their subordinates. They tend to foster a view that implies, if not actually state, that those who are appointed to positions of dominance are somehow free of culpability – an implied moral ascendancy. In other words, blame for the breakdown of 'normal functioning' is to be found 'elsewhere'. Such a view clearly disavows the possibility that protest may be motivated by injustice, still less by principled disapproval.

Similar explanations are sometimes advanced for the breakdown of order in military organisations, but they are harder to sustain. James comments that:

> **... the official mind in its obsession with hidden hands behind mutinies always assumed that the ordinary soldiers and sailors were somehow incapable of making up their own**

minds or thinking for themselves about matters which affected their daily lives. (James, 1987, p 22)

This is amply borne out by the historical record. For example, when towards the end of the First World War there was widespread unrest among troops in the British and Dominion Forces (Dallas and Gill, 1985; Gilbert, 1994; James, 1987; Rothstein, 1985), Sir Douglas Haig, Commander-in-Chief of the British Expeditionary Force, was in no doubt about what, and whom, to accuse. He put the blame firmly on the shoulders of 'troublemakers' in the ranks; men from the urban working class, who "come from a class which like to air real or fancied grievances", and, with their "habits" of trade unionism, voiced unrest and discontent (Dallas and Gill, 1985, pp 73-4). But, comforting though this explanation may have been for Haig, it does not bear even casual scrutiny – unless one subscribes to the view that 'other ranks' are somehow irretrievably stupid.

The punishments for insubordination in the armed forces, let alone open rebellion during wartime, are potentially of the harshest severity (James, 1987). During the First World War, for instance, British soldiers could be condemned to death "by a handful of captains and lieutenants, gathered perfunctorily in a tent" even for simple acts of insubordination. On at least one occasion, for example, a soldier was shot for refusing to put on his cap (Dallas and Gill, 1985, pp 38, 146 note 24). All military forces have at their disposal similar sanctions to help them keep order, greatly to be feared even when they fall short of the death penalty. The notorious 'Field Punishment No 1' is a particularly unpleasant example which, under a variety of names, has been used by military authorities throughout history the world over. It entailed tying a man to a cart wheel or gun carriage and leaving him there without food or water, sometimes for days.

The scale of the problem confronting members of the military wanting to protest should not be underestimated. Insubordination and mutiny are terms with very wide parameters in the face of which service personnel are practically defenceless in support of their rights (Dallas and Gill, 1985). James (1987) spells out the extent of this defencelessness under British military law: in the 1879 Army Discipline and Regulation Act, still in force, "a combination of two or more persons to resist or to induce others to resist lawful military authority" defined 'mutiny', a definition which also applies to naval and air force personnel. Similar laws exist in all military forces, regular and irregular.

Making a complaint anonymously was illegal, as was "any other method of obtaining redress for grievance real or imaginary". James cites two cases illustrating the point. In the first a private serving with a Lancashire regiment wrote an anonymous letter to a newspaper criticising his officers and was sentenced to six months by a court martial in South Africa in 1901. In the second example, after a rating serving aboard HMS *Repulse* wrote to his MP complaining about arrangements for his leave, "He was traced and given 28 days detention". Furthermore, private conversations among servicemen commenting on their superiors' conduct were forbidden, and "disloyal or insulting words about the royal family, a serviceman's ship or regiment or officers were punishable":

> **A private of the Seaforths who spoke abusively about his regiment was given twelve months in 1901, but the coarse nature of an Irish soldier's remarks about Queen Victoria in 1900 were thought to be too much for Her Majesty so his sentence was not passed to her for confirmation. (James, 1987, p 11)**

Similar restrictions and punishments also applied in the United States forces. For example, one officer was sentenced to two years in 1945 for remarking that Roosevelt was a 'son-of-a-bitch' (James, 1987, p 11).

It is clear from these examples that even simple peaceful protest was liable for punishment as mutiny – "a grave and dishonourable crime". Unfortunately, servicemen did not always understand this, and left themselves exposed for what they thought were reasonable actions. A sailor involved in the naval mutiny at Invergordon in 1931, for example, commented: "We were not disloyal or mutinying but fighting for our rights" (James, 1987, p 9; also Ereira, 1981).

This chapter is not intended as a criticism of military authorities, in general or particular. The important point is that the scope for dissent within a military context is severely constrained even today, and even those forms of protest that are taken for granted within civilian life are liable for severe punishment especially during a war.

Under such circumstances it is not credible that those serving under military law would casually confront the constituted authorities, or allow 'troublemakers' to expose them to such sanctions on a trivial pretext. Indeed, explanations that rely on blaming troublemakers are, most often, simply an admission that those in charge are fundamentally incompetent.

This is the key to this chapter. Dissent, or even open reluctance, within a military context, during wartime, cannot simply be dismissed as trivial or wanton given the possible severity of punishment. It follows that when military authority is challenged in such circumstances, the issues must be *particularly* important for those who are taking action. Examination of such situations in which relations of 'leadership' have evidently broken down, together with the reasons given by the actors involved, can shed important light on processes of leadership and, especially, followership, with implications for our understanding of such relations in everyday life.

Defining leadership

Leadership as an idea has always been a problem. On the one hand the word is a perfectly ordinary one, and most people can discuss the subject without any difficulty (Kelvin, 1970). On the other, it is a term which, even in ordinary discourse, can evoke conflicting interpretations and even strong emotions (for example, Freeman, 1970; Levine, 1974). Attempts to define the concept soon founder on a welter of contradictions, exclusions, special cases and distinctions of mind–numbing subtlety.

Cartwright and Zander (1953; 1968) observed that there was "little consensus about what leadership is or what it should be", and Stogdill, in his monumental and definitive *Handbook of leadership*, commented that there:

> ... are almost as many definitions of leadership as there are persons who have attempted to define the concept.... (Stogdill, 1974, p 7)

He also lamented that despite many years of research:

> It is difficult to know what, if anything, has been convincingly demonstrated by replicated research. The endless accumulation of data has not produced an integrated understanding of leadership. (Stogdill, 1974, p vii)

Nearly 10 years later Bass (1981), in his update of Stogdill's handbook, felt compelled to repeat the comments, and Quinn (1984) added:

> [The] ... seemingly endless array of unconnected empirical investigations is bewildering as well as frustrating. (Quinn, 1984, p 10)

Stogdill gives what he calls a "rough scheme of classification" showing the variety of approaches devised by researchers and theoreticians (Bass, 1981, pp 7-16). This includes definitions given in terms of group processes (for example, Cooley, 1902; Bernard, 1927); influence (for example, Nash, 1929; Tead, 1935; Stogdill, 1950); persuasion (for example, Schenk, 1928; Copeland, 1942) and power (for example, French, 1956; French and Raven, 1959; Gerth and Mills, 1953). He also gives definitions of leadership in terms of personality (for example, Bingham, 1927; Kilbourne, 1935); the induction of compliance (for example, Munson, 1921; Bennis, 1959); and leader behaviour (for example, Carter, 1953; Hemphill, 1949; Fiedler, 1967).

Nevertheless, notwithstanding the difficulties, there is a general convergence of emphasis. Overall these definitions are of two general types: those which emphasise *leaders*, and those which concentrate on *leadership*.

Structurist theories

The dominant approach to leadership emphasises 'leaders'. 'Leaders' in this tradition are identified a priori on the basis of established order and appointed position within a hierarchical structure, hence the designation *structurist*. Leadership is more or less synonymous with what leaders do and is considered a personal quality rather than a social relation. These approaches assume, or rely on, dependency of 'followers' on leaders, and conflate leadership with control. They are essentially static models, because the relationships between actors are defined by formal structures, which remain fixed whatever the quality of dynamic social, psychological, moral and political processes that exist between them (Kelvin, 1970). Even when relations break down, and followers are in dissent, the 'leader' is still leader by virtue of position.

Fiedler's comments about his own 'contingency theory of leadership effectiveness' are interesting in this context:

> **By leadership behaviour we generally mean the particular acts in which a leader engages in the course of directing and coordinating the work of his group members. This may involve such acts as structuring the work relations, praising or criticising group members, and showing consideration for their welfare and feelings. (Bass, 1981, p 10; see also, Fiedler, 1964; 1967; 1978)**

This is essentially a paternalistic position scarcely distinguishable from Fayol's 'classical management' (Fayol, 1949). Indeed it is significant that this strand of 'leadership' theory tends to use the terms 'leader' and 'manager' almost interchangeably (see Bass, 1981; Graumann and Moscovici, 1986; Hunt, 1991; Hunt et al, 1984; Syrett and Hogg, 1992; Yetton, 1984 for examples).

But it contrasts sharply with real life examples. Hastings (1984) describes attitudes among the allied air chiefs in the run up to the D-Day landings in 1944. Air Marshall Sir Trafford Leigh-Mallory had been appointed Air Commander-in-Chief for Operation Overlord (the codename for the invasion of northern France), but was widely considered to have achieved the position illegitimately by intriguing to supplant Air Marshals Dowding and Park in the wake of the Battle of Britain. For this he aroused considerable personal animosity and, despite his position, bomber commanders "flatly declined to accept their orders from him and would acknowledge only the mandate of [Air Marshall Sir Arthur] Tedder" the Deputy Supreme Commander of Overlord.

> **The fighter commanders also made clear their dislike of and lack of respect for the Commander-in-Chief. The American [Major General Lewis Hyde] Brereton, an officer of limited abilities commanding IXth Air Force, and the New Zealander [Air Marshall Sir Arthur] 'Mary' Coningham, commanding the British 2nd Tactical Air Force, united in their antagonism to Leigh-Mallory, while General Elwood R. 'Pete' Quesada, commanding the close-support squadrons under Brereton, was a bewildered spectator of the wrangles: 'I just didn't know people at that level behaved like that. Nobody wanted to be under Leigh-Mallory, even the British.' (Hastings, 1984, pp 52-3)**

Despite this description, a structurist model of leadership would still have to consider Leigh-Mallory a 'leader' because, as noted before, these particular approaches take as their starting point situations of de jure authority and concentrate more or less exclusively on the workings of that authority. The 'leader' is simply the person in charge, with authority over a group of others, usually appointed by some authority outside that group (see Fiedler, 1964, p 171, for an explicit definition to this effect). But as the example above makes clear, this leaves a conceptual gap in what might reasonably be expected from a concept like leadership as opposed to, say, management. It is clear that some people are good at being in charge, and others not. It is not by chance that theorists and researchers in the structurist tradition are forced to distinguish between 'effective' and 'ineffective' leadership, because their focus is not really on leadership at all, but on leaders – that is, on representatives of the political status quo. But leaders, by their definition, may well owe their position to factors irrelevant (or even damaging) to leadership relations, such as luck, nepotism, intrigue, incompetence or purchase. The case of Leigh–Mallory puts this into high relief, as do the many, well-known, historical examples of incompetent officers in positions of command simply by virtue of 'birth', connections or purchase (see Dixon, 1979; Foote, 1992; Guttridge, 1992; James, 1987; Macksey, 1988; Regan, 1991, for extensive examples).

The real problem here is the embedded assumption within structurist models that legitimacy, and therefore the goodwill of subordinates, follow necessarily from the fact of appointment to position. But again, the example makes it clear that legitimacy is based on the judgement of subordinates – it is not something that can be imposed.

There remains the problem of leadership itself, and how it relates to leaders. Structurist models define leadership simply as the 'position' of a leader, what leaders do or, bizarrely, something leaders *have*, much like a virus or personality defect. But as Gibb (1969b, p 210) pointed out, while this might seem like an obvious and convenient starting place for studying leadership, "it embraces such a wide variety of relationships" that, for research purposes, it is largely useless. Part of the problem is to identify what is or is not relevant to leadership. For example, if a particularly good leader is in the habit of wearing a pink woolly cardigan, are there any good a priori reasons for supposing that this is not essential to their success? After all, Field Marshall Montgomery's sartorial eccentricities, especially his habit of wearing two cap badges in his beret (contrary to regulations) have often been cited as a partial reason for his success with his troops. Moreover, these approaches tend to have a *universalistic* objective in common. They are largely attempts to crystallise the essence of leadership abstracted from all particular circumstances – to identify what is sometimes called *the one best way*. Necessarily, therefore, they gloss over the importance of context, especially the role of 'followers'. But context cannot be excluded in this way.

To take an illustrative example. Leadership personality theorists concentrated early on the task of identifying significant personality traits which distinguished leaders from 'followers'. These were later called leadership traits to avoid the problem that many of them could not reasonably be considered aspects of 'personality', but seemed to have broader behavioural aspects. Among defining traits – those which leaders allegedly had to a more marked degree than 'followers' – studies identified, inter alia, intelligence, judgement, knowledge, fluency, adaptability, aggressiveness, assertiveness, enthusiasm, independence, self-confidence, achievement drive, initiative and enterprise (Bass, 1981, p 76).

These are undeniably admirable characteristics and one can easily see how people with such qualities might well become influential. But, as Stogdill notes, a person so endowed might or *might not* rise to prominence, because an individual's upward mobility often seems "to depend to a considerable degree upon being at the right place at the right time" (Bass, 1981, p 82). Keegan (1987) makes a similar point:"... leadership ... is, like priesthood, statesmanship, even genius, a matter of externals almost as much of internalities" (p 11). In other words, personal characteristics cannot be taken apart from context and, as Stogdill further notes, conceptions of desirable traits are culturally coded (Bass, 1981). What is admirable and praiseworthy in one culture, may be irrelevant or even repulsive in another (Hofstede, 1994; Trompenaars, 1993).

The traits identified above are not really objective categories of individual characteristics. They are, on the contrary, moral, social or political judgements of *approval* – that is to say, judgements, made by people of others whom they admire. There are other, equivalent but negative, words available in the lexical armoury for the same qualities when they are *disapproved* of. For example, a person regarded as knowledgeable and intelligent in a context of approval could be labelled a 'know-it-all bore' or 'too clever by half' in a context of disapproval. An adaptable individual could be seen as inconsistent, spineless and uncommitted. Judgement may be called judgementalism; fluency called garrulousness; enthusiasm called hotheadedness; and self-confidence called hubris, bumptiousness, pomposity, vanity or pride. Napoleon, for example, was widely admired for the confidence with which he conducted his battles – while they were victories. But the same characteristic was called over-confidence when he lost, especially after his final defeat at Waterloo in 1815 (Cronin, 1990).

How a particular characteristic is labelled depends critically on the context in which the judgement is made. Furthermore, any specific characteristic of a particular individual could be *simultaneously* labelled both positively and negatively, depending on the different moral, social or political standpoints of the observers. Thus a trade union leader who is seen as firm and committed by his or her members, might be seen as stubborn and backward-looking by opponents in management. This is a perfectly well understood phenomenon and history is replete with examples. Napoleon was simultaneously revered by his supporters and reviled by his enemies for the same characteristics (see, for example, Cronin, 1990). The same is true for Adolf Hitler (for example, Keegan, 1987), Abraham Lincoln (for example, Foote, 1992), Oliver Cromwell (for example, Fraser, 1973), and indeed anyone else who achieves similar prominence. That the labels for 'leadership' traits are used in a quasi-scientific setting does not alter the fact that they are moral judgements – in this case of approval. They cannot therefore be made, and nor can they have any force, when abstracted from the context in which leaders operate or are viewed – 'followers' being a crucial part of that context.

At issue are questions of dependency and interdependency. Definitions emphasising leaders imply a one-way dependency of 'followers' on leaders and, by extension, characterise 'followers', insofar as they are considered at all, merely as unthinkingly reactive to circumstances created by leaders. There is a hidden prescription here, one that structurism holds in common with all entitative models of organisation: that there is only one paramount model of reality – the one adopted by the 'leader'. Descriptively, of course, this is nonsense, as the following example from the American Civil War shows:

> **The story went round how General Wigfall, commanding Texas troops, came across a guard reclining on a pile of boxes, his musket leaning against a nearby tree. 'What are you doing here, my man?' asked the General. 'Nothin much, jes kinder takin care of this hyar stuff,' replied the private without moving from his reclining position. 'Do you know who I am, sir?' 'Wal, now 'pears like I know your face, but I can't jes call your name – who is you?' 'I'm General Wigfall.' Without rising, the soldier stuck out his hand. 'General, I'm pleased to meet you. My name's Jones.' (Katcher and Youens, 1975, p 16)**

Whatever world General Wigfall looked out on, it was clearly not the same one that Private Jones inhabited. Within a structurist tradition there could only be one conclusion – that Private Jones was mistaken.

Phenomenologically, of course, this is nonsense, but people like General Wigfall have at their disposal the means to impose their world view on those of others with less institutional power. Structurist models of leadership imply, as much by omission as anything else, that this is as it should be – the 'leader's' perspective being the only one of real interest to them.

The implied model of person is a familiar one, a simple input-output model or, in psychological terminology, a stimulus–response model (see Figure 3).

The principle of this model is that inputs, in the form of leader behaviours or initiatives, enter the system, and responses, usually measured as productivity of some kind, appear at the other end as outputs. 'Effective leadership' is measured, indeed *defined,* by a high output from 'followers' (see Fiedler, 1964; 1978 for a good example). The box in the middle (the 'followers') which economists and engineers would refer to as throughputs, is seldom if ever examined. It is as if the leader's inputs are magically transmuted into productivity via mysterious, but essentially uninteresting *mechanical* processes inside the black box which, like a lathe or a computer, is not itself aware of what is going on and therefore plays no major role in the process. Leadership therefore becomes little more than an exercise in resource management, capable of being performed by any clerk who knows the rules. The human 'resources' (subordinates) become like any other resources at the disposal of management – passive lumps – in this

Figure 3: A structurist model of leadership

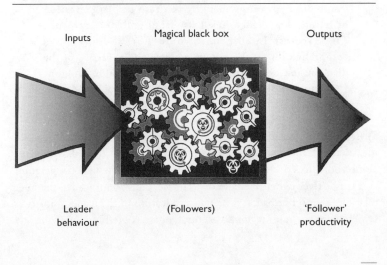

Inputs   Magical black box   Outputs

Leader behaviour   (Followers)   'Follower' productivity

case of human flesh: hired hands, heads or legs, but certainly not brains (Braverman, 1974). Apart from all other considerations, this flies in the face not only of common sense, but also of every development in the understanding of what it is to be human, whether psychological, sociological or anthropological. Note, however, that this view is, within these models, applied solely to 'followers'; leaders in contrast are clearly thought to be endowed with that intelligence which is the defining characteristic of what it is to be human (Schein, 1970).

To summarise so far. It has been argued that concentrating solely on what 'leaders' do, or on what personal characteristics they might have, is simply not good enough as a basis for understanding what *leadership* is, or how it impinges on human existence – even at work. The picture is both incomplete and distorted. Because 'followers' do not figure in these models, they present at best a partial perspective on a complex social situation which, in the final analysis, cannot credibly be conceptualised in terms of 'follower' passivity. They distort the situation because they imply, by omission, that 'followers' have nothing of value to contribute. This undoubtedly leads to, or is based on, various forms of self-serving ideological constructions about the context of work, specifically the implied moral ascendancy of those in positions of power – captured, in short, by vacuous slogans such as 'management's right to manage'. But, more importantly, such models necessarily imply that *all* responsibility for the functioning of a working context must reside with 'leaders' alone, which is a bizarre notion to say the least. As Bakunin remarks:

> **I am conscious of my inability to grasp any large portion of human knowledge in all its detail and developments. The greatest intelligence would not be equal to a comprehension of the whole, whence the necessity of the division and association of labour. (Bakunin, in Dolgoff, 1971, pp 229-30; also Bakunin, 1916, pp 32-3; Woodcock, 1977, pp 312-13)**

Structurist models scarcely have room, and give less credibility, to the idea that a 'leader' may not even be *liked* by his or her 'followers', yet alone room to consider more troublesome concepts like cooperation and trust. Even when Fiedler, for example, talks about leader-member relations as good or bad, it is merely as a feature of the leader's situation which he or she must take into account, not as something involving any active responses of 'followers'. These are essentially static models of leadership, because relations between the various actors, 'leaders' and 'followers' alike, are predefined by a formalised structure which remains more or less invariant whatever the quality of dynamic, social, psychological, political and cultural processes that exist between them.

Relational theories

In contrast to structurist models, those emphasising process and context take as their starting point considerations of leadership (not leaders), based on a quite different model of person – the intelligent actor. Some representative examples of this approach were mentioned earlier, under the headings group processes, power, influence and persuasion (Stogdill, 1974; Bass, 1981). Two things stand out as particularly interesting about these groups of definitions. First their vintage – many date from the earliest years of this century and are at least as old as the structurist theories considered above. Despite this they are consistently overlooked in the literatures, particularly those of management. Second, these definitions have an overall sophistication lacking in the structurist models, locating leadership within broadly social processes and explicitly recognising that leadership, however defined, does not occur in a vacuum. Stogdill notes, for example, that:

> **The influence concept recognizes the fact that individuals differ in the extent to which their behaviours affect activities of a group. It implies a reciprocal relationship between leaders and followers, but not one necessarily characterized by domination, control, or induction of compliance on the part of the leader. It merely states that leadership exercises a determining effect on the behaviours and on activities of the group. (Bass, 1981, p 10)**

The important point here is the explicit recognition of power and influence, and by extension also politics, as a significant aspect of leadership phenomena, as it is for other human relations (Foucault, 1979; Lee and Lawrence, 1991; Lukes, 1974; 1986; Thompson and McHugh, 1990).

> **Persuasion is a powerful instrument for shaping expectation and belief – particularly in political, social and religious affairs.... Power is regarded as a form of influence**

> relationship ... many of those committed at one time to
> trust building, openness, and participatory approaches ...
> have come to acknowledge the importance of power
> relations in understanding leadership. (Bass, 1981, pp 11-
> 12)

Such definitions tend to emphasise *inter*dependency and other relational factors between leaders and 'followers', in contrast to the dependency relations emphasised in the structurist models. For this reason they are referred to here as relational models. An illustrative comment is given by Merton (1969), who regarded leadership as: "An interpersonal relation in which others comply because they want to, not because they have to." This has considerable echoes in the views expressed by Michael Bakunin in 1871:

> In the matter of boots, I defer to the authority of the
> bootmaker; concerning houses, canals or railroads, I consult
> the architect or the engineer. For such specialist knowledge
> I apply to such a 'savant'. But I allow neither the bootmaker
> nor the architect nor the savant to impose his authority on
> me ... I recognise no *infallible* authority, even in special
> questions; ... I bow before the authority of specialists because
> it is imposed upon me by my own reason.... I receive and
> I give; such is human life. Each directs and is directed in ...
> turn. Therefore there is no fixed and constant authority,
> but a continual fluctuation of mutual, temporary, and above
> all voluntary authority and subordination. (In Dolgoff, 1971,
> pp 229-30; also Bakunin, 1916, pp 32-3; Woodcock, 1977, pp
> 312-13)

This is essentially an expression of contingent, or bounded, trust, based on reflection and sentiment. Such formulations draw a sharp distinction between cooperation and coerced compliance, although in practice the lines between persuasion, influence and coercion on the one hand, and therefore cooperation and mere compliance on the other, are not so easy to draw (Cartwright, 1959; French and Raven, 1959; Lukes, 1986; Prince, 1988; Wrong, 1979). This is why it is so important to have a firm understanding of power and its dynamics in relation to leadership phenomena (Thompson and McHugh, 1990). Nevertheless, theorists from this perspective take a clear stance on the important differences between leadership and coercion, arguing they are not at all the same phenomena. On the whole leadership in this tradition tends to be viewed as the *outcome* of interaction, rather than the prime determinant of it. Copeland (1942), for example, states:

> ... leadership is the art of ... influencing a body of people by persuasion or example to follow a line of action. It must never be confused with drivership ... which is the art of compelling a body of people by intimidation or force to follow a line of action. (Bass, 1981, p 11)

Structurist theories on the whole do not make this distinction or, when they do, fail to encompass the full implications. Stogdill, in reviewing definitions of leadership as the effect of interaction, says:

> This group of theorists was important in calling attention to the fact that emergent leadership grows out of the interaction process itself. It can be observed that leadership truly exists only when acknowledged and conferred by other members of the group. (Bass, 1981, p 13)

In this quotation Stogdill is reiterating the same point as Bakunin, quoted earlier. Leadership by this view is not solely a function of appointment (de jure authority), but is crucially dependent on the reactions and responses of the 'followers', and the relations between leaders and 'followers' (de facto authority). By this view leadership is *always* emergent leadership (Prince, 1988), with an essential basis in trust (Bass, 1981, p 12).

This principle currently enjoys the status of a platitude. It is routinely quoted in chapters on leadership in general management textbooks (for example, Buchanan and Huczynski, 1985; Child, 1984; Gordon, 1987; Handy, 1993; Wilson and Rosenfeld, 1990). But once the basic principle has been annunciated, it is then just as routinely ignored and the emphasis quickly shifts back to leaders. Although the relational tradition has always coexisted, in one form or another, alongside the structurist tradition, for inscrutable reasons it has generally been overlooked in terms of research and public exposure. The management texts, as the main conduit through which research in these areas is transferred to 'users', illustrate this point very well, concentrating almost exclusively on the structurist tradition (for example, Hunt, 1991; Syrett and Hogg, 1992). And yet that tradition does not sit well with the principle that leadership exists only when accepted, conferred and conceded by 'followers', if only because structurism does not acknowledge any part for them.

However, the principle of follower participation has exquisitely important consequences, with far-reaching implications. First it implies *choice* – not that 'followers' are always in a position to choose who is placed in charge of them but, more critically, *who and what they will willingly follow*. This further implies choice about who and what *not* to follow. In other words, in circumstances which one might define as leadership (as opposed to, say, headship (Gibb, 1958; 1969b), drivership (Copeland, 1942) or simply command (Watson, 1980), 'followers' have the choice and ability to say *no* – the choice and ability of *dissent*. Furthermore, this is not something which can be conferred or denied by authority as a privilege, any more than constituted authority can legislate for what people will or will not like. As an aspect of individual and group sentiment it is entirely outside formal authority's remit. That this principle is at odds with the so-called 'new managerialism' is beyond dispute – dissent having been practically 'criminalised' in formulations emphasising managerial prerogatives over and above those of other groups within a working environment (Lee and Lawrence, 1991; Pollitt 1993). Here again, there are several historical examples which illustrate forcefully the importance of the principle of choice.

As is well known, after his defeat at Leipzig in 1813 Napoleon was forced to abdicate, and was subsequently exiled as 'Emperor, and Sovereign of the Isle of Elba' (Cronin, 1990, p 374). In 1815, however, he escaped from Elba with around a thousand followers and landed in the south of France at the start of what became known as the 'hundred and thirty six days', culminating in the Battle of Waterloo. The Bourbon king, Louis XVIII, despatched the army to intercept Napoleon's small force and bring him to Paris under arrest. This presented an interesting situation for those involved because the army opposing Napoleon's return was the same one he had led through many wars and campaigns. Whatever the final verdict of history most of the soldiers revered him practically as a deity and, furthermore, the soldiers they confronted were former comrades.

Near Grenoble, Napoleon's force was opposed by a battalion of the 5th Regiment of the Line. Napoleon walked alone towards these soldiers until he was within pistol range. A Captain Randon gave the order: 'There he is. Fire!', but there was silence:

> **After taking a few steps, Napoleon stopped and drew apart the lapels of his overcoat, exposing his white waistcoat. 'If you want to kill your Emperor,' he called in a loud voice, 'here I am.'... Back came a tremendous shout of 'Long live the Emperor!' The men of the 5th, waving their shakos on bayonet tips, rushed cheering towards him. 'Just see if we want to kill you,' shouted one soldier, rattling his ramrod up and down the barrel of his empty musket. In a matter of minutes the soldiers had whipped from their haversacks the old tricolour ribbons they had been obliged to remove eleven months before and stuck them in their hats, while on to the grass fell a litter of white cockades [symbol of the Bourbons]. (Cronin, 1990, pp 391-2)**

Meanwhile, Louis XVIII's brother, the Comte d'Artois, had travelled to organise the defence of Lyons. He had at his disposal three line regiments and around 1,500 National Guards under the command of the very able Marshall MacDonald. Under the Bourbons MacDonald, who had been promoted by Napoleon, had received considerable favours and, unlike the soldiers, was not about to give up his privileges for his former Emperor. At a parade of the troops in the Place Bellecour, he gave a rousing speech and called upon them to show their loyalty by giving the cheer 'Long live the King!' There was silence.

> **Then Artois walked along the lines in pouring rain and spoke in a kindly way to a veteran dragoon. He invited the dragoon to give a lead by shouting 'Long live the King!' Again there was dead silence. Artois left the parade, jumped into his berlin and took the road to Paris. That evening the people of Lyon welcomed Napoleon into their city. (Cronin, 1990, pp 392-3)**

From a relational viewpoint, leadership is *characterised* by choice and commitment on the part of 'followers' to act or not in accordance with proposals for action, thought or ends put forward by would-be 'leaders'. Clearly, by this principle, neither Captain Randon, Marshall MacDonald nor the Comte d'Artois were leaders because 'their' soldiers *chose* not to follow them, despite their evident seniority.

By extension, leadership entails the engagement of opinions favourable, or at least *indifferent* but not hostile, to what is intended, how it is to be done and to what ends. This is a principle of 'acceptable influence', involving the engagement of values and sentiments about means and ends (Brown and Hosking, 1984; Hosking and Morley, 1991; Prince, 1988) – what MacGregor-Burns (1978) calls modal and end values, that is, values about what is to be done and how. It further implies relations of mutual positive interdependence – which Deutsch (1968) called promotive interdependence – between *all* the actors in a situation, rather than one-way dependence of 'followers' on 'leaders' (Brown and Hosking, 1984; Gibb, 1958, 1969a,b; Hollander, 1964; Hollander and Webb, 1955; Hosking and Morley, 1991; MacGregor-Burns, 1978). In sum, this tradition emphasises choice rather than constraint (Prince, 1988), and trust rather than coercion. It recognises that while it may be possible to coerce the body (of followers), leadership is really about engaging hearts and minds (Dixon, 1979).

This highlights the fundamental basis of relational approaches to leadership, which take it as axiomatic that people are most appropriately considered as intelligent actors (rather than passive human resources). This means that even institutionally unimportant people are active in trying to understand their environment, make judgements about it and attempt to influence it in some way (Burrell and Hearn, 1989; Hosking and Morley, 1991; Lee and Lawrence, 1991). It necessarily draws attention to questions about values and interests – those who seek to influence their environment generally do so on the basis of particular values and interests that they wish to protect or promote. In turn it highlights the importance of cognitive, social and, above all, *political* processes within organisations (Hosking and Morley, 1991). This model of the intelligent actor is quite at odds with the 'passive lumps' characterised in structurist theories as 'followers' and its importance is far reaching when taken seriously.

Negotiated social orders

The social contexts within which intelligent actors operate are, necessarily, social orders based on understandings of that context which may or may not be commonly shared (for example, Berger and Luckmann, 1976; Hosking and Morley, 1991; Kelvin, 1970). Part of this will be based on shared cultural codes and assumptions, but a further contribution to establishing shared understandings can be characterised properly as an aspect of 'leadership'. By this view leadership, as opposed to 'command' (or its synonyms), becomes a process by which a social order becomes established and maintained within, and responsive to, a context of choice understood in relation to values and sentiments about ends and means (Prince, 1988).

There is an issue of creativity here. Within structurist traditions, because it is assumed that people in subordinate positions simply respond to their contexts, of which managers and 'leaders' are key components, there is implied a one-way change process, with the context (managers) shaping subordinate members of staff to fit. What is left from this account is the other side of the equation. People not only respond to their contexts, they shape them. This is obvious when one considers the physical environment (for example, Simon, 1982), but it is also true of the social environment, as some of the examples already given demonstrate. Organisations may shape people, but people also shape organisations, whether as individuals or in groups. Something of this point can be seen in the following passage from Hastings (1984), which also clearly highlights the important role of trust. He describes what happened in an action on 11 June 1945, involving the British troops around Cristot in France during the Overlord offensives following D-Day:

> **A sour sense, not of defeat, but of fumbled failure overlay the British operations on the Western flank.... Lieutenant-Colonel Robin Hastings of the 6th Green Howards was mistrustful of the reported lack of opposition – he anyway lacked confidence in his elderly brigadier – ... Hastings remained bitter about the losses his men had sustained in an attack that he believed was misconceived – that was simply 'not on'.... Before every attack, most battalion commanders made a *private decision* about whether its objectives were 'on', *and thereby decided whether its purpose justified an all-out effort, regardless of casualties, or merely sufficient movement to conform and to satisfy the higher formation.* Among most of the units which landed in Normandy, there was a great initial reservoir of willingness.... Thereafter, following bloody losses and failures, many battalion commanders determined privately that they would husband the lives of their men when they were ordered into attack, *making personal judgements about an operation's value.* (Hastings, 1984, pp 164-5; emphasis added)**

A shared social order enables action. It is not, however, something that can be imposed (any more than an organisational culture can) but is essentially negotiated, whether tacitly or overtly, between 'leaders' (those whom followers choose to follow) and 'followers' (those who, for whatever reason, are not leaders). It should be noted here that negotiation implies the opportunity for achieving something by all participants, related to their values and interests. Those who believe they cannot achieve something of value from the process will not negotiate, and will probably withdraw (Hosking and Morley, 1991; Morley and Stephenson, 1977).

Such social orders are not, however, static, but dynamic and changing, although the rate of change will depend on many factors internal and external to the context. This suggests that the process of negotiating a social order is never completely finalised, but will be ongoing within any particular set of relationships. It further implies that processes of *leadership* and therefore trust are never finalised, but are negotiated and renegotiated in successful relations as circumstances change. Complacency and leadership do not mix.

Values and interests

The principles of choice and the intelligent actor elaborated earlier draw attention to the importance of values and, by extension, interests. Management literatures are full of discussions about values but, as one might expect, these discussions tend to focus only on those values promoted, and protected, by management – that is, by those with institutional power (Hosking and Morley, 1991; Lee and Lawrence, 1991). Much more important, however, are the values, and concomitant interests, of subordinates within organisations, because it is these that determine cooperation and resistance.

It is something of a platitude to say that people's values and interests are shaped by much more than the context within which they work. However, one could be forgiven for believing that it is no longer true once someone walks through the office door, when one considers all the recent talk about 'organisational goals', as if these were the sole focus of importance. Of course, people vary in the extent to which they elaborate or hold to different sets of values and interests. Nevertheless, when they enter *any* context, whether work, or warfare, or whatever, they do so with some basis on which to understand and judge that context – and this basis is properly and necessarily considered as a value base, regardless of the extent to which the values are held or elaborated. Judgement, of course, implies approval or *disapproval*.

Values can be grouped, crudely, into three overlapping sets: personal, professional and institutional (called by Morgan [1997], extramural, career and task). Personal values include strong religious, political or social values, including those relating to protection of family and home. Professional values are pretty much self-explanatory, and include codes of conduct and ethics imposed by the professions. Institutional values are those relating to the job in hand, that fleeting moment of employment in a lifetime of much else. Unfortunately much of the management literature, including structurist models of leadership, focuses only on institutional values, to which they accord privileged status. Hence the hysteria about 'whistle blowers' who, having found the tension between personal morals and what they are asked to do at work intolerable, 'blow the gaff' (Clinard, 1990; Punch, 1996).

But it is clear that personal and professional values are equally, if not more, important to explain a person's motivations. Certainly the different sets of values and interests can come into tension or conflict, and therefore may be possible grounds for dissent. In particular, a person who is asked or required to do something that fundamentally contradicts deeply held values is likely to feel considerable tension, or cognitive dissonance, which will have to be resolved one way or another (Festinger and Aronson, 1968), often by some form of dissent. There are some excellent historical examples of such situations.

Lieutenant William Douglas-Home, brother of the future British Prime Minister Sir Alec, and later a celebrated playwright, had made it clear to his fellow officers that if he disapproved of something done on the battlefield, he would say so. During the Allied offensives in northern France in 1944, he served as a troop commander of 'Crocodiles' – a particularly odious weapon, being a flame-throwing tank. The Allies had planned a massed air bombardment of a town in order to induce its garrison to surrender, and this so appalled Douglas-Home he immediately "set out on his own initiative to parley the Germans into giving up, declining to have anything to do with the attack himself" (Hastings, 1984, p 254). For this he was court-martialled and sent to serve a term of imprisonment in Wormwood Scrubs.

Another, more recent example, throws an interesting twist on the same situation – an officer who argued that he actually 'followed' orders, but was still dismissed from the service for doing so. Captain Lawrence

Rockwood was an intelligence officer with the US Army specialising in Central America, by all accounts a man of very high principle. On one occasion, for example, he spoke in defence of a colleague who had been disciplined for expressing misgivings about US policy *to a priest* (Katz writing in *The Guardian*, 30 May 1995).

Rockwood was posted to Haiti in September 1994 as part of the American occupation force following the coup by Raoul Cedras. According to a speech made by President Clinton, that force was there to prevent brutal atrocities being carried out by supporters of the coup against those of the ousted President Aristide. Although Rockwood's primary role as a counter intelligence officer was to collect intelligence about possible threats to US troops, he said that he immediately began receiving reports about brutality in the island's prisons: "This information was coming in through intelligence channels. I didn't go out looking for it". Some of the information came from US soldiers – including one report of a man who had been chained to a wall for so long the skin on his back had rotted.

In addition, Rockwood also received a report from the Pentagon expressing concern about possible brutality in the Haitian prisons. He argued later that, as far as he understood the situation, he was required by international law to investigate these reports and prevent any brutality he discovered. Accordingly he asked his superiors to investigate, but was told it was not a priority. Later he asked for permission to investigate himself, but was refused on the grounds that regulations demanded a Military Police escort, but the Military Police were refusing to supply one.

Mindful of the fate of Lieutenant General Yamashita, who had been found guilty of *failure to prevent* war crimes during the Second World War and was subsequently executed in 1946, and of the fates of the war crimes defendants at Nuremberg in 1945-46, Rockwood wrote a letter of complaint, alleging that his superiors were subverting the President's 'mission intent' for Haiti: "The President is my commander-in-chief. I looked hard in Haiti but I couldn't find anyone that outranked him" (*The Guardian*, G2 30 May 1995, p 5). Subsequently he broke into the prison at Port au Prince to look at the conditions for himself. His inspection was cut short when he was escorted from the building by a US military attaché.

It says something about the military authorities' view of Rockwood's protest that he was later sent for psychiatric examination. At his trial, he was portrayed as a headstrong and arrogant figure. It is significant that the authorities asked for a prison sentence of six years – five for arguing with a senior officer when he allegedly said: "I am an American military officer, not a Nazi military officer". His final comment after his court martial is particularly illuminating: "You can't leave the military in the hands of cynical people who believe that might is right" (*The Guardian*, G2 30 May 1995, p 5).

As Rockwood himself pointed out, the treatment he received for acting on his own ethical initiative contrasts very sharply with judgments at the Nuremberg war crimes trial in 1945. Field Marshall Wilhelm Keitel, for example, argued in his defence that he only obeyed orders, but this was rejected and he was executed in 1946 (Keegan, 1995, p 87).

The psychological contract

An important aspect of working relationships that links discussion of values and interests more closely to that of trust, is the psychological contract (Handy, 1993). In formal terms this does not exist, but insofar as employers and employees are located within a common cultural nexus, then the psychological contract comprises what one might call the *implied* terms of the formal employment contract which set limits on what is and is not acceptable.

When people enter any context they have expectations about concepts such as fairness, justice and equity. Admittedly these may be loosely formulated, if at all, but they provide the basis from which a person will make judgements and decisions to commit, or otherwise, to a situation, another person or an organisation. It is on the basis of such judgements as fairness that trust is built or destroyed (see Coulson, Chapter Two). In relation to leadership, these are the judgements that define a relation as one of leadership or something else.

It must be emphasised that such judgements are not necessarily, or even very often, based on expectations of freedom from difficulty, hardship or effort. It all depends on the context and the nature of the contract. For example, during the American Civil War, the soldiers of General Thomas 'Stonewall' Jackson were notable for their willingness to accept great hardships despite being poorly fed, clothed and equipped. During the Shenandoah Valley Campaign of 1862 in particular, Jackson's soldiers marched nearly 500 miles in 30 days – an average of nearly 17 miles a day *on foot* – skirmishing daily. They fought five battles, defeated four numerically superior armies, completely routing two in the process, and captured large quantities of stores and prisoners (Foote, 1992; Selby and Roffe, 1971). The soldiers revered Jackson, and yet he was not noted for his leniency, or even for his overt friendliness. On the contrary, many of his soldiers (and colleagues) thought him rather odd, and he had something of a reputation for harshness in meting out punishments (Foote, 1992; Katcher, 1994). The key to Jackson's success was not his mildness, but his ability to deliver victories. For the soldiers under his command the Civil War was being fought on home ground, and more than anything most wanted the invading Northern armies defeated and chased out. To achieve this they willingly followed someone who could *help them* to win battles, meanwhile accepting the hardships entailed by the process.

In a similar vein, there is an account given by Lieutenant Andrew Wilson of the Buffs during the run-up to D-Day in 1944 (Hastings, 1984). After joining up he and the other young officers spent months in a relatively peaceful routine dominated by mess life. At the beginning of 1944, however, things changed abruptly, and this was replaced by training and exercises which took them and the rest of the regiment to "the very limits of its endurance: 'We suddenly knew we were going to be put through the full Monty treatment'." (Hastings, 1984, p 55). But far from resenting the change, Wilson and his colleagues welcomed it as preparation in earnest for what they had to do once they were in France.

The psychological contract, together with the values and interests that a person brings to a context, and those that develop within it, form a web of evaluation. On this basis people make judgements, cognitive and affective, about their situation and whether or not it is acceptable.

Acceptability

In a world viewed through the managerial lens, questions of acceptability apply only to subordinates, with those holding de jure position judging those inferior to them in institutional status: acceptable performance; acceptable commitment; acceptable behaviour; acceptable goals. Within such a framework, protest, withholding assent or objecting to managerial prerogative is generally treated as pathological, or at least something that must be overcome in order that the managerial prerogative is preserved (Lee and Lawrence, 1991; Thompson and McHugh, 1990). The demonisation of dissent in the managerialist perspective is manifestly part of the same tradition as the entitative models of organisation and structurist theories of leadership. The standpoint is solely that of those with institutional power - the status quo – with the perspective of subordinates or 'followers' being almost entirely ignored. But, judgements of acceptability are *also* made by subordinates – of themselves, their colleagues and, above all, of their 'leaders'. Subordinates can and *will* make judgements about their contexts, including judgements about those in charge of them and of what they are expected to do for those people. As one of Hastings' respondents put it, when talking about the situation in Normandy in 1944:

> **In the end we all became 'canny', and would obey orders only to the extent that there appeared a reasonable expectation of carrying them out. (Hastings, 1984, p 228)**

A person put in charge of others can, *when it is part of the psychological contract between them*, expect a certain level of cooperation. But there are important limits imposed not by those in charge but by the 'followers' themselves. These are set in relation to the implied terms of the psychological contract and developed within their frameworks of values and interests, some of them shared, some not.

The situation can be conceptualised very simply, as in Figure 4. This is based on comments made by Barnard (1938) and Sherif (1967) and shows a continuum running from 'acceptable' to 'unacceptable', with a broad zone in the centre labelled 'indifferent'. Broadly speaking, the behaviour and demands of anyone in charge of others will be evaluated along this continuum *by their subordinates*.

Those things judged to be *acceptable* are clearly not going to give grounds for resistance. Followers' values and interests are not threatened, and may even be served. There is, therefore, a basis for full, perhaps even willing, cooperation, as in the cases of Stonewall Jackson's soldiers and Lieutenant Andrew Wilson cited earlier, who clearly judged what was asked of them to be acceptable *in the circumstances*.

Judgements of indifference are slightly different. Here fundamental values and interests (of the 'followers') are not threatened, but neither are they served. But – and this must be emphasised – no one has strong feelings about *everything* they are asked to do, and much of the time will be more or less indifferent to it, particularly if already implied by the psychological contract. This 'zone of indifference' represents a large reservoir of latent goodwill. But violations of that goodwill can, and will, make it shrink.

Judgements of unacceptability on the other hand give firm grounds for resistance and opposition, whether psychological or behavioural. When something is judged to be unacceptable by 'followers', this implies a perceived threat to fundamental values and interests, an undermining of trust, and vigilance – monitoring the behaviour of those in power to identify further threats. Both ends and means may be considered unacceptable – what is done, and how it is to be achieved – as well as the person promoting them, which includes judgements of incompetence. The examples given above make it clear that people in subordinate positions can, and do, make such judgements. Whether they choose to act on them is, of course, a different matter. The following are examples to illustrate the point further.

In the early stages of the American Civil War soldiers of both sides were able to transfer between units, or even arms of service. Unpopular officers, particularly those with a reputation as martinets, frequently found that their units had transferred en masse elsewhere. The result of this was that appointed officers were often left with nothing to command, except on paper (Katcher and Youens, 1975).

Figure 4: Acceptability and the psychological contract

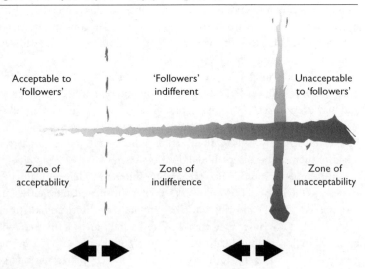

Acceptable to 'followers'	'Followers' indifferent	Unacceptable to 'followers'
Zone of acceptability	Zone of indifference	Zone of unacceptability

As is well known, the British Army was sent to intervene in the early stages of the Russian Revolution. This was extremely unpopular, particularly with soldiers who thought they were to be demobilised at the conclusion of the First World War. Accordingly, in 1919, the 6th Battalion of the Royal Marine Light Infantry mutinied and refused to go into action against the Bolsheviks. All mention of them was later excised from official records of the so-called North Russian Campaign (James, 1987).

During August and September 1946, 258 soldiers from the 13th Battalion The Parachute Regiment were court martialled for mutiny. Earlier in the year, on 14 May, they had held a demonstration at the edge of their camp in Malaya, protesting about the poor conditions they were expected to live in. They were addressed first by a divisional general, later by a colonel, and warned that their actions or, more precisely, their *in*actions, were mutinous. They were ordered to fall in, but refused. Apparently the response was some indecisive shuffling and contemptuous whistles. By and large the demonstration was relatively good-natured. They saw nothing wrong in what they were doing, but considered they were only standing up for their rights (James, 1987, p 8). The army, of course, saw it differently, but the sentences meted out at the court martial were later quashed.

The situation becomes more complex when one considers that the three zones identified above will probably be set differently by different people, and will shift for a particular individual according to circumstances. For example, someone who has just received a large gas bill is probably going to be less tolerant than if they had received a large cheque through the post. Similarly, soldiers who are well trained and fresh are likely to be more tolerant than those who have just returned from arduous campaigning. Hastings gives a very good example of this. Discussing veterans returning from the fighting in the Mediterranean, who were expected to take part in the D-Day landings, he comments:

> **Many of the men from the Mediterranean, above all the old regular soldiers, were bitter that, after fighting so hard for so long, they were now to be called upon once again to bear the brunt of the battle. A staff officer described the difficulties with one unit recalled from the Mediterranean for the invasion: 'The 3rd Royal Tank Regiment were virtually mutinous just before D-Day. They painted the**

> walls of the barracks in Aldershot with such slogans as "No
> Second Front", and had it not been for their new
> commanding officer, ... I really think they might have
> mutinied in fact.' Lieutenant-Colonel Michael Carver of
> 7th Armoured's 1st Royal Tank Regiment found some of
> his senior NCOs appearing before him to protest about
> their role, and echoing complaints from their wives, who
> demanded to know why those who had sat in England for
> four years and had not 'done their bit' could not now take
> over the burden. It was a sentiment shared by the Prime
> Minister. (Hastings, 1984, p 57)

Quite how psychological dissent becomes translated into behavioural or
active dissent is difficult to say. Certainly it is not possible to identify *all*
the necessary conditions and triggers, and much will be determined by
features of the overall context. Indeed, in some examples of mutiny, it
can be a relatively small spark or irritation that precipitates the whole
thing (Dallas and Gill, 1985; James, 1987; Rothstein, 1985). Psychological
dissent can be disguised, so that mere grudging compliance can appear
to be cooperation, especially in circumstances of extreme threat. But, as
several of the examples quoted earlier show, gaining behavioural
compliance is not at all the same thing as 'winning hearts and minds',
which is why the military examples are so important.

The key point in all of this is that the parameters of acceptability are
set not by those with institutional power, but by those who are subordinate.
In matters of leadership it is 'followers' who concede leadership, who
choose whether to follow willingly. This is not, however, to suggest that
institutional power and position are totally irrelevant. On the contrary,
from the examples of dissent given above, it is quite clear that in some
cases those protesting often thought of themselves as taking legitimate
actions similar to their civilian counterparts (James, 1987), only to fall
foul of different definitions of their actions – they being in the relatively
weak position, and therefore having their own explanations and
understandings dismissed as 'inaccurate'. This is what has been described
as the hegemony of power – the ability of those with institutional power
to define, in the face of all opposition, situations to suit themselves or
their rules (see for example, Lukes, 1974; 1986; Wrong, 1979). But the
point remains that *willing cooperation*, as opposed to mere behavioural
compliance, is a matter of *follower choice*.

Concluding comments

Full understanding of leadership needs an acknowledgement that it is contextual. Despite the dominance of structurist theories which concentrate on leaders rather than leadership, it is clear that to focus simply on people 'in charge' is not a sufficient basis on which to understand the complex dynamic processes that underlie relations between 'leaders' and 'followers'. Contexts, critically, are set and developed by sets of actors in interaction with one another, in a cycle of mutual creation and influence – interdependencies rather than dependencies. People adapt themselves to their surroundings, including other people, and their surroundings subtly alter themselves to adapt to them. The distinction is well captured by the slogan: the "organisation of production" (structurist models) versus the "production of organisation" (relational models) (Burrell and Hearn, 1989).

When people interact, they structure their interactions. These structuring processes have cognitive, social and political dimensions (Hosking and Morley, 1991), and, perhaps most important, evaluative dimensions. Intelligent actors in interaction judge situations and one another, especially those who are apparently in charge. The basis of these judgements is to be found in the various values and interests that participants bring to the situation, and which they use to structure their own lives. Some of these will be shared, particularly those derived from a common cultural heritage. Others will be diverse. Indeed diversity is probably considerable in any social situation. But such differences do not matter if the situation is one in which diverse values, interests, goals and judgements are in consonance, that is, where interdependency is recognised and respected by actors in a situation, especially those with power.

The issue of recognised interdependency is important. What it demonstrates is that leadership, far from being a simple unidimensional feature of life, with a well established set of rules easily applied, is actually a phenomenon of considerable complexity. To understand it fully requires consideration of other factors and processes such as power, influence, authority, legitimacy, trust and status, all of which are themselves difficult concepts. But what it also draws attention to is the importance of relational issues, and consideration of the broad context within which leadership takes place. This requires a diagnostic turn of mind, and a willingness to accept that social situations are fluid, often contradictory, and even paradoxical at times (Morgan, 1997).

Examples of dissent, or open mutiny and rebellion, underline the role of choice, specifically the irreducible element of follower choice in leadership – that leadership is conceded by those who follow, not taken by those who lead. They also highlight the critical role of values, interests, and relations of trust, the last being understood in terms of the various values and interests of actors within a situation, especially those who are expected to trust others with institutional power. That this trust must be earned is apparent, and is at least partially a matter of not violating the values and interests of those in subordinate positions. This does not imply that those in positions of power must be liked, however. On the contrary liking is an entirely independent issue. It is perfectly possible to like someone without trusting them, and to trust someone that is not liked. The important point is that trust is fragile, and, following the quotation from the head of the chapter, once lost is likely to be irretrievable.

Leadership can be defined as the construction, development and maintenance of frameworks for action, in particular collective or joint action. This raises issues of intersubjectivity. If people are to act together, they need to have consonant frames of reference, although these need not be identical. The process by which these frames of reference are established is what has been called leadership here.

In conclusion, it is clear that 'followers' cannot, and should not, be dismissed merely as passive pawns in a game of leadership played only by those in positions of institutional power. On the contrary, it is 'followers' *not* leaders who set the most important parameters. Leaders are simply those to whom 'followers' concede leadership, those whom 'followers' *choose* to follow. 'Followership', far from being passively reactive, is an *active* role in leadership relations. Perhaps, in the final analysis, it is *the* active role. To discover the 'rules' of leadership, therefore, we need to study 'followership' and 'followers' rather than 'leaders'.

Author's acknowledgements

I would like to thank Professor Gibson Burrell and Simon Baddeley for their kind comments and helpful suggestions on earlier drafts of this chapter. I would also like to give special thanks to Dr Andrew Coulson, who not only made helpful and useful suggestions, but also bullied me into completing this piece. In this case, Andrew, I judged your 'influence attempts' to be more than 'acceptable in the circumstances'.

Part Three

The trust of individuals in organisations

SEVEN

Trust and the competence of the welfare consumer

Marian Barnes and David Prior

Introduction

In this chapter we consider the ways in which trust between providers and recipients of public services is a factor in the operation of hierarchical and contract-based systems of welfare. We identify contradictions and limitations in the role of trust within these systems based on an ambivalence about the perceived 'competence' of users, and suggest points at which a reciprocal notion of trust is needed if public trust in welfare services is to be renewed. We have developed our ideas concerning *how* 'public trust' in welfare services might be renewed elsewhere (Barnes and Prior, 1996).

The creation and extension of choice for individual users of public services was one of the key ideological underpinnings of Tory government policy in its mission to expose public services to the dynamics of the market. In an earlier article we criticised this emphasis on consumer choice, arguing that an examination of the circumstances in which people actually use public services indicates that, in many situations, the availability of 'choice' is unlikely to be regarded by users as beneficial (Barnes and Prior, 1995).

There are circumstances of service use, especially encountered by the users of welfare services, that are characterised by uncertainty, risk and confusion. In such cases, the requirement on users to make a choice about the type of service they want, or who they want to provide it, may actually be experienced as disempowering. Trust is a significant factor affecting the confidence with which people make use of services in such contexts. However, trusting the experts to know best is no longer an option. Here we explore what a reciprocal and dynamic concept of trust might mean in the context of relationships between users and providers of welfare services.

Trust and the development of welfare services

The postwar welfare settlement was intended to banish the five 'giants' defined by Beveridge: ignorance, want, disease, idleness and squalor. Fifty years on, we know that these giants have not been vanquished (Commission on Social Justice, 1994). Questioning of the form and scope of the welfare state which started under the Tory government is continuing under a New Labour government which has set its face against redistributive policies and increases in taxation to resource welfare provision. This questioning is not just about the relative costs and benefits of welfare: it addresses the moral basis of the idea of 'welfare' itself, which rests on the respective rights and responsibilities of individual citizens and government. Our focus on welfare services, rather than public services generally, is intended to reflect on particular characteristics of those services and the way in which they are used at a time when the welfare state is subject to potentially radical review.

We begin by considering the significance of 'trust' in changes in patterns of welfare provision, particularly in the transition from hierarchical to contract-based forms of management and organisation. Hierarchy was the dominant principle of public service management in the 'classic' phase of the British welfare state from 1948 to the 1970s. This was an era when the public and private sectors were clearly demarcated. Although hierarchical management was dominant in both sectors, they were distinguished by different structures of ownership and public accountability. These differences had an effect on management and organisational processes. Thus the public and private sectors were also distinguished by different operational forms through which hierarchical management principles were expressed.

Hierarchy in the public sector was characterised by:

- large-scale, vertically integrated service delivery organisations;
- direct control of all functions from policy formation to service delivery;
- upward accountability to local or national political authorities;

- political authorities accountable to the public through the electoral process;
- operations governed by a combination of bureaucratic and professional expertise;
- resource allocation and organisation designed to ensure uniformity of outputs.

These general characteristics were subject to considerable variation within different public service settings. Key variables included the nature and extent of political control over different services, and the balance of power between bureaucratic and professional expertise within different services (Newman and Clarke, 1994). Professional power was predominant in the NHS, for example. At a local level neither bureaucrats nor politicians could challenge the authority of doctors. In contrast, local government housing services had a weak professional base and were subject to strong political control. Education occupied a position somewhere between the two. The power of teachers was strong in the classroom, but had little impact within local authority decision-making structures.

Collective trust (the trust of society, or the public in general) was an implicit rather than explicit feature of the institutional formation of the welfare state. The foundation of the welfare state itself can be seen as enhancing the trust of citizens in the state as a source of protection from the ravages of Beveridge's giants (see Deakin, 1987). In practice, trust in the state was dependent on direct experience of those public service organisations responsible for delivering welfare services, but was underpinned by consensus around the principles on which the welfare state was founded. Chief among these was the principle of equity: that everyone who received services from welfare state organisations would be treated in the same way, regardless of differing economic and social characteristics and of individual preferences. The public's trust was that the professional or administrative class which ran the welfare state would do so in order to best meet the general needs of society. The principal guardian of collective trust was the democratic state itself, exercising its guardianship through a range of regulatory powers and mechanisms of political accountability. As importantly, however, guardianship was also provided through the self-regulating mechanisms adopted by key professional groupings within the welfare state.

Collective trust was grounded in the individual experience of trust in the particular experts (the individual professionals and officials) with whom service users came into contact. This involved personal trust in the professional or the official with whom the user was dealing, who was seen as engaged in meeting the public interest, rather than serving a profit motive or other personal interest. It also involved an impersonal trust in the authority (often scientific or legal) of the expert knowledge held by those who, through their control of this expertise, provided access to the resources and services of the welfare state: GPs, social workers, school teachers, housing officials and others.

The way in which collective trust and individual trust interacts in the institutional framework of hierarchy generates two dynamics which help sustain the framework:

- If an individual welfare professional or official abuses a service user's trust in him or her, this does not necessarily destroy trust in the expert system: experience of a rogue doctor would not usually invalidate the patient's acceptance of the authority of medical knowledge.
- If the expert system malfunctions, the user's trust in the particular professional or official with whom they are involved would not usually be damaged: repeated cancellations of appointments for hospital treatment, or lengthy delays, would not undermine trust in the individual GP. Trust at the interpersonal level can survive even a failure of prescribed treatment: the doctor is seen as having done his or her best (see Giddens, 1990, on the distinction between 'trust in persons' and 'trust in systems').

Within the traditional model of hierarchical organisation in the public services, the trust of service users, both collectively and individually, in the welfare system is significant but implicit. It can remain implicit because there is little requirement for *reciprocal* trust: the system does not need to have trust in the users in order for it to work. The user's role is a passive one of following administrative rules and accepting professional or bureaucratic judgements.

Trust and the welfare consumer

This configuration of trust relationships began to break down with the ending of the 'postwar consensus' on the welfare state. As political concerns became focused on the crisis of financing welfare services, so the state as the guardian of collective trust began to *distrust* the self-regulating professionals and officials. They were accused of failing to meet the public interest by squandering resources and ignoring the real needs of users, who paid for public services through their taxes and were therefore entitled to get value for their money. The remedy was the application of principles derived from marketplace economics and managerial practices transferred from the private sector (Pollitt, 1993; Walsh, 1995a).

Two major features of this are significant for a consideration of public trust. First, the bureaucratic elements of the welfare state's expert systems began to be replaced by management techniques of contract and performance measurement. Quality and flexibility came to be prioritised over uniformity of provision. Secondly, the state would no longer be a monopoly provider. Competition between providers within the mixed economy reintroduced the prospect of profit considerations affecting the provision of services.

Within the new market-based institutional framework of the public services, collective trust effectively disappears from the relationship between users and providers. It is replaced by systems of performance measures and targets, achievement of which is controlled through contracts (or contract-like arrangements) with detailed procedures for monitoring and for the imposition of sanctions in the event of failure. The role of guardian of collective trust, previously undertaken by the democratic state, is given to regulatory systems, distanced from direct political control and with little accountability to users, designed to supervise provider competition (Walsh, 1994). Rather than trusting the providers, consumers are asked to place their collective trust in the regulators: somewhat ambiguously, both for their impartiality and for their ability to have consumer interests at heart.

For the individual user, the transformation is from having trust in the expert system to having consumer rights in relation to the system. Users are themselves transformed into 'customers'. Most of these customers will, as before, have little technical understanding of the system, but they are no longer required or expected to be passive – if things go wrong, they are empowered as consumers to take action (Prime Minister, 1991).

In this construction the relationship between the citizen and the state is usurped by that between the consumer and the provider and/or regulator. Collective considerations are marginalised; the individual customer is assumed to know best. The authority of expert knowledge is challenged by the authority of the consumer (Keat et al, 1994). The deployment of consumer 'rights and entitlements' is one aspect of this confrontation.

The institutional framework of the welfare state can be challenged in this way because users have also come to question both professional and bureaucratic knowledge and authority. Their experiences of welfare services have often confirmed the criticism that services are dominated by producer interests, and that they are expected to receive what is offered without question. The access of consumers to a proliferating range of alternative knowledges, which challenge the hegemony of professional, scientific and official knowledges over the identification and interpretation of people's personal and social needs, has brought into question trust in the experts.

Historically, the development of these alternative knowledges, discourses and material practices is bound up with the disintegration of the postwar consensus on welfare and the wider consumer revolution that characterised Western economies from the 1960s onwards. The development of alternatives is, in part, the response of the market creating new products for consumption. Globalisation and the development of an increasingly multicultural society within the UK has further opened up access to a wider range of knowledge systems from which to 'choose' (see also Chapter Three by Newman on the relevance of diversity).

But, more significantly for our argument, they are also in part the result of the development and validation of *experiential* knowledge: alternative ways of responding to need that emerge from people's engagement in processes of self-discovery and understanding, articulating what they know intuitively about the world or uncovering through discussion and analysis of shared experiences knowledge that has previously been hidden (Wainwright, 1994).

Women's groups are a well-documented example of the process at work, but it is a characteristic of 'new social movements' generally. The development of experiential knowledge invariably involves a critique of established knowledge-based authority, some of which feeds into general public awareness. Thus there has been a partial transfer of awareness and understanding about women's needs in relation to health services – and a consequent dissatisfaction with aspects of health service provision for women – from the women's movement into wider public discourse.

In assessing the impact on the public services of people's awareness of 'other knowledges', it is helpful to distinguish between alternatives which claim an intellectual authority comparable to those knowledge systems which currently dominate (for example, holistic medicine), and alternatives which counter the authority claims of *any* 'abstract system' with assertions of the primacy of knowledge arising from personal experience. Such assertions are a political challenge to the status quo rather than a rival intellectual challenge. Both, however, while quite different from the challenge that is based in notions of consumer rights, contribute to a weakening of professional authority and to the undermining of trust in the 'expert'.

This is not to deny that trust in the functioning of expert systems may still be present. Trust in medical knowledge remains widespread, and the knowledge-based authority of doctors is widely accepted (Calnan and Williams, 1992; Lupton, 1996). This trust in certain kinds of expertise may be psychologically necessary: much medical treatment, such as surgery and various drug therapies, involves risks, and those contemplating treatment need to have trust in the outcome. But this is a separate issue from the particular trust requirements of a contract-based, market-oriented management culture.

Within this culture, the issue of users' trust in individual professionals or officials remains important. This is well recognised in the theory and practice of the 'new public management'. Thus the emphasis on customer responsiveness and user-friendliness (ranging from the 'Have a nice day' syndrome to making accessible personal records on users) has, as one of its aims, the building and maintenance of trust in the service, which is necessary if the service is to be effective and successful in a competitive environment. Good public relations is a central part of public service delivery in the age of the empowered consumer; correspondingly, high value is placed on professional interpersonal skills as against more traditional technical skills.

However, the trust relationship between user and professional or official is different from that in the hierarchical model. The professional or official tends to be seen not as the interface between the user and the expert system (and therefore someone who can be trusted in spite of the system) but as a representative of the system. The dynamics noted earlier are therefore altered:

- Failure on the part of the individual professional or official is more likely to be seen as indicative of general failures in the expert system: loss of trust in the individual contributes to (or reinforces) loss of trust in the system.

- Failure on the part of the system generates loss of trust in the individual system representative. This is likely to be heightened when individual professionals are taking responsibility for overall management of the user's involvement with the system: it is not unreasonable that a GP who purchases treatment for a patient in a specific hospital is held responsible by the patient if the hospital makes an error.

Contract-based management, like hierarchical management, does not require trust to be placed in users. Unlike hierarchical management, however, it does not assume users to be passive in the face of professional-bureaucratic authority. Rather it sees users as active in pursuit of their individual rights to receive what they are entitled to and in exercising their private choices.

Contradictions of public service consumerism

Underlying this assumption of the active consumer is a series of tensions which arises from an ambivalence concerning the perceived competence or incompetence of users. Freedom to pursue private choices implies either that the user is regarded as sufficiently competent to know what she needs (that is, to choose what is in her best interests – the assumption underpinning the model of the rational economic actor) *or* that it does not matter, from the point of view of the service, if the user is not sufficiently competent to understand her needs and may therefore make a 'wrong' choice. However, for a number of public services – which are public because they serve collective as well as individual interests, and therefore have to balance multiple objectives – this second assumption is problematic. This is recognised in the formal limitations on freedoms to exercise choice in relation to services placed on certain 'incompetent' users: people with mental health problems, older people and children, for example.

Thus when people with mental health problems are assessed as endangering either their own health or others' safety, they can be compulsorily admitted to hospital and required to receive medical treatment. This is justified on the grounds of both public safety and the interests of the patient. Public discomfort at older people living in conditions of squalor and neglect authorises forcible removal from such situations. Individual autonomy (that is, freedom to choose), is subordinated to a social requirement for minimum standards of self-care, thereby justifying the intervention of welfare professionals.

For many other services, the consequences of the consumer making a 'wrong' choice matter because the consequences extend beyond the individual to affect others, or indeed society as a whole. Examples here could include: a parental decision not to allow a child access to available nursery education, a decision to leave school immediately this is legally possible rather than undertake further education, or a decision to discharge oneself from hospital against doctors' advice. However, current judgement is that individual autonomy should not be overtly constrained in such circumstances. Within a liberal state, much policy is concerned with the search for *acceptable* means of constraining the exercise of choices such as these. Similarly, decisions about the kinds of situation within which coercive action is justifiable form the substance of much political debate regarding welfare policy.

A second tension is generated by uncertainty about whether users can be trusted with information about the system whose services they are consuming: information concerning rules and procedures, performance measures, allocation criteria, professional competencies, reasons for political decisions. The economic model requires that all participants in a market have equal access to information, but professional-bureaucratic assumptions about public interest and user 'incompetence' have frequently prevented access of individual users to information about how public services and their professional practitioners operate.

Thirdly, there is a tension about whether users can be trusted not to make unreasonable or inappropriate demands on a public service once they are given fuller information on what it does and how it can be accessed. This problem arises from the clash between the anticipated behaviour of people who are encouraged to think of themselves as consumers in a market, leading to an expansion of demand, and service provision which is restrained by public resource allocation decisions and is unable to meet increased demand. The frantic policy reversal on the explicit identification of 'needs', following the implementation of the 1990 NHS and Community Care Act, is an example of this. Once a 'need' was identified through a formal assessment process involving both provider and user, the fear was that social services authorities could become legally obliged to meet it by users appealing to the courts. Hence advice from the Department of Health cautioned against defining as 'needs' the difficulties of users identified during community care assessments.

Within the market-based system of public welfare, therefore, the issue of trust between consumers and providers is highly problematic. It is a site of contradictory forces, as people are both trusted as private agents in a market ('the customer is always right') and not trusted as users of public resources. This 'trust/distrust' duality is configured in different ways within different services. The state, in pursuit of specific policy objectives, shapes the separate public services according to different balances of consumer choice and citizen obligation.

Thus there is currently some consumer choice over which school a child may attend, but a requirement that all children follow the same National Curriculum. Parents are trusted to make choices about educational quality but not trusted as competent to make choices about educational content or, indeed, about whether it is in their or their child's interest to undergo education (Ranson and Thomas, 1989). With health services, similarly, people have some choice over health service quality, but little or none over content. They may choose which GP to attend, but it is the GP who chooses which drugs to prescribe or whether to refer elsewhere for treatment.

Unlike education, people are implicitly trusted to make choices about their actual usage of prescribed healthcare. With the exception of treatment under the Mental Health Act, there is generally no explicit element of compulsion about service use and people may choose not to accept the treatment offered, for example, refusing to undergo an operation or not taking prescribed medicines. While some do exercise such rights to refuse treatment, the complexity of relationships between patients and their doctors suggests that to view such choices as indications of autonomous consumerism is a simplistic and inappropriate analysis (Lupton, 1996; Meredith, 1993). In spite of this, concerns are increasingly being expressed about 'untrustworthy' patients who do not attend appointments or who do not take prescribed medication. At the time of writing expected revisions to the Patients' Charter are likely to include emphasis on the responsibilities of people as consumers of healthcare as well as on 'rights'.

With community care services, the situation is still more complicated (Barnes, 1997; Lewis, 1994). Community care policy is based on a necessary and implicit trust in the competence of 'informal carers' (family members or neighbours of the person requiring care) to provide the principal care resource; formal services are increasingly seen as existing to support the informal care role. But access to these formal supports relies on a complex, and arguably confused, system of assessment of individual needs and selection of appropriate provision by professionals. Steps have been taken to increase the degree of user and carer influence over both needs assessment and service choice, but the lack of trust in users to make appropriate decisions about what is right for them is reflected in the official refusal to accept that the definition of need should necessarily determine the allocation of service.

Housing is different again (Clapham et al, 1990). Perhaps because housing is more obviously a 'commodity' and because, unlike education, health and social care, private sector provision far outstrips the public sector, there is less equivocation about the state's acceptance of the consumer's competence. Current policy implies a high level of trust in that it is geared towards encouraging people to become homeowners: people are to be trusted to meet their own housing needs and, through incentives, are assisted in so doing. However, this predisposition towards trusting the user has also increasingly shaped policy in the residual public housing sector, with much of the recent development being concerned with passing control and responsibility for a range of housing and estate management issues over to tenants.

By contrast, social security policy demonstrates little or no trust in benefits recipients. Operational procedures are geared towards the prevention of fraud. Entitlements are governed by officially defined criteria and much of the service effort is concerned with 'policing the boundary' of those criteria. Other officials, for example doctors, are called on to determine whether criteria are met; users are not trusted to make this judgement themselves. This tends to reinforce a 'dependency' status, which contributes to the official view of recipients as 'incompetent' (Ling, 1994). However, recent policy shifts indicate a view of welfare recipients as 'potentially competent' workers. For instance, the imperatives underpinning the Welfare to Work policy are to reduce the numbers of those claiming benefit, which, in turn, requires an assumption that recipients have to be encouraged to recognise their competence beyond their status as 'welfare dependants'.

These illustrations suggest that the identity of the 'welfare consumer' operating in a market for welfare services is by no means fully established. Moreover they point to a considerable variation in the nature of this identity between different services (Harrow and Shaw, 1992). This variation underpinned our earlier analysis of the contradictions in the notion of 'choice' as a universal principle of public service provision. If we accept the description of the new economic and political configuration

of the public services as 'quasi-markets' (Le Grand and Bartlett, 1993) –
that is, as displaying some of the key characteristics of conventional markets
(competing suppliers, consumers making choices) but differing from them
in other ways (competing suppliers who are not necessarily profit-seeking,
consumers not expressing their choices with cash purchases) – then
perhaps what we are describing here are characteristics of the 'quasi-
consumer'. The varying position of the public service user along the
'trust/distrust' axis is, we would argue, one of these key characteristics.

Conclusion: trust beyond consumerism?

Our analysis has focused on the relationships between users and providers
within hierarchical and market systems of welfare. Under hierarchy, trust
operates explicitly in one direction: the user trusts the provider. The
trust relationship is coherent but limited. In the current market-oriented
system, trust relationships are more complex and less coherent. The user
increasingly relates to the provider through a framework of rights and
entitlements rather than trust. In neither system is there substantial
evidence of reciprocal trust: the user is not seen as sufficiently competent
to determine the nature of the service to be provided, nor to contribute
to collective decision making about welfare policies.

However, the neo-liberal philosophy underpinning current policy does
emphasise individual responsibility for behaviour and choices intended
to reduce 'dependence' on state welfare. Examples include exhortations
to adopt healthy lifestyles to minimise the need for healthcare, to take on
paid work in addition to the work of bringing up children and to take
on family responsibilities for the care of older relatives. This should alert
us to be cautious about what Newman (in Chapter Three) refers to as
the promiscuous application of the concept of trust. Simply turning the
equation around and advocating trust in individuals to meet their own
needs cannot provide what we have referred to elsewhere as 'a new social
basis for welfare' (Barnes and Prior, 1996). If we are advocating the
development of a reciprocal notion of trust which recognises the
contribution to be made by the diversity of knowledges and competencies
of welfare consumers then, as Newman argues, we need to address issues
of power within the provider–consumer relationship.

Typically, users are constructed as customers, in competition with each
other for the acquisition of scarce resources. Welfare consumerism focuses
on the relationship between individuals and services, rather than that

between citizens and the state. It tends to erode trust *between* users and to limit their capacity to identify a collective interest in ensuring high quality public services; its emphasis is on private action for personal gain rather than collective action for public benefit. Consumerism offers little incentive for users to identify themselves as members of groups of people with common experiences. By individualising users as self-interested competitors, consumerism restricts the possibilities for users to support and learn from each other and, thereby, to become more effective participants both in decision making about services and in social life more generally. Lack of 'competence' among users is reinforced, and providers remain, at best, ambivalent in their willingness to trust users to make appropriate decisions. A shift in the balance of power to enable relationships of mutual trust to be established is not really possible.

The potential for an alternative and more constructive approach is evident in the development of certain organisations of users. Through activities of self-help, consciousness-raising and campaigning, these demonstrate an awareness of the value of trust between users themselves and of the limitation of the model which constructs users as competing consumers. This approach moves from a two-way relationship of provider and consumer, to a triangular relationship of provider, individual user and user group.

This has a number of significant effects. Participation in user group activities helps develop the competence of individual users in understanding their own needs and in responding to providers. It makes explicit the value of alternative knowledges and experiences and gives validity to them. It thereby helps redress the power imbalance between users and providers at both individual and collective levels (see, for example, Barnes and Shardlow, 1997). By developing relationships of trust with each other, users demonstrate to providers their capacity to be trusted partners in relations of co-production. Moving from the competitive individualism assumed by market systems of welfare, to forms of cooperative organisation established by user groups, creates opportunities for the development of reciprocal relationships of trust between users and providers which have been conspicuously lacking in the development of public welfare services to date.

This is not to ignore the tensions evident in relationships between user organisations and provider organisations – particularly as these too become increasingly mediated by contracts. The significance of user self-organisation (in the context of our consideration of trust as a means of analysing new social relationships between citizens and state, and public service users and providers) is that the development of trust is no longer solely dependent on the nature of the relationship established between the *individual* user and provider and/or the system they represent. The possibility of trust becoming a dynamic process within a developing relationship, rather than a static prerequisite underpinning continuing dependence on provider good faith and competence, is thus enhanced.

EIGHT

Quality and citizens

Lucy Gaster and Nicholas Deakin

The quality of services is part of democracy

The trust of citizens in their institutions of governance is vital to the health and stability of a democratic society. Government has a duty to respond to, and have a care for, the 'public good', the needs of individuals and of society as a whole (Stewart and Walsh, 1989). It is also the recipient of public funds, for which it acts as 'steward', and is accountable to the voters and taxpayers without whose support it would not survive. If that support is withdrawn locally or nationally, the case for public services to exist at all is under threat. In the last two decades, when all aspects of the welfare state have been under attack from central government, public support for its continued existence, albeit in new forms, has been essential. Yet how strong is this support? Is it based on a reluctant recognition that at least some services can only be provided for the common good or to protect the weak through public institutions? Or is it more positive, seeing public institutions, especially those which are elected, as the guardian of rights and citizenship, as the organ of accountability in an increasingly unaccountable world, as an institution people would fight to save?

Public expectations of government, as a democratic institution and as a provider of services, are currently not very high. Recurring incidents of 'sleaze', infighting and misuse of public funds (Committee of Public Accounts, 1994), together with the experience of poor and uneven services and the continuing funding crisis in public services lead the public to wonder whether it is worth voting in elections (or even registering to vote) and to ask whether resources are being used as effectively as they should for the public benefit. Can the public, in other words, *trust* government to deliver services that are appropriate, fair and efficient? Can they trust government to listen to and learn from the public? Does 'government', through the remaining public sector of local government, the health services and central government 'Next Steps' agencies, or through the widening range of quangos, private companies, contractors and voluntary organisations now delivering public services, reinforce or deny people's role as citizens? And, whichever the answer to this question, how is this done?

There are, of course, many kinds of relationship between organs of government and the public. As mentioned above, the electoral process is one such relationship. The service relationship is another. It is increasingly argued that the two are closely interlinked, and that a good service relationship – in other words, a good experience of services as they are planned, designed, delivered and monitored – is a foundation upon which new 'citizen' roles can be built (Corrigan, 1996). People will not even exercise their rights as citizens, far less perform their duties, if they feel that the institutions which are set up to protect and enable them to exercise those rights are themselves flawed and weak.

The premise of this chapter is that the quality of public services is (or should be) an integral element in the policy and practice of democracy. The actual quality of *particular* services experienced by individuals, families, groups and communities is a practical symbol of a *general* relationship: that between service providers and the public as a whole. If service quality is 'good', it increases the credibility of the organisation and the trust of citizens in its ability to fulfil its public purposes. If quality is 'bad' – and we come to definitions later – then mistrust is almost certainly present, as both cause and effect. This in turn decreases the credibility of the service provider and, in services delivered through contracts, of the purchaser as well.

Relationships between provider and consumer or public service and citizen exist in several dimensions. Using its knowledge of political, professional, managerial policies and practice, the public makes a judgement as to whether to have trust in, say, a local authority, a hospital trust, or a central government agency such as the Child Support Agency or the Benefits Agency. Such knowledge may derive from direct experience or be mediated through press reports, public relations and word of mouth. It is one of the influences on what people expect of public service organisations and what, as citizens, they feel they have a right to.

But the day-to-day relationship of service provision is possibly the most immediate influence. It is this, the experience of policy in action, that tells the public whether a particular organisation is sticking to its principles and fulfilling its promises (and duties). And feedback from the public – through studying patterns of use, complaints, survey findings and direct communication – can inform the organisation about whether and how it needs to change. An organisation that listens to its public needs to consider what kind of organisation it is and how it interprets its role as a public service provider. The key question becomes: what is the business we are in, and how should we develop and put into practice policies to improve service quality?

Practical policies to differentiate more clearly between consumer needs, and to develop more consistent and reliable services, may be a spin-off from market testing, quasi-markets, compulsory contracting and the like, as is discussed in the preceding chapter and elsewhere in this book. In the sense that such policies have forced public service organisations to rethink their services and, to some degree at least, to consider how these are received and perceived from the point of view of service recipients, this shift has been important for consumers. However, as we see it, one important effect of contracts, performance measures and internal markets has been to divert institutions away from thinking more clearly about the needs of the public. Enormous tensions now exist between what ten years ago was strikingly encapsulated as the 'public service orientation' (Clarke and Stewart, 1987) and the 'business orientation' of current management thinking. Fulfilling quantitative targets, winning market shares, controlling contracts, even making 'profits', all lead only too easily to 'cream-skimming' or 'cherry-picking' (concentrating on the easy things) and to thinking of 'quality' merely as a technical process to ensure standardised 'conformance to specification' (Gaster, 1995).

By playing the contractual game, the players (clients and contractors, purchasers and providers) can find themselves neglecting the real needs of consumers and, in particular, the wider public of 'citizens' (Walsh et al, 1997). 'We know best' is coming back in a new guise.

Services as complex, interactive processes

Service delivery is a complex activity. Like manufacturing, services are the outcome of a whole series of interdependent activities but, unlike manufacturing, they are not the result of a technical or mechanical process, and the end–product is not generally one that can be standardised. For some routine private services, in banking, hotels or insurance for example, the service providers try to routinise and prescribe the details of the service transaction as closely as possible. Customers know what to expect and can choose a different supplier next time if they do not like what they experience. However, consumers of public services cannot be equated with 'customers' in a supermarket. They often cannot choose whether or not to receive the service and they cannot go to another supplier if they do not like their first experience. In many services, the first experience is the decisive one, and after that it is too late to change (childcare interventions, community care assessments, healthcare interventions, housing allocations are simply the tip of the iceberg).

For some public services, for example, environmental services such as street cleaning, refuse disposal, street lighting and grounds maintenance, explicit outputs can be specified in advance. It may appear to the service providers, the professionals and the managers, that not much debate is needed about what these outputs should consist of. However, recent debates around Agenda 21, plans for new roads and better understanding of community safety underline that even in these apparently 'simple' services, a technical specification is not the end of the story. As direct consumers and as citizens and members of communities, people feel strongly and are willing to make their feelings known, sometimes in radical ways.

Once an overall specification or standard has been debated and agreed, some level of flexibility will almost certainly be needed. Even in apparently routine services, this will be necessary if the service is not to be rigid and, from the point of view of the customer or consumer, unsatisfactory in character (form and frequency). Acknowledging the differing needs of individuals, groups or localities could well lead to differences in how, or how often, the service is delivered. Actual examples from environmental services, to continue that particular theme, have included: helping disabled people put out their bins; taking on a reporting and communication role in remote rural areas; giving priority to cutting the grass in children's play areas; working with women's groups to decide priorities for street lighting.

In many services, the situation is still more complicated. Sometimes it is impossible to tell what the 'product' is until well after the service transaction has taken place – in the case of medical intervention, for example, or providing training for unemployed people. In many personal services, life-changing events take place which, while subject to general principles determined by law, contract or local rules, must nevertheless be decided through local discretion, influenced by the particular circumstances of the case and the interaction between the main interested parties.

Public service quality has, then, to take account of many more factors than private products. As Kieron Walsh and John Stewart pointed out (Stewart and Walsh, 1989), public services not only have to try to meet users' requirements, they also reflect the wider needs of society, aiming to meet public purposes which in some cases will override individuals' preferences and needs.

The questions then become: how to define the users' needs and the public (citizens') purposes; and how to reach the best accommodation between them.

Balancing individual and collective needs

In the past, certain people – elected representatives, professionals, managers – have taken it on themselves to define what services they felt the public needed, what was in the public interest and what was not. At least as far as elected representatives were concerned, at local or national level, such views were influenced both by political belief and by actual knowledge, acquired through public surgeries and letters, of what mattered to their constituents. Many councillors still feel that they 'know' what is needed and that, once elected, they can speak for the wider public. And they do indeed have the responsibility of making decisions, basing these on a judgement of what is legal, acceptable, affordable and consistent with overall policy.

However, we would argue that not only councillors, but all those responsible for the delivery of public services, including quango appointees, management committee members, managers and professionals can make better decisions if the public directly affected by services or with a democratic interest in them are involved in helping to make decisions.

Long experience of poor, insensitive and inappropriate services have undoubtedly led to low public expectations and a lack of trust in the service providers. This is mirrored by service providers' apparent lack of respect for the public and lack of faith in their own product. The professionals 'knew best' and there was no one to challenge them. This could be a cause for pessimism. However, the increasing complexities and fragmentation of service delivery, the loss of trust in both politicians and professionals, and the increased ability of individuals and groups to acquire knowledge, form their own views and challenge long-standing professional practice have reduced the certainty, acceptability and credibility of one-sided decision making (see Barnes and Prior, Chapter Seven, and 1997).

At a time when the public no longer trusts the decision makers to make decisions in the interests of the public, and when 'equity' can no longer be equated with 'uniformity', service providers feel under an increasing obligation to respond to this mixture of complexity, 'consumerism' and demand for democratic accountability. At the same time, they feel nervous about (as they see it) raising expectations too high.

So how can the complexities of decision making about services be managed? The right of *individuals* to complain and to receive redress, while they always existed in theory, have now been highlighted by central government through the Citizen's Charter (at the time of writing subject to consultation by the new Labour government, but unlikely to be abandoned). At the same time, many local authorities have been struggling since the early 1980s to become more open, accountable and accessible to their *communities* (Gaster and Hoggett, 1993). New and different structures and processes have been established, generally, it has to be said, on local government's terms, to involve the public in a more active way (Stewart, 1996b; Stoker 1997). However, structural solutions are not enough on their own. The old attitudes can persist unless a culture exists to support new relationships between public service agencies and the public, fostering mutual knowledge, respect and influence.

The level and indeed quality of the dialogue between public service providers and their public, not only with current users, as was urged on us through the Citizen's Charter policy, but also with citizens in a much wider sense, is thus vital to achieving a more even balance of power between providers and citizens. It is this, we argue, that is the potential starting point for generating individual and collective mutual trust (and it does have to go both ways) in the context of day-to-day service delivery and the much wider arena of democracy and citizenship.

Consumers, citizens and quality

In thinking about quality, citizens have two relationships to public services.

They can be *consumers* – active users (willing or not), past users, and people wishing or needing to consume but excluded from doing so because of rationing, discrimination, inaccessibility or other causes. This is a direct relationship.

At the same time, they can have a broader interest in service quality because they are members of the wider community – an indirect relationship derived from the rights and duties of *citizenship*.

> **Citizenship as a status derives from membership of a particular political community and gives expression to the relationship between individual members and the community's institutions of government, and between individual members themselves. The status of citizen locates the individual within a body of reciprocal rights and obligations. (Prior et al, 1995, pp 5-6)**

Both these relationships, as consumers and as citizens, give rise to a right to speak about service quality *and* to be heard. Consumers have procedural rights, deriving from their immediate relationship with the state, mostly but not exclusively expressed in the form of redress. Citizens have substantive civil rights derived from their status as residents, voters and taxpayers. Civil rights enable citizens to influence and shape society and to participate in the state's decision-making processes (Taylor et al, 1992).

The freedom to exercise these substantive rights is important for all citizens. It is vital for those who have in practice been excluded. Reasons for their exclusion include rationing (failure to meet increasingly stringent eligibility criteria), inaccessibility, discrimination, poverty, ignorance or because inclusion of 'difficult' cases makes it more difficult to achieve the numerical targets required by current contractual practice. Recently publicised examples of the latter type of exclusions include patients of non-fundholding GPs; children with lower examination achievement levels; the chronic sick, or old people with expensive illnesses; older long-term unemployed – the list has become alarmingly long.

We therefore see the notion of citizenship as inclusive. People are both citizens *and* consumers, self-evidently so in the case of 'universal' services provided for all individuals (social security, for example) and whole communities (roads, refuse collection, police), possibly so for other services which, even though we may not need them now, may be needed in the future. Also, as John Stewart points out,

> **Citizens have views on education, on the care of the elderly and indeed the welfare of communities, irrespective of whether or not they are users of particular services. To restrict an authority's concerns to customers is to deny citizens their right to be heard and beyond that to participate. (Stewart, 1996a)**

If, as we suggest, citizens not only could but should be actively involved in the development of public services – and in improving their quality, as suggested by the current 'Best Value' policy – the relationship needs to be as straightforward as possible. Policies to improve quality, including the insertion of 'quality clauses' in contracts (Walsh, 1991b), have so far tended to be top-down and over-complex. Whether through Quality Assurance accreditation, Total Quality Management approaches or in the struggle for supremacy between clients and contractors, purchasers and providers, the democratic element has tended to be squeezed out.

So is it possible to change direction, to redress the balance in some way and to take a more 'bottom-up' approach? Is it technically feasible for citizens to become actively involved in defining and implementing quality improvement?

Defining quality

Quality can be defined as a collection of characteristics, decided through a process of bargaining. These reflect, explicitly or covertly, the prevailing sets of values, professional, managerial or political, and the service objectives that derive from them. Expressed as a written standard, as a contract condition, or through 'custom and practice', these characteristics of quality should reflect the notion of 'fitness for purpose': what is the 'technical' or 'objective' quality the organisation is aiming to achieve? The other extremely important dimension – without which the 'technical' quality is unlikely to be achieved – is the 'non-technical', subjective quality that expresses the relationship between the service and the public (Pollitt and Bouckaert, 1995). Interpersonal and environmental quality is what demonstrates, verbally and non-verbally, whether mutual respect, knowledge or understanding exists between service providers and the public.

In an organisation that acknowledges and values the participation of citizens (as 'users' *and* as 'citizens'), defining quality can become part of the democratic process. This is not necessarily straightforward, as we show below, but it contrasts with the situation prevailing in organisations where there is no such acknowledgement or valuing, no bargaining and no negotiation. In such organisations, quality is merely another technocratic (ticking boxes) and managerial ('we [still] know best') approach to service delivery.

We do not propose to analyse in any detail the forces that affect processes of consultation and participation in general. This we have both done elsewhere (for example, Gaster and Taylor, 1993; Deakin et al, 1995), as have other writers interested in the processes of participative and representative democracy (Hambleton and Hoggett, 1990; Lowndes and Stoker, 1992; Stewart, 1995; 1996a; Stoker, 1997). We would simply reiterate three broad findings from the considerable amount of research on this question:

- The need for honesty as to what the consultation is about and the extent to which the public's views and suggestions can realistically be expected to affect the result.
- The need to recognise that 'success' will not be instantaneous or necessarily based on consensus: time is needed to demonstrate the match between words and action (small but symbolically significant actions can help here) and bargaining will be needed to decide what that action is.
- The need for the process to be supported, practically and psychologically, removing barriers to participation so that the public feels empowered to express real views, without the fear of being shouted down or patronised if they challenge existing practice.

Bargaining and negotiating about quality – an analytical approach

Bargaining can take place through direct consultation with and participation by citizens' groupings of various kinds (interest, community or identity) and through elected representatives. However, it takes time and effort, and there are many forces to prevent even the most committed organisations from fully supporting the process. It is only too easy to fall into tokenism, which in turn leads to loss of trust and lack of public credibility and legitimacy.

Therefore, so as to bring the democratic approach to quality to the fore, not as an 'add-on' gesture, but as a normal part of everyday working, we suggest a 'force field analysis' (Lewin, quoted in Hicks, 1991, p 290) as the starting point for action. This useful device helps to disentangle the influences that are either preventing or potentially helping an organisation move forward to achieve defined goals. In this case, the goal would be involvement of citizens in the steps required to improve public service quality so as to produce real changes. Once analysed, choices can be made as to whether to try to reduce the 'negative' forces or to strengthen the 'positive' forces.

Negative forces would be those that increase the complexity and remoteness of organisations and individual services, making people (staff and the public) cynical about quality and unwilling to become involved in discussing it. Positive forces would be those that increase the credibility, simplicity, accessibility and accountability of the organisation in the eyes of citizens, encouraging a feeling that invitations to participate are genuine – can be *trusted* – and will have a real effect on the outcome.

> **The more there is trust then the easier it is to develop long term relationships that are self-reinforcing.** (Walsh, 1995a, p 50)

Negative forces preventing democratic involvement in quality

Each public service organisation setting out to involve citizens in quality improvements will need to make its own analysis of local factors affecting their ability to become involved in practice. We can predict that in such analyses some of the factors arising from recent changes in the processes of service production are likely to have negative consequences:

- the development of internal markets ('marketisation'), if driven solely or largely by commercial concerns;
- citizen's charters (if based solely on the notion of the citizen as individual consumer);
- legalistic and confrontational contractual relationships;
- quality assurance systems, quantitative performance indicators and performance related pay, if insensitively introduced and mechanically applied;
- the undervaluing of front line staff – the vital tip of the organisational iceberg by which the rest of the organisation will be judged.

These consequences are 'negative' if they reinforce departmental, professional or hierarchical divisions, and/or exclude the public and lead organisations away from a public service orientation. However, we do not see the negative experience as inevitable. Discussion in this book and elsewhere (Prior et al, 1993; Walsh, 1995a; Gaster, 1995; Deakin and Walsh, 1996; Walsh et al, 1997) demonstrates both the desirability and the possibility of developing different kinds of contracts, quality systems, charters and even internal markets.

If the underlying values are those of mutual trust and cooperation, not confrontation, the right start can be made on developing contract specifications and service standards with the help of consumers and citizens. 'Expert' knowledge can be combined with 'experiential' knowledge to develop a powerful and workable definition of the services to be provided (see Chapter Seven by Barnes and Prior). Once in place, such contracts and standards can be jointly monitored and in some cases co-produced, leaving room for flexibility and citizen involvement in the production process. And while purchasers and providers of, say, community care may compete for the right to consult the public, as sometimes seems to be the case (Harrison, 1993), this is surely better than excluding them altogether. Conscious or unconscious exclusion is very easily achieved in negotiations between, say, health authorities, health trusts, social services and voluntary organisations (Martin and Gaster, 1993). Nevertheless, imaginative and committed organisations and departments can and do include citizens – or, more often, current users – as key and active 'interests' or 'stakeholders' in relation to service quality (Stewart, 1996a; Audit Commission, 1997, para 1).

The weakness of consumer-based models of action, like the (so-called) Citizen's Charter, is that they exclude in another way, by admitting only half the concerns of citizens as legitimate (those affecting them in their capacity as individual users of services) but do not recognise the accountability of service providers to the community at large (Deakin, 1994). This is the real citizenship dimension. Some of the gains made recently as a result of the introduction of charters in the standards of services to consumers are genuine and welcome. But the charters confer no rights upon citizens and therefore contribute little to inclusive dialogue or participation.

Public services can consider and respond to the 'citizen question' (Gaster, 1996) at three levels. There is the 'macro' level of service priorities and overall planning: what services need to exist and what shape should they take? There is the 'meso' level, where consideration of specifications and standards, of implementation and public participation can be debated for particular areas of service and need; and there is the 'micro' level of the day-to-day experience of the public receiving, applying for or being refused particular services. All these need to be brought into the frame. The consistency of approach at all three levels would be one indicator of a real culture shift towards the inclusion of consumers and citizens in service quality.

Once the principle of 'inclusion' rather than 'exclusion' is adopted, it is easy to see that it needs to apply within the organisation as well as in its external relations: staff, too, need to be treated with respect and valued for what they can contribute. Indeed, as innovators tend to find, underestimating the 'human resource factor' (which includes the role of trades unions) can put a policy on or near the rocks (Ashrif, 1993; Homa and Bevan, 1996; Gaster, 1997).

Positive forces assisting democratic involvement in quality

As with 'negative' forces, so in the analysis of 'positive' forces, we would expect individual organisations to come to their own conclusion, based on their local circumstances. Again, however, some factors are likely to be present in many, if not most, situations where active inclusion of citizens in quality developments seems to be possible. They are, on the whole, the converse of the negative factors discussed above, but distinguished from them by the creative approach to policy interpretation and the existence of political and managerial values which sustain the idea of *public* services in the face of pressures not to do so.

Thus the positive forces could include:

- Any move towards new kinds of relational, trust-based, output-oriented contracts, encouraging negotiation and bargaining and enabling active involvement of citizens.
- Quality policies that start from what citizens need and want, balancing that with legal, financial or technical requirements and capacity, and covering both the 'technical' and the 'non-technical' dimensions of quality.
- Organisational values, structures and cultures that reinforce the legitimate and active role of residents as (collective) citizens, for example, equalities policies, non-hierarchical, non-departmental

cultures, localised and devolved decision-making structures (decentralisation).

> Investment in trust ... is self-reinforcing. There are likely to be vicious and virtuous circles of distrust and trust. Repetitive interaction between social actors will lead to conventions which in turn become established in institutions. Trust then becomes built into the system because one can rely on institutional conventions. (Walsh, 1995a, pp 51-2)

Conclusions

As Andrew Coulson underlines in Chapter Two, trust can easily broken and is not easily mended. One consequence of broken trust is a reliance on rules and procedures – something that we have witnessed in the last decade of 'new public management' (Deakin and Walsh, 1996). As Coulson points out, this approach adds greatly to the transaction costs – for consumer as well as producer – of any service. At the same time it reduces flexibility and responsiveness. Alternative responses to broken trust are withdrawal from the system (rarely possible in public services), avoiding it whenever possible (a common reaction), or actively complaining. Complaints have been increasingly encouraged by government, but they are just as traumatic, difficult and confrontational as they ever were for the dissatisfied consumer. How much better it would be if there was no reason to complain in the first place – getting it right first time.

Collective action, through citizens and service users coming together to protest, negotiate and bargain, is clearly one way forward. The development of more positive relationships – working together to solve joint problems – is even more desirable. The aim must be to reassert the trust of the public in the institutions of governance, working at the macro, meso and micro level to ensure that citizens have a say in what is delivered, know what to expect and receive what is their right. As a counter activity to the negative and alienating experiences of the last decades – some the fault of the public services themselves, some reinforced by central government action – this is all highly necessary.

It is even more necessary when the dangers of exclusion are considered. Citizens have a right to public services, but there are many who do not currently exercise those rights. 'Social exclusion' is an issue exercising the minds of government at central and local levels across Europe. By this we mean exclusion from normal life caused by poverty, discrimination, lack of access or knowledge about services and fear and stigma arising from the past experience of public services. Exclusion cannot be eliminated merely through increased access to labour markets: there are many people who, temporarily or, because of disability or age, permanently, will not be 'included' in this way. Programmes of empowerment and quality improvement – focusing on the relevance, accessibility, sensitivity and flexibility of public services – would go a long way to include people both to exercise their rights as citizens and to experience 'citizenship' in its widest meaning.

Conditions therefore need to be created where a real dialogue with the public as citizens can be achieved. If this is not done, talk about 'quality improvements' descends to jargonistic and alienating management-speak. It may be difficult to measure all aspects of a democratic approach to quality, but this does not mean that it should not be assessed – by citizens themselves as much as, if not more, than the service producers. An essential element is that the relationship between the organisation and the public is based, not on confrontation and/or traditional arrogance and remoteness, but on a more equal mutual appreciation of what each has to offer. This is a democratic dialogue where quality, evolving over time, is the result of negotiation, bargaining and the agreement of what needs to be 'traded off' in order to achieve a generally acceptable (and not necessarily populist) result.

Such negotiation and bargaining must be founded on mutual respect, knowledge, openness and, above all, trust. Consensus is not necessarily the result. It may be necessary to agree to disagree. But if trust, derived from both experience and instinct (see Chapters Two and Three), is not developed and carefully nurtured by all those involved, any hope of developing credible, achievable service quality is severely diminished. And where is the democratic legitimacy of the public service organisation if the quality of its services is unacceptable?

Part Four

Trust between organisations

NINE

Trust and competition: blue-collar services in local government

Howard Davis and Bruce Walker

This chapter is concerned with the issues of trust and competition as they relate to a number of services provided by British local government. The first section outlines the changing policy context of competition for local authority services and is followed by a discussion of the nature of trust under contracting, drawing primarily on elements of economic theory to identify the features of contracting which we would expect to find in a 'low trust world'. We then ask whether these features appear to be present in contracting in local authorities and point to some features of the compulsory competitive tendering (CCT) legislative framework which may help to explain this. After raising the question of whether the sorts of activities subject to CCT would be likely to be subject to competitive tender in the private sector, we outline some aspects of contracting in that sector. This leads us to investigate whether these aspects of private sector contracting could be replicated under CCT and to consider the extent to which it is desirable to do so.

Competition for local authority services – the policy context

There is a long history of the use of competitive tendering processes in British local government, but before the 1980s this had largely been in connection with the procurement of goods and materials and with large capital investment projects. However, two pieces of legislation introduced by the Thatcher-led Conservative government brought about dramatic changes in the way that local government services are organised and represented a major extension of the influence of competition.

The 1980 Local Government Planning and Land Act introduced CCT for highways maintenance and construction and for building maintenance and construction. The 1988 Local Government Act extended CCT to a further seven 'defined activities'. These were refuse collection, street cleaning, schools and welfare catering, other catering, vehicle maintenance, building cleaning and grounds maintenance. The management of sports and leisure facilities was later added to this list. Further extensions of CCT to, predominantly, white collar services were under way at the time of the 1997 General Election, but are not explicitly examined in this chapter.

The essence of CCT under this legislation was that local authority workforces could only continue to undertake the provision of defined activities if they had been successful in winning the work in open competition. They were required to maintain financial accounts separate from the rest of the authority and to achieve minimum financial rates of return. The government reserved to itself a number of powers to regulate the competitive process and to take action against local authorities and their workforces transgressing its interpretation of the legislation.

As a number of writers have discussed (for example, Grayson et al, 1990; Walsh, 1991b; Walsh and Davis, 1993), the impact on the conduct and organisation of local government has been profound. An early need was to establish an organisational divide between the client and contractor sides of services. The client side would be responsible for producing and letting the contract and for monitoring the work of the successful contractor. Where local authorities' own workforces secured the contracts, these became known, following the legislation, as direct labour organisations (DLOs) or direct service organisations (DSOs), for example, those employees and their immediate supervisors who actually empty the town's dustbins.

Labour's landslide victory in the 1997 General Election has brought with it major changes in the policy agenda for local government. Not least among them, and most significant for our purposes, is the intention to replace "the failure of compulsory competitive tendering" (DoE, 1997, p 1) with a requirement for local authorities to achieve 'Best Value' in service provision.

Shortly before the election, Hilary Armstrong MP, who subsequently became the Local Government Minister, had explained Labour's position in the Spring issue of *Progress* as follows:

> **Labour will challenge the compulsion to uniformity that
> [the Conservative] government has attempted to impose.
> CCT is a clear example of this drive to bland uniformity.
> CCT is driven by legalistic rules and regulations drawn up
> by the centre. It is anachronistic, failing to reflect the modern
> relationships which have been developed by forward thinking
> councils and forward looking companies. It isn't only local
> government or direct labour organisations who don't believe
> that the current CCT regime works, it is also many of the
> contractors.**
>
> **A Labour government will abolish the compulsion because
> it has come to stifle innovation and imagination.... We
> believe that it is the requirements of the public which should
> be the overriding factor in determining when and how
> services are provided. What we need therefore is not a new
> model created by ideological dogma, but a new dialogue
> about what framework best assists in deciding what forms
> of delivery are appropriate to which forms of service.**

Competition will remain "an important management tool" (DoE, 1997,
p 2), but local authorities will be able to explore different arrangements
and new processes in their search for efficient and effective service delivery.
In answer to a parliamentary question on 21 November 1997, Hilary
Armstrong indicated that:

> **Competition will remain a vital element of Best Value but
> we are keen to use it in a more flexible and constructive
> way.**

It is against this background that we seek to assess the existence, feasibility
and desirability of trust-based contractual relationships between clients
and DLOs/DSOs under future contracting arrangements.

Trust: some implications for contracting

Lewis and Weigert have suggested that trust:

> **... involves a degree of cognitive familiarity with the object**

> of trust that is somewhere between total knowledge and
> total ignorance. (Lewis and Weigert, 1985, p 970)

In respect of economic relationships in particular, some would see apparent trusting behaviour as being, in reality, based on a careful calculation of likely risk (for example, Williamson, 1996a, Chapter 10 and Coulson, Chapter Two above, p 14). It can nevertheless be argued that the existence of trust between the two or more parties to a transaction is necessary both for that transaction to be entered into in the first instance and for it to be completed successfully. As Arrow has pointed out:

> There is an element of trust in every transaction: typically,
> one object of value changes hands before the other one
> does, and there is confidence that the countervalue will in
> fact be given up. (Arrow, 1973, p 24)

Frankel similarly points to the significance of trust in arguing that:

> ... trust can be said to be based on the belief that the person
> will honour an obligation, and he will keep a promise under
> all circumstances under which he has control. *It is trust in
> this sense which is the binding cement of all contractual relationships.*
> (Frankel, 1977, p 36; italics added)

If this is accepted, the key questions then become, not whether some degree of trust is necessary for contracting and for the conduct of economic activity more generally, but rather what degree of trust is necessary in specific cases and how this affects both the nature of the agreements made and how, subsequently, those agreements function.

There are many interesting approaches to the analysis of contracting and of contracting behaviour, particularly from legal and socio-legal perspectives (see, for example, Macneil, 1980; Zucker, 1986; and, for a perceptive summary, Seal and Vincent-Jones, 1997). Concentrating specifically here on the economics literature on contracting, however, the degree of trust assumed to be present among the contracting parties appears to be of a particularly low order. The likelihood of the parties indulging in opportunistic behaviour, defined by Williamson (1985, p 47) as "self-interest seeking with guile", is seen to be one of the major problems with which any set of arrangements for the governance of economic relationships has to contend. Given the difficulties of drawing up contracts and other agreements covering every eventuality – that is, contracts will almost certainly be 'incomplete' – opportunities are likely to arise for one of the contracted parties to gain at the expense of the other. Williamson argues (1985, p 48) that if people were not opportunistic it would be possible to have a general clause in any agreement to the effect that both parties would openly and honestly share all relevant information between them and would cooperate in activities to their mutual benefit, with those benefits being divided between them in a pre-agreed manner.

Principal-agent theory highlights this issue of information and information disclosure as a particular problem which affects arrangements under which one party (the principal) contracts with another (the agent) to carry out certain tasks for them. Summaries of this theory can be found in, for example, Ricketts (1987, Chapter 5), Sappington (1991) and Petersen (1995), but for our purposes we can summarise the salient features as follows. The principal first faces the problem of choosing the right agent when, arguably, only the agent is fully aware of their own skills and capabilities, and of the objectives that they wish to pursue. Secondly, while the principal may be able to observe the outcome of the agent's work on his or her behalf, they may not be able to observe the effort applied, the assiduousness with which it is undertaken or any surpluses (in cash or in kind) appropriated by the agent as a result of undertaking the work.

This may not be of concern to the principal if the outcome is as required, although the information would be invaluable for the design of any subsequent contracts. The main problem arises when the outcome is different from that specified. The agent is likely to be in possession of superior information as to whether this is due to their own (lack of) effort or whether it is due to external factors genuinely beyond their control. In any event, however, the agent is likely to claim the latter if taking an opportunistic stance. Thus, the information asymmetry as between the parties, both before and after the contract is entered into, is likely to work in favour of the agent. Consequently, the problem, for principal-agent theorists at least, becomes the design of that set of incentives which will militate against both the dangers of choosing the wrong agent ('adverse selection') and those of the agent's subsequent opportunistic behaviour (a form of 'moral hazard').

Local authority contracts under CCT do not in general appear to be characterised by provisions of the sort outlined above relating to the open sharing of information and its subsequent benefits. This may be taken to indicate that the danger of opportunistic behaviour is recognised, or perhaps assumed, in practice. Certainly, if there is a relative lack of trust we would expect there to be certain observable features of the contracting process which might point to this, as the client attempts to avoid the adverse selection of a contractor and to reduce the problems of moral hazard once the contractor is chosen.

These features would include extensive and detailed checks on the contractor's previous performance, together with checks on finances and other matters of integrity at the pre-tender stage to avoid the problems of adverse selection. Further, short contract lengths, indicating low commitment on the client's part, would, as Laffont and Tirole (1993, Chapter 16) point out, allow the client to rectify relatively quickly an inappropriate choice of contractor and reduce the difficulties associated with incomplete contracts.

The nature of the contract would also reflect the lack of trust between the parties. Specifications would be tight and detailed, and procedures for agreeing variations would be clearly laid down. Variations arising in the course of operating the contract would be tightly controlled. Comprehensive monitoring of the contractor's compliance with contract conditions, and extensive inspection of the work undertaken, would also be a feature of the relationship. Poor performance in respect of either would immediately attract financial penalties. The anticipation of disputes arising, because of the assumed opportunistic behaviour on the part of both parties, would require a clear arbitration procedure, which would be likely to be resorted to frequently in practice. These considerations would also tend to lead to highly formalised client–contractor relations more generally. In this low trust environment, taking the word of the contractor as to the amount and quality of the work completed, allowing occasional lapses in performance to go unpunished, or assuming that disputes could be readily settled by negotiation and goodwill would be deemed naive.

We would also expect the contract in such a world to contain incentives to encourage effective and efficient contractor compliance. Fixed price contracts, with those prices set at the beginning of the contract period and with the contractor as residual claimant to any surpluses, are argued to contain such incentives. These can be contrasted with cost-plus contracts, for example, where the client agrees to pay the contractor's outturn costs plus an agreed sum or percentage of those costs, which offer low powered incentives for efficiency and clear possibilities for opportunistic behaviour (for example, Laffont and Tirole, 1993, p 10ff). The generation of surpluses as a result of fixed price contracts may, however, be expected to lead to difficulties between client and contractor where the former perceives such surpluses as arising from overcharging or where the client regards them as his or her money. These difficulties are likely to be particularly acute within a local authority where the contractor is a DLO/DSO, the surpluses of which in accounting terms accrue visibly from transfers from the client account.

It can be argued that many of the features of contracting in a low trust world which we have identified above would also be observed in any context where there is uncertainty, or where due regard is paid to prudence and financial probity, particularly in respect of other people's (that is, taxpayers') money. Leaving aside the point that in a high trust world these would not be problems, as people could be trusted to act appropriately, the main argument here is one of degree. For example, it is not the presence of penalty clauses which might indicate the absence of trust but rather the degree to which they are invoked and their severity. It is also the extent to which variations appear to be the cause of frequent conflict between client and contractor that is significant, not the fact that variations arise and have in some way to be agreed upon.

In examining the extent to which contracts drawn up under CCT appear to exhibit low or high levels of trust between client and contractor, it is thus not solely the formal contract provisions that concern us – it is also the way in which contracting arrangements operate in practice that is of importance. Empirical studies in both the public sector (for example, Vincent-Jones and Harries, 1996) and the private sector (for example, Deakin and Wilkinson, 1996) have reinforced the importance of this distinction between the formal provisions of a contract and the realities of its day-to-day operation. Seal and Vincent-Jones have suggested that:

> **… trust and the recourse to formal contracting are not *necessarily* mutually exclusive. The real task, therefore, is empirically to specify the conditions under which formal … contracting processes are supportive of, or compatible with the development of trusting and cooperative long-term relations; and to distinguish these conditions from others under which the effect of such processes is indeed inimical to, or destructive of, trust and cooperation. (Seal and Vincent-Jones, 1997, p 4)**

In our contribution to this debate on contracting practice we draw upon our empirical studies of contracting between local authorities and their DLO/DSOs. We limit our attention to two aspects of such contracting – monitoring and the question of contract detail.

Trust under contracting in practice

In the context of a low trust world, attempting to draw up a detailed and complete specification of the work to be done can be taken to indicate an attempt to reduce both the uncertainty for the client and the possibility of opportunistic post-tender price increases on the part of the contractor. In practice, under CCT, detailed specification has been the norm. Contracts for most services will stand several inches in height when placed on a table top. Nevertheless differences in interpretation still arise. Walsh and Davis cite a respondent from one authority who described client–contractor relationships early on in the contract:

> **The problems were based on fear on the client side that the specification was open to exploitation and that you could find costs increasing. The fear from the DSO was that control would be too tight and they wouldn't make the rate of return. Both sides thought the other would 'stitch them up'.... (Walsh and Davis, 1993, p 9)**

Such fears are often compounded by the view that if differences of interpretation cannot be resolved at an operational level they will escalate to the highest levels of the authority where:

> **If it goes to the chief executive it just comes down to who presents their case best or who shouts the loudest.... (research respondent cited in Walsh and Davis, 1993, p 12)**

A frequent response to such difficulties is that, once differences of interpretation are discovered, attempts will be made to tighten future contracts and thus limit the scope for future disagreements. Contracts thus have a tendency to grow and become ever more complex. One of our research respondents took the view that "a lot of petty games have been institutionalised".

It is in the so-called responsive building maintenance field that some of the most detailed specifications of work subject to CCT are to be found. Those which appear to be most commonly used take the form of Schedules of Rates (SORs), identifying individual or closely linked jobs which the tenderer is expected either to price on a per job basis or to indicate deviations from the prices stated. Such SORs can run to hundreds of pages containing thousands of jobs. SORs also contain high powered incentives for efficiency in the presence of extensive monitoring and control of variations.

In practice, Walker (1993, p 20ff) discovered that SOR-based specifications were popular with clients and in-house contractors under responsive building maintenance CCT since they assisted the budgeting of both parties, and offered significant time savings in comparison to a situation in which each job would have to be priced as it arose. In contrast, private sector contractors were, in a small number of cases, believed to have been disadvantaged by the use of SORs, since the one-off pre-pricing of a large number of jobs was not held to be characteristic of the work that those contractors undertook as a normal part of their business.

It is perhaps inevitable that in building maintenance work specifications are incomplete, and that allowance has to be made for variations from the specification and from the individual task as ordered by the clients. It is here that the possibilities for opportunistic behaviour abound. Walker (1993, para 5.15) reports the case of one authority in which the client had, for certain jobs, initially allowed an 'excess' of up to £100 on the invoice as compared to the SOR price, without prior authorisation. Forty per cent of such jobs were invoiced by the contractor at higher than the original estimate. On deciding to query all such work invoiced at more than £25 above estimate, the contractor subsequently submitted only 10 per cent of invoices above the SOR price. In a second authority, difficulties in agreeing variations after the event had led the DLO to over-print all repair order cards relating to SOR tasks with the warning of 'No additional work without authorisation'.

Next we consider the issue of contract monitoring by the client. We suggested above that the absence of trust would manifest itself here in the form of regular and extensive monitoring of the contractor. In their case study of refuse collection and cleansing, McIntosh and Broderick (1996) point to the much closer supervision and surveillance of the workforce which took place after the 1988 legislation. Walsh and Davis (1993) show in Table 3 that across a range of services subject to competition under the 1988 Local Government Act the proportion of work inspected by client officers almost doubled, on average, following competition, with no tendency for the pattern to vary by type of authority.

Table 3: Proportion of work inspected

	Before competition %	After competition %
Refuse collection	16	21
Street cleaning	26	28
Building cleaning	29	44
Schools and welfare catering	41	59
Other catering	38	44
Vehicle maintenance	38	40
Grounds maintenance	36	53
Sports and leisure management	15	40
Average	24	42

Source: Walsh and Davis (1993, p 99)

In Walker's study of building maintenance under CCT (Walker, 1993, especially para 5.5ff), all client side respondents agreed in principle that post-inspection of work was important and wished to undertake it. Some managed in practice to inspect work and monitor contract compliance in the manner that they desired, even if this appeared excessive to the contractor. In general, however, because of resource constraints on the client side, formal inspection was limited in the main to cases where there were expensive variations, where particularly complex jobs were involved or where there were end-user (for example, tenant) complaints. Indeed, end-users themselves were effectively the monitoring agents in most cases. Refuse collection is another activity which relies almost wholly on householders and property owners to 'monitor' the service provided. Complaints by them are generally the trigger for action by the authority.

This raises an interesting point about who exactly is the client and what constitutes the appropriate remedy when, as is the case with all services provided by a local authority to the public, the authority's client side is not the end-user of the service. As one building maintenance DLO manager observed:

> The client has raised expectations among tenants and has
> promised them more than is written into the contract and
> more than they are prepared to pay for. That's where most
> of our complaints come from. (Walker, 1993, para 5.9)

Given the nature of the CCT regime such a 'problem' is unsurprising.
At its simplest clients will be seeking the greatest amount of work for
the smallest amount of money whilst contractors are broadly seeking the
opposite. Both are likely to be seeking an ever better deal – from their
own perspective. Walsh and Davis cite an example from another authority:
in this case it is the contractor causing difficulties for the client:

> The business plan of the catering DSO includes an objective
> of increasing the number of school meals served and sold.
> But as each meal includes a subsidy, the more successful
> they are, the more they push up the client's costs. (Walsh
> and Davis, 1993, p 62)

The evidence presented above would suggest then that, on balance, the
world of blue collar CCT has not been characterised by a high degree of
trust between clients and contractors. The next section begins to consider
why this might be the case.

Trust under compulsory competitive tendering

In considering this issue, it is important to recall that competitive tendering
for the defined activities was *compulsory* in the event that the authority
wished its own workforce to have the opportunity of competing for the
work. Thus, irrespective of the authority's own judgement of the merits
of the competitive process or the adequacy of its in-house suppliers of
particular services, the law required that it should put certain of these
services out to open competition. If local authorities were assumed to
be motivated primarily by the desire for efficiency, in the sense of seeking
the most cost-effective way of providing a service at the required quality
level, then there would be no need to legislate in order to ensure that
they have recourse to competition. Authorities would themselves put
services out to competition where it was deemed likely to result in more
cost-effective services.

The clear assumption behind the legislation was that local authorities
could not be trusted to act in the most efficient manner. In pursuing

political or bureaucratic objectives, whether benevolent or self-serving, the local authority, it was assumed, would seek to supply directly goods and services which, while requiring collective organisation in their supply, are more efficiently provided through competition. Proponents of this view can point to some evidence on cost savings, albeit with certain caveats, which are believed to have resulted from services being subjected to a competitive tendering process (Domberger et al, 1986; 1995; Walsh and Davis, 1993).

Further, the Conservative government assumed that, even in the presence of the CCT legislation, authorities would still attempt to act opportunistically by exploiting loopholes in the legislation to favour their DLOs/DSOs. Indeed, it is interesting to note that Labour's Hilary Armstrong has revealed that one of her concerns about CCT was that:

> ... the best and brightest in local government have been employed to undermine and go round the legislation. (*Local Government Chronicle*, 20 June 1997)

Certainly some authorities have quite explicitly set out to favour their in-house organisations when awarding contracts. For example, one authority's CCT policy includes among its "specific key objectives", the desire:

> ... to ensure services subjected to CCT are retained in-house [and] to provide services by directly employed staff except where there are over-riding operational or financial reasons.

It is for such reasons that additional requirements were placed upon authorities in respect of competition. These included:

- the requirement that DLOs/DSOs make a specified rate of return on their capital and the introduction of rules as to what is to count as capital in that calculation;
- the proscription of various forms of behaviour deemed to be anti-competitive;
- the requirements as to contract lengths;
- the prohibition of the authority recontracting with the DLO/DSO at the end of a contract without a further round of competition.

Central government was attempting to impose on local authorities the sort of market disciplines which are believed to encourage efficiency in the private sector. For the purposes of this chapter this means that two key questions need to be addressed. The first is whether the type of local authority services subjected to CCT would be put out to tender by a private firm. The second is whether, in the presence of contracting, private firms would manage contracts in the same manner as local authorities. In the light of the answers to these two questions, it should be possible to determine which factors might explain the low trust features of some client–contractor relationships discussed above.

Contracting for private and public services

Consider first the decision that a private firm might make in respect of in-house or external sourcing of services. Much analysis of the theoretical and empirical aspects of such a decision has stemmed from Coase's original observation that:

> ... there is a cost of using the price mechanism. (Coase, 1937, p 336)

When the costs to the firm of carrying out transactions through the market to secure, say, necessary inputs exceed those associated with an alternative form of organisational arrangement, such as in-house or within-enterprise production, then the cost minimising firm will choose that alternative arrangement. Such 'transaction costs' vary with the nature of the transaction under consideration. Among the features of a transaction which materially affect the costs associated with it are the frequency of the transaction, the degree of uncertainty surrounding future requirements, the ability to measure the quality of the good or service being purchased (that is, whether it is possible to ensure that we are getting what we pay for) and the specificity of the assets involved in producing the good or service (Williamson, 1985; Milgrom and Roberts, 1992, Chapter 2).

As a generalisation – but one that is by no means uncontroversial – the greater the frequency of the transaction, the more likely the parties are to enter into some form of longer-term contractual, rather than simply a 'spot' market, relationship. This is likely to be the case also when there is uncertainty concerning the pattern and level of demand, and when one party, usually the supplier, has to invest in assets which are specific to the requirements of the purchaser. The difficulties of measuring quality and performance are likely to result in special arrangements for purchaser supervision of the production process, or particularly close supplier – purchaser working relationships, which also require the drawing up of an appropriate contract.

Any contracts drawn up in response to these features are almost inevitably incomplete, in the sense outlined above. In respect of asset specificity in particular, they also lead to the possibility of opportunistic behaviour. This may manifest itself in 'hold up' as one party attempts to exploit the other's dependency which has been brought about by the latter's specific investments. Even where 'hold up' does not occur, there is the possibility of 'lock in', given the investment in both physical capital and human and organisational relationships which has occurred during the course of the contract and where, at the end of the contract period, one or both parties have little opportunity in reality to recontract with a different party. In such situations, where 'hold up' is again possible, there may be a case for supplier and purchaser to merge, thus replacing the external contracting arrangement with one of in-house production under hierarchical control.

The question of whether some, or even all, of the services that local government has had to subject to CCT exhibit the features that would have encouraged out-sourcing by a similarly situated private firm is difficult to answer. This is partly because there are no private firms in a position directly analogous to that of a local authority, although it is interesting to note that a government report has used the terminology of industrial organisation analysis when referring to CCT in housing management as "unbundling vertical integration" (Department of the Environment, 1992, Appendix G). The preceding discussion does suggest, however, that particular services may have features which make their provision under contractual arrangements, rather than through integrated in-house provision, problematic in practice.

For example, the ownership of assets, such as refuse collection vehicles, may be an issue that carries with it the possibility of 'hold up', both where the assets are the responsibility of the contractor and where they are leased or rented from the client. As we have noted above, there can be problems in operating contracts in the case of building maintenance, where the range of work cannot be fully anticipated in the contract and individual jobs are inevitably difficult to specify accurately before the contractor arrives on site. Additionally, the frequency of client-contractor interaction in such contracts suggests that a truly arm's-length relationship between the two parties may be both difficult to sustain and, in the end, inefficient. For example, there can be around 2,500 repair requests a week in a typical Metropolitan District (Audit Commission, 1986, para 36). Similarly, cleaning standards are notoriously difficult to agree and detail in a contract specification. After all, what is 'clean'?

None of the above is sufficient in itself to demonstrate that exposing local authority blue collar services to competition, as opposed to producing them hierarchically in-house, is inappropriate or ill advised. However, it does lead to the second question posed above as to whether, given the requirements of CCT, local authorities are in a position to operate contracts in the manner that appears to be common in the private sector.

Managing contracts in the private sector

The reality of much private sector contracting appears to be an acceptance of incompleteness in contract specification. One reason for this may be the high transaction costs of attempting to achieve greater completeness. As Klein has put it:

> ... attempting to fix contracts by writing down all elements
> of intended performance under all contingencies is costly
> ... most real contracts, as opposed to the contracts described
> in economic theory, are imperfect in the sense that they are
> intentionally structured to leave many elements of intended
> performance unspecified ... transactors choose to use
> incomplete contracts that permit them to wait until future
> conditions emerge before determining economically what
> should be done. (Klein, 1992, p 153)

Other mechanisms are then used to facilitate mutually beneficial behaviour, given the danger of 'hold ups' and opportunism, once these future conditions arise. These include the possibility of contract termination by either party, should the actions of the other be outside the spirit of the original contract, or a commitment to further developing or extending the relationship should the other's actions fall within that spirit. The effects on a party's "reputational capital", as Klein (1992) puts it, are also likely to be significant in the event of an attempted 'hold up' or other explicitly opportunistic behaviour. In this respect, it is important to remember that contracting is not a one-period game – one or both parties to a contract may wish to renew on reaching the end of the original contract period. Past behaviour may be an important influence on the possibility of renewal. In any event, both parties will need to be aware of the effects of having a reputation for 'holding up' or being aggressively self-interested on their ability to secure other contractual partners in the future.

Evidence on the implications of this for the nature of contracting in the private sector, for example in respect of the Japanese motor industry, is provided by, among many other writers, Milgrom and Roberts (1992, p 566ff). Toyota, for example, uses very few suppliers and does not make extensive use of competitive bidding among potential suppliers. Rather, suppliers tend to be evaluated on past performance and, when chosen, enter into long-term arrangements with the company. Suppliers are often chosen before the precise nature of the components to be supplied are known, with the contracted company offering its expertise to Toyota as part of the product development process. This contractual relationship is characterised by extensive two-way flows of information and significant post-contract client-contractor cooperation.

The Co-operative Bank provides a second example of this approach, even though some might object that this is not a *private* sector organisation per se. It has been stated that the Bank recognises:

> ... that, in business as in nature, short-sighted self interest cannot result in sustainable development. Long term success can only be achieved by enterprises that embrace both competition and co-operation. Both are essential ... and neither is good or bad in itself. What is healthy is a balance.... In all kinds of ... organisations, interdependence provides the key to success.... [In] business and society at large we all ultimately depend on each other. (The Co-operative Bank, 1997, p 5)

The recognition of such mutual interest and dependency facilitates, indeed requires, a move to a more relational form of contracting, one under which "the contract becomes the basis on which continuing relations are negotiated" (Walsh, 1995a, p 42). The contract then serves "to structure a relationship ... set common expectations ... and ... establish mechanisms that will be used to make decisions and allocate costs and benefits" (Milgrom and Roberts, 1992, p 132). Such relational contracting has of necessity to be underpinned by mutual trust which, as Vincent-Jones and Harries (1996, p 205) comment, "can only develop and be sustained on the basis of long-term relationships".

If private business is to be the model for the delivery of services in the public sector, and contracting in the former is indeed increasingly trust-based and relational, then contracting in the public sector should be encouraged to develop in the same way. Yet we have observed above that, at least in respect of monitoring and contract specification, CCT appears to be operating in a comparatively low trust environment. We thus need to consider the factors to which this apparent divergence between private and public sector practice can be ascribed.

Constraints on trust-based contracting in local government

If the evidence as to whether the services concerned are suitable for contracting is unclear, then it is similarly unclear that it is unsuitability which accounts for the low-trust manner in which clients and DLOs/DSOs operate. It might be argued that it is the nature of the services themselves which engenders a low-trust mode of operation, yet it is not immediately obvious why this should be the case. While anecdotal evidence abounds concerning 'cowboy' builders, mechanics and gardeners, certainly most households, and undoubtedly many firms, attempt an assessment of such potential contractors' (and sub-contractors') reputational capital. In other words, as a minimum they 'ask around' before entering into what might be a quite general agreement as to the work likely to be necessary and the approval of any later variations.

In part the low trust features of some relationships are likely to be due to the wider aspects of public service accountability. We return to this below. It is also possible that they are attributable to excessive cautiousness, particularly on the part of clients. This may stem from relative inexperience in contracting. Although with the passage of time that explanation becomes less plausible, it is possible that the inevitably different objectives of clients and DLOs/DSOs under CCT may still at present cause friction, given that previously they adhered to, at least in principle, the same organisational objectives.

However, we would argue that the absence of significant trust-based relational contracting with DLOs/DSOs is largely ascribable to its effective prohibition by the Conservative government's legislation. For example, the ability to commit to positive future working relationships was not possible outside the term of the existing contract, given the requirement that any new contract must be subjected to open competition if the DLO/DSO was involved. Post-contract negotiation is a feature of private contracting yet such negotiations over key elements such as the prices posted in the original tender were not allowed unless other tenderers were also included. Selecting a DLO/DSO on the basis of its past performance was very likely to be judged as anti-competitive behaviour. Similarly after tendering, treating the DLO/DSO leniently during the early stages of contract operation would be likely to attract allegations of favouritism.

A DLO/DSO is arguably more directly answerable for its financial performance than private sector companies are to their shareholders. Not only is the private sector option of 'low balling' (submitting loss leading tenders) a very dangerous strategy for DLOs/DSOs in this context, but the legislative requirement to make a specific rate of return may override client needs and lead to accusations of an excessive DLO/DSO concern with appropriating taxpayers' money, a view expressed by some respondents in the Walker (1993) and Walsh and Davis (1993) studies. Finally, the relationship between the client and a DLO/DSO is likely to be more heavily weighted in favour of the former than in the case of a private contractor. The DLO/DSO has, in effect, only one choice of client, its own local authority, and any contract that the DLO/DSO has with the client is not enforceable through the courts since, strictly speaking, a local authority cannot have a contract with itself. Such 'dependency' is likely to generate particular problems in any attempt to encourage a more relational style of contracting between clients and a DLO/DSO.

In sum, then, we would concur with Seal and Vincent-Jones when they argue that:

> **The CCT programme is, by its nature, inimical to the development of trusting and long-term relationships. (Seal and Vincent-Jones, 1997, p 28)**

The desirability of trust-based contracting in local government – a cautionary note

If relational, trust-based, contracting is seen in many circumstances to be an efficient way of organising contractual relationships outside the public sector, then it could be argued that by relaxing some of the constraints on contracting in the public sector more efficient client–DLO/DSO relationships could be established. While we would suggest that, in general, this argument is valid, it is nevertheless necessary to sound a cautionary note.

Seal and Vincent-Jones have summarised one set of concerns as follows:

> **[The] positive image of trust that emerges from the literature is based on an implicit assumption that trusting relationships are somehow welfare enhancing. Less obvious are the negative aspects of trust – trust between members of self-serving elites which may flourish within bureaucracies whether they are located in town halls or Communist Parties. (Seal and Vincent-Jones, 1997, p 7)**

We would also stress the importance of the observation that, with contracting, motivations change – indeed, they have to. The first objective for a contractor has to be to survive. For local authority services one consequence of this is that a contractor's staff, especially where that contractor is a DLO/DSO, quickly have to learn that they are not there to provide the best possible public service, they are there to provide the best possible public service *according to the contract*. A contractor cannot afford to do too many things without charging and survive financially. Ultimately it is the client who must decide what services are to be provided, and how, and provide the necessary resources for them.

This can be argued to work against traditional ideas of public service, as the Committee on Standards in Public Life recognised. The Committee commented that:

> **Decentralisation and contracting out have varied the format for organisations giving public service. There is greater interchange between sectors. There are more short term contracts. There is scepticism about traditional institutions. Against that background it cannot be assumed that everyone in the public service will assimilate a public service culture unless they are told what is expected of them and the message is systematically reinforced. The principles inherent in the ethic of public service need to be set out afresh. (Committee on Standards in Public Life, 1995, p 17)**

The Committee set out 'Seven Principles of Public Life' – selflessness, integrity, objectivity, accountability, openness, honesty and leadership (p

14). The first of these, 'selflessness' ("holders of public office should take decisions solely in terms of the public interest") is undoubtedly undermined by contracting. Openness, honesty and integrity cannot be assumed but must be demonstrated. Consequently, very close client–contractor relationships in which taxpayers' money is involved run the risk of being interpreted as, if not actually becoming, corrupt. This is something that history tells us is far from being a purely theoretical concern. Financial probity and the fiduciary duty that authorities owe to their taxpayers is enhanced and made visible by clients and contractors being able to demonstrate that relations between them are conducted according to clear financial requirements and standards. Too 'cosy' a relationship between clients and contractors can sit uneasily with these requirements.

None of this is to deny, of course, that a greater degree of trust between client and contractor would be beneficial to taxpayers and service users. However, there is little likelihood that the looser, more informal, contracting that characterises some parts of the private sector would prove acceptable when set against accepted and expected standards for the conduct of public life.

Conclusions

There are a number of perceived benefits flowing from the competitive tendering process:

- an increased focus on service definition;
- an increased focus on service performance;
- an increased clarity of responsibilities (at least in principle);
- an increased emphasis on 'the right to manage' ('you have been given your task, get on and do it');
- an increased focus on the 'customers' of the service.

Much of this results from having to write a contract document. If services are to be put out to contract, then it is necessary to specify what is required and who is responsible for particular aspects of the service. Wherever contracting has been applied these issues have had to be worked through. In some cases activities are being managed as services, effectively for the first time – building cleaning provides a good example. In many authorities this was previously an activity that just 'happened' after premises were closed. In all cases it has been necessary to clearly answer the question, 'What are we trying to do here?'

As we have noted, however, CCT also tends to bring with it an increased complexity and formality in relationships, because of the need to work to the contract and to determine whether or not that is in fact being done. Flexibility can be reduced (or at the least it now comes at a very clear price) and there is a danger of service ossification. A contract may freeze the service in aspic at the time that it is written and there may be no incentive for anyone to seek to change it. Long-term planning and security of the service become more difficult when it is not known who will be the contractor in X years' time. Successful performance on a contract by a contractor is no guarantee of being re-awarded the contract when it is up for renewal. Thus, neither the client nor the contractor are really able to take a longer view.

One of our research respondents emphasised that contracting in local government has been very much governed by:

> **... that 12 o'clock feeling when you're opening tenders and you either exist or you don't....**

Welsh puts it rather more colourfully, in a fictional context (and a Scottish dialect):

> **We dinnae win contracts, there's nae direct labour organisation. Endy f—in story. (Welsh, 1995, p 78)**

This, of course, has important implications for personnel. The previously secure nature of local government employment has in any case been changing in recent years, but contracting adds a new dimension. If the DLO/DSO loses the contract most of its current employees will lose their jobs. Some may be successful in obtaining a post with the incoming contractor, but long-term continuity of employment with the same employer seems less likely than previously. This is a never-ending treadmill. Every time a contract is up for renewal there will be uncertainty. There also tends to be an increased use of part-time, temporary and casual labour. An Equal Opportunities Commission survey of compulsory competitive tendering in local government reported that this too has created "a climate of uncertainty and insecurity" and a widening inequality in pay and conditions (*Financial Times*, 29 March 1995). None of this is likely to be good for morale and low morale in the end impacts on service delivery.

Further, the financial effects of contracting can be very variable. In some services savings have been achieved (although not necessarily in the total cost to the public purse); in others costs have actually increased. Efficiency (at least in the narrow financial sense) should improve, but may not, whilst the scope for innovation may also be reduced depending on how contracts are written.

Martin, in considering the challenges raised by CCT, suggests that the major issues are:

> ... about how to construct a new ethos combining the essential and special role of public service with new forms that improve its performance. How to transform the relationship with service users from one in which they are passively cared or provided for to one in which they can actively participate in designing their service if they wish? How to release and reward individual initiative while strengthening rather than undermining collective security and responsibility? How to respond readily and quickly to the aspirations of service users while ensuring, through an appreciation of the wider needs of the community, and accountability to it, that unrepresentative groups do not capture the 'user' constituency? How to balance competition with co-operation and ground it in values that encourage its creative potential while containing its destructive power? How to meet the ever-growing demands on public service without an ever-growing share of society's resources? How to mobilise the professionalism of public service specialists without succumbing to a tyranny of the professional? (Martin, 1993, p 175)

Clearly, some of these points go beyond the contracting question. Relational contracting, however, does go some way to meeting a number of the concerns expressed and to developing a more partnership-based approach. It allows flexibility to change the nature of a service or a relationship as needs and circumstances change. It allows long-term partnerships to flourish. We have suggested that full relational contracting is not a feature of CCT , is probably not feasible in the existing legislative context, and is not necessarily desirable in the context of the new government's policies, given expectations about accountable public services. There is, however, a widespread desire for a move away from the straitjacket approach that has characterised CCT. One of our interviewees put it thus:

> **I'd like to see more of a teamwork approach ... where everybody shared the problem.**

Sonnet and Wakefield of UNISON, a trade union with 800,000 members in local government, have commented that:

> **There is a desperate need to reconstruct a public service ethos in place of the crude commercial imperatives that have come to dominate CCT. (Sonnet and Wakefield, 1997, p 71)**

Speaking from a private contractor's perspective, Hawkey also expresses the desire for,

> **... a radically different approach from the conventional 'handle turning' of a CCT programme.... The effective use of competition in a public sector organisation should be seen as a strategic rather than a tactical issue. (Hawkey, 1997, p 76)**

He notes that 'partnership contracts' seek to achieve balance by transcending the adversarial relationship within 'traditional' contract management, requiring the parties to the contract to "own and develop a common agenda" and to share risks and rewards commensurate with the contribution by each party (p 80). Nevertheless,

> **... the 'glue' that maintains partnerships is the trust generated by a set of clear rules that underpin a common purpose. (Hawkey, 1997, p 80)**

Some local authorities have begun to develop such arrangements. Hertfordshire County Council, for instance, has developed a 'partnering agreement' with Amey Facilities Management Ltd (AFM) for the delivery of professional property services which has as a 'principal objective' that,

> **Both parties will approach the relationship in a spirit of openness and trust such that each keeps the other fully**

> informed of developments (both good and bad) at all times
> ... neither party shall have a monopoly on best practice,
> initiative or solution. (Hertfordshire County Council and
> Amey Facilities Management Ltd Partnering Agreement,
> no date)

Turning developments such as these into a wider reality will be one of the major challenges for any new scheme of contracting for local government services.

Authors' acknowledgements

This chapter represents an extension and refinement of the arguements which we presented in an article published as Davis and Walker, 1997. We are grateful for helpful comments received from academic friends and colleagues. We would also like to thank the ESRC which, under award number R000 23 6498, has been financing our research and that of our colleagues into local government contracting.

TEN

White-collar services in local government: competition and trust

Peter A. Watt

> **Better trust all, and be deceived,**
> **And weep that trust and that deceiving,**
> **Than doubt one heart, that if believed**
> **Had blessed one's life with true believing.**
> **(Frances Anne Kemble, 1809-93)**

White-collar compulsory competitive tendering (CCT) was initiated by the Conservative government in 1994 with the first dates for implementation in 1996. The new Labour government is pledged to abolish CCT and replace it with a requirement for local authorities to seek 'Best Value' in the provision of services. However, at the time of writing, white-collar CCT remains in force for local government and the competitive mechanism will continue to be important:

> **Competition remains one of the key mechanisms to deliver**
> **best value in the transitional period. Indeed in Best Value**
> **terms, some form of market testing or tendering is likely to**
> **remain appropriate for each professional service. (DETR, 1997)**

Research has indicated that in total between 250,000 and 300,000 professional and technical staff are working in areas that could in principle be subject to a competitive tendering exercise. The annual cost of their activities exceeds £5 billion (DoE, 1991) and the amount of work involved is about equal to that involved in blue–collar competition. Table 4 gives details.

Table 4: Professional and technical staff in local government (England, Scotland and Wales, 1990)

Corporate services	
Corporate and administrative	49,000
Finance	67,300
Personnel	11,100
Legal	7,850
Computing	14,250
Construction services	
Architecture	18,700
Engineering	50,250
Property management	14,600
Regulatory services	
Planning	26,650
Consumer protection	4,700
Environmental health	17,150
Direct public services	
Libraries and museums	34,550
Overall total	316,100

Source: Burton (1992) and Carnaghan and Bracewell-Milnes (1993) using unpublished material prepared for the DoE

A distinction can be made between white-collar departments that supply services direct to the public, and those that supply services to other parts of a local authority. Staff in libraries and museums, consumer protection, environmental health and planning supply services direct to the public.[1] Central service departments, in contrast, provide services almost entirely to other departments and hence only indirectly to the public.[2] Because of this more complicated route for service delivery, central service departments in many ways generate the most interesting questions about white-collar competition. This chapter will therefore focus in particular on the issues that arise from applying CCT to these departments.

The services provided by central service departments fall into the broad categories of support and corporate regulation. Table 5 shows the main activities they usually undertake. Although in principle the two roles of central services – support and corporate regulation – are analytically distinct, in practice and traditionally, the two functions have often been intertwined.[3]

Table 5: Central service functions in local authorities

Financial	Financial planning/advice, internal audit, exchequer services and cash collection, payroll administration, accountancy services, pensions administration, treasury fund management, benefits administration, local taxation
Computing	IT strategy, procurement, software development, systems operation, telecommunications
Personnel services	Human resource planning, employee relations, welfare, health and safety, equal opportunities, organisational development, training, recruitment
Legal services	Corporate advice, ensuring propriety, advocacy and litigation, commercial and contractual work, conveyancing
Administrative services	Corporate strategy, committee administration, member services, elections, information, public relations, land charges, purchasing, printing, secretarial and clerical support

Sources: DoE (1991) and Audit Commission (1994)

The overall move towards the use of market-like mechanisms in local government in the last decade (Walsh, 1995a), with the introduction of blue- and white-collar CCT and an increasing use of internal markets, has raised fundamental questions about the need for central services and the form in which they are provided. At the same time, these market-like mechanisms can provide a new analytical perspective on the organisation of the local authority.

The first question to ask about central services is: what are they for? This can then be split into a question about the need for central *support* and a question about the need for central *control*, both of which can be examined from an internal-markets perspective. Of the two questions, that of the need for central support functions is the more straightforward. Central support services are an input to other departments in the local authority and the growth of internal markets has made them increasingly dependent on pleasing their customers. If these customers prefer external suppliers then they will exert pressure for a voluntary competitive tendering (VCT) or compulsory competitive tendering (CCT) exercise preferably with them as the client.

In practice such outsourcing decisions are usually made by the centre as one of its control and regulation functions. This leads on to the second half of the question posed above: what is the need for the central-service role of providing corporate control and regulation? An illuminating way of answering this question can be provided by referring to the arguments on the need for government set out in the public finance literature. This takes as its starting point a fully laissez-faire economy and argues that the role of government is to provide intervention to correct market failure (Musgrave, 1959; Atkinson and Stiglitz, 1980). By analogy, the reason for the existence of the local authority corporate centre can then be seen as a response to 'internal market failure'.

Under this analogy, therefore, the centre provides government-like control functions to the rest of the local authority. Seen in this framework, a spectrum of possibilities for the role of the centre can be set out, depending on the enthusiasm for central planning. At one end of the spectrum, a minimalist corporate centre would restrict itself to distributing resources according to political decisions about outcomes sought in the community and policing free operation of the internal market. Any support roles for the centre would then arise from the play of 'internal-market forces'. For instance, if use of a central payroll function would lead to reduced costs, then the operation of an internal market[4] would bring it into existence. The internal market would also determine whether the central supplier was an in-house unit or an external contractor. Likewise, departments would buy central coordination on the internal market where it was worth more than it cost.

Beyond this minimalist concept, movement can proceed towards the other end of the spectrum by further pursuing the analogy with the public finance market failure literature. A series of reasons for central intervention can be put forward. Firstly, the internal market may fail to secure economies of scale in the provision of support services. In response, the centre may intervene to institute and regulate a single internal (or external) contractor, in preference to a multiplicity of small contracts. Again the provision of payroll services is a relevant example. Secondly, there may be externalities between different units of the authority, and the centre may impose on them a requirement for joint working. Thirdly, a role for the centre arises if the internal market fails to provide what are in the nature of public goods within the local authority (Leach et al, 1994, p 126; Watt, 1996a, p 108). Examples of such public goods would include: overall strategy, corporate information systems, public image, personnel policies, an 'atmosphere of trust and reciprocity' within the organisation (Lorenzoni and Baden-Fuller, 1995), financial probity, well-managed relations with central government and the shouldering of corporate responsibility. The role of the centre would then be to 'tax' or 'top-slice' internal units to provide the funds for provision either directly in-house by the centre or through contracting with an external contractor.[5]

Analogy with the 'merit wants' argument for government intervention provides a final role for the centre (Musgrave, 1959). This role arises when the centre believes it knows best and wishes to impose its views on units within the authority. One aspect of this is performance management. Another is the pursuit of 'green' technologies throughout an authority if these are judged to be appropriate.

The above analysis demonstrates that a major role for the centre lies in coercively imposing outcomes on departments of the authority. These are outcomes that would not arise by the free interaction of those departments. The centre *adds value* by correcting internal market failure. However, as has been pointed out in the public finance literature, just as markets may fail, governments may fail. The cure may be easily worse than the disease (Sidgwick, 1887, p 414; Coase, 1964, p 195). In the same way the corporate centre can destroy value by issuing the wrong directives (Goold et al, 1994; Hungenberg, 1993; Ackoff, 1993).

The corporate centre is therefore a powerful vehicle for creating or destroying value and, when necessary, acts by *overriding* the views of managers in the component departments or trading units of the local authority. The support function of the centre, by contrast, essentially survives by *responding* to the preferences of the managers of other units rather than by overriding them.

This has important implications for the question of outsourcing these functions, either by CCT or VCT. It implies that a local authority should view the possibility of outsourcing central corporate control – an essentially coercive function – with much more caution than the possibility of outsourcing support functions. Corporate control, with its role of overriding the views of sub-managers, has powerful potency for adding value to the organisation. But this potency also offers powerful scope for *destroying* value if the centre imposes the wrong corporate policies. For instance, an important source of value destruction could be *opportunism* (as defined in Chapter Two) by central service providers. It seems plausible that if a corporate control function is provided, as is usual, by an in-house unit, its possible selfish gains from such opportunistic behaviour are likely to be more constrained than they would be if provided by a private contractor[6] and that in-house provision is therefore to be preferred. Another reason for preferring in-house provision for such services is that any value destruction by an in-house strategic centre is likely to come closer to *self-destruction* than is likely to be the case with a private contractor. This is probably the essential reason why discussion of what activities might be suited to CCT (see for example DoE, 1991) generally treats activities concerned with corporate strategy as being *least* appropriate.

It is concluded from this discussion that the support functions of the centre are more likely to be suited to external provision through contracts than its control functions. However, a further perspective on the whole issue of outsourcing white-collar central services is provided by the new literature on organisational design already drawn on in Chapters Two and Nine of this book. This chapter now turns to these questions.

Issues of organisational design

The 1980s saw a major sea change in thinking on the organisational structure of local authorities, stimulated by CCT itself and the concept of the 'enabling authority' (Ridley, 1988; Clarke and Stewart, 1988; Leach et al, 1994). This thinking put a fundamental, but previously neglected, question of organisational design on the agenda for local authorities: why are some services bought in and some services made in-house? The collection of ideas originating with Coase (1937) and developed in particular by Williamson, as set out in Chapter Two of this book, greatly illuminate the question. For the purposes of this chapter the precise form of the question is: why make central services when you can buy them? The new institutional economics provides an extremely powerful way of examining this question by focusing on the question of how easy (in a wide interpretation of the term) the product or service is to *buy*.

Buying is done through contracts – in many ways a hazardous process as Williamson and others have documented. As a result:

> ... the prediction is that 'make' eventually supplants 'buy' as
> contractual hazards build up. (Williamson, 1996b, p 140)

What are the relative attractions of buying in a service as against 'making' it in-house? Buying in a service is at its most simple if the service is available in an industry-standard form from many alternative suppliers. Purchasing from such suppliers or 'discrete market transacting' as it is labelled in the literature (Macneil, 1974; Williamson, 1979) is a relatively simple process. However, interest in this process is limited as, in practice, most local authority white-collar services are not required or provided in a simple industry-standard form.

Even if a simple standard product *does* exist, a judgement needs to be made on whether buying a tailor-made specialised product is nevertheless preferable, despite the extra price and contractual difficulties likely to be entailed (Evans and Grossman, 1983, p 116; Holmström, 1982, p 338). Sometimes the industry-standard product will be chosen on the grounds of its lower cost, even if the product is not entirely appropriate to the task. For example, there has been a notable movement in this direction in the IS/IT field in recent years. Products such as computer packages are now much more frequently bought off the shelf rather than developed in-house.

In many instances, however, the off-the-shelf product is spurned and a judgement is made that a non-standard product is worth the extra cost. In such a case, a process of contracting, with all the possibilities of the contractual difficulties outlined in Chapter Two, will then be required. Among the difficulties of contracting are that bounded rationality, uncertainty and complexity mean that all issues cannot be dealt with explicitly and in advance in the contract and opportunism means that omission to do so is likely to cause problems for one party or the other.

Opportunism in contracting can take two basic forms. Firstly, there is deviation from a given contract (hopefully undetected). Secondly, there are efforts to *change* the contract, either before it is agreed, or, by staging a 'hold up' after it *has* been agreed (Klein et al, 1978, pp 297-326; Masten, 1996, p 7; see also Davis and Walker in Chapter Nine). Further problems of contracting are that asset specificity makes both parties vulnerable to 'hold up', and uncertainty and complexity mean that a given contract will never take all contingencies fully into account (Schwartz, 1992, pp 80-1). Furthermore, parties to the contract may understand terms differently, and any court of law involved in enforcement may have a limited understanding of what is meant. Contracts are therefore *incomplete* and are likely to need adaptation as circumstances develop.

White-collar professional services in local government present all of the contractual difficulties mentioned above, often in particularly problematic forms. A major area of difficulty lies in setting out a specification of requirements in the contract, and in monitoring what is actually provided – usually involving a series of complex judgements. One of the first judgements to be required is *how much* of the service is needed. On this question, users frequently find themselves in the hands of the providers (Wolinsky, 1993, p 380), and this is only the beginning of the problems they face. White-collar services in local government are largely professional services provided by 'experts'. Their product is intangible and cannot be held in inventory (Sharma, 1997), and quality is not easy to judge:

> **It is difficult to state the nature of the work for most professional services, indeed professionalism frequently exists precisely because it is difficult to state the nature of the work to be performed. (Walsh, 1995a, p 127)**

As well as it being difficult to specify the service in advance, users may still not be clear on what they have received even after receipt of the service.[7] For example, it may not be easy for a local authority to know that it is receiving *excessively cautious* rather than *good* legal advice. Similarly, while the users may be clear that they have received a poor service this may not be verifiable in court at any worthwhile cost (Schwartz, 1992, p 81). In such situations, when quality is not easy to judge or verify, there is a possibility of opportunistic behaviour by providers, and buyers may react defensively by "assuming the worst on matters of quality" (Williamson, 1985). If this happens, high-quality suppliers will not be able to charge more than low-quality suppliers. As a result, a functioning market for high-quality services may not exist despite the existence of effective demand (Akerlof, 1970, p 488; Leland, 1979).[8]

In addition to problems of specification and monitoring, white-collar contracting is subject to the problems of asset specificity as defined by Williamson (1983) and discussed in Chapter Two. A white-collar contractor will need to make a number of specific investments in order to supply to a local authority which will have little alternative-use value if the contract is terminated. They will need to invest in special equipment, to locate some of their operations near to or in the local authority's premises and to acquire human capital in the form of skills and knowledge relevant only to working with the particular local authority (Williamson, 1983). Of these, the specific human knowledge skills – for example, the need for contractors to know the working methods of the local authority – are of particular relevance in white-collar contracting. Asset specificity means that it is not easy for either partner to break off a contract once it is let, and this introduces room for opportunism.[9] Terminating a contract for collecting council tax, for instance, would not be a matter to take lightly:

> **Once the relationship has begun, the supplier will be isolated to some degree from competition and will be in a position to 'hold up' the consumer. A simple example would be the automobile mechanic who agrees to fix a car, takes it apart, and then says he will put it together again at three times the originally agreed upon price. (Goldberg, 1976, p 439)**

Techniques for the restraint of opportunism

The above discussion suggests that the users of professional services confront a formidable array of problems in obtaining true information about the need for and quality of the services contractors try to sell them. They also face these problems when evaluating in-house services. What can the users do to mitigate these problems? A possible minimal approach is for users to trust to self-regulation by professionals:

> **Recipients of expert services are not themselves adequately knowledgeable to solve the problem or to assess the service received. Who then controls the experts?... The answer in the functionalist model is bafflingly simple: the experts themselves. Individually and, in association, collectively, the professions 'strike a bargain with society' in which they exchange competence and integrity against the trust of client and community, relative freedom from lay supervision and interference, protection against unqualified competition as well as substantial remuneration and higher social status. (Rueschemeyer, 1983, p 41)**

This self-regulation model, as Rueschemeyer points out, "coincided to a large extent with the interpretations advanced by these privileged occupations themselves", which "stirred doubts" about its validity. Reliance on professionals' self-control is therefore usually supplemented by some form of bureaucratic control within an organisation or by some other third party. However:

> **Even in bureaucratic employment or under third-party supervision expert practitioners derive from the special character of their services a core of autonomy which, though different from profession to profession, is greater than the irreducible autonomy found in other occupations. (Rueschemeyer, 1983, p 48)**

So should professionals be trusted to do what is in the purchaser's interests? Cynicism on this point considerably antedates George Bernard Shaw's line that "all professions are conspiracies against the laity" (Shaw, 1906, Act 1; Corfield, 1995). Halmos argues that sociological opinion is "radically and bitterly antiprofessional":

> **The claim for so-called 'service-ethic' specific to the professionals is a sheer mystification of status claims and a device to silence the critics of monopoly, privilege and power. (Halmos, 1973, p 6)**

Suspicion of the efficacy of self-regulation by professionals has also been expressed by a number of economists who have argued that the main effects of professional bodies are to restrict entry into the profession and consequently drive up members' remuneration (Friedman and Kuznets, 1945; Friedman, 1962; Kessel, 1958). Friedman (1962), for example is "persuaded that licensure has reduced both the quality and quantity of medical practice".

The conclusion to be drawn on the merits of professional self-regulation is that buyers of white-collar services are not advised to be too trusting of this method of controlling opportunism. Fortunately, a number of other possibilities for restraint of opportunism exist (Sharma, 1997). Firstly, the competitive mechanism itself is a major tool for generating information about services as pointed out inter alia by Niskanen (1971, p 217). A competitive tendering exercise is a powerful tool for assembling the views of a range of rival experts.[10]

> **Competing sellers will often happily compare the relative merits of their own products against comparative defects in the competing product which the other seller would be unlikely to emphasise. (Milgrom and Roberts, 1992, p 186)**

This method may in fact be more useful when buying a manufactured product than when buying professional services, where criticism of a rival's product may be inhibited by defamation laws. A further limitation of this technique arises when the competing parties share some common interests that work against the buyer's interest (Milgrom and Roberts, 1992, p 186). For example, competing professional service providers are all likely to at least agree that their service is *needed*, even if it is not. Furthermore, competing providers may occasionally be partners on other projects.

A second useful technique for reducing opportunism is to split up the task so that one provider has the task of deciding *what* is required and a different provider has the task of *actually supplying it* (Darby and Karni, 1973; Wolinsky, 1993; Sharma, 1997; Emons, 1997). Such a split removes the incentive to recommend unnecessary services that can be a factor present when one supplier carries out both tasks. A very fundamental application of this technique is the use of the familiar client–contractor split with an in-house client and an internal or external contractor. A less familiar possibility is the use of an *external* client, independent from the contractor.[11]

A problem with this approach of splitting up the service into 'diagnosis' and 'treatment' is that it may be much cheaper to do the diagnosis and treatment tasks together. For example, in the case of both car repair and medicine:

> **... it is easier to repair any damage while the transmission or belly is open to see what is wrong, than to put everything back together and go elsewhere to repeat the process for the actual repair. (Darby and Karni, 1973, pp 67-8)**

A judgement may be made that the cost savings gained by putting diagnosis and treatment together are likely to outweigh possible losses arising from provider opportunism.

A third sanction against provider opportunism is to attack the reputational capital of the provider if substandard service is received (Darby and Karni, 1973, p 82; Walsh, 1995a, p 51; Wolinsky, 1993, p 381; Kreps,

1990; Sharma, 1997). This sanction may well be more powerful against an external contractor as they are likely to be more concerned about their reputation than the traditional in-house team. (However, a beneficial effect of the increasing possibility of the use of external contractors is to make the in-house team more concerned for their reputation). A related control mechanism lies in the fact that professionals belong to professional associations that will wish to protect their reputations – a situation that will apply to both in-house and external contractors' professional employees. The importance of reputation can be increased if there is networking between the clients of professionals.

Lastly, but most straightforwardly, an obvious route for seeking to control provider opportunism is through the specification and monitoring of the contract. Ideally specifications for a service to be provided by a contractor will focus upon the output or outcome that is desired rather than the inputs and methods used. The reason from this springs from the principle of not hiring a dog and barking oneself. The more a purchaser moves towards specifying inputs the more the they become involved in the production process, avoidance of which was presumably the reason for contracting-out in the first place. However, although it is in theory preferable to specify outcomes or outputs, as has been pointed out above, these may often not be clear or only become clear after a certain amount of time has elapsed. It is difficult, for example, to define 'good legal advice' in a contract for the supply of legal services. If this is the case, it may often be necessary to fall back on specifying the inputs and/or the processes used.[12] These may be expressed in either qualitative or quantitative terms (see Walsh, 1995b). Thus, for example, a specification might stipulate the percentage of professionally qualified staff that the contractors would use on a contract and set out some of the methods to be used in some detail.

Relational contracting and trust

The above discussion indicates that precise control of white-collar professionals will be difficult. It is likely, therefore, that a range of approaches will need to be brought to bear on the problem, none of which is likely to offer a complete solution by itself. In addition, as has been noted, contracts will in general be incomplete. An approach to this collection of problems that is frequently found between commercial parties is to move towards a system of 'relational contracting'.

Development of the academic concept of relational contracting partly stems from an early discussion of the actual use of contracts by Macaulay (1963) which pointed out that in practice businesses paid very little attention to the legal terms of the contract. As one of his interviewees put it:

> **You can settle any dispute if you keep the lawyers and the accountants out of it. They just do not understand the give and take needed in business. (Macaulay, 1963, pp 55-67)**

Macaulay argued that "although parties fail to cover all foreseeable contingencies, they will exercise care to see that both understand the primary obligation on each side". In relational contracts, emphasis shifts "from a detailed specification of the terms of the agreement to a more general statement of the process of adjusting the terms of the agreement over time – the establishment of a 'constitution' governing the ongoing relationship" (Goldberg, 1976, p 428). These effects were clearly discerned by Walsh (1995a) in a survey of current British experience:

> **The more difficult it is to specify the service to be provided, the more interest will tend to shift to the contract conditions, and the structures and processes they lay down for the management of contracts. In some more complex contracts, public organisations will only settle the detail of the service to be provided after the contract has been let, through a process of negotiation with the contractor. (Walsh, 1995a, p 115)**

A related reason for not insisting obsessively on the detail of contracts, but for focusing more on the general relationship, stems from Holmström and Milgrom's work (1991). Here they point out that if some tasks are measurable and others are not, pinning things down tightly in the observable areas is likely to shift the productive energies away from important but non-measurable tasks.

Because of the complex nature of the contractual issues involved, white-collar services are particularly suited to relational contracting, an important element of which is the development of trust. The costs generated by the problems outlined in the previous section can be greatly reduced by the presence of warranted trust. For instance, adapting a contract in the face of unforeseen circumstances is easy:

> How to effect these adaptations poses a serious contracting dilemma, though it bears repeating that, absent the hazards of opportunism, the difficulties would vanish – since the gaps in long-term, incomplete contracts could be faultlessly filled in an adaptive, sequential way. A general clause to the effect that 'I will behave responsibly rather than seek individual advantage when an occasion to adapt arises', would in the absence of opportunism, suffice. (Williamson, 1979, p 241)

If a party to a contract truthfully abjures opportunistic behaviour on their side, costs are lowered for the other side. Seen in the game theory terms outlined in Chapter Two, the problem is that the other side can then choose to either (a) play them for a sucker by behaving opportunistically or (b) cooperate by also truthfully abjuring opportunistic behaviour. The local authority is in a Prisoner's Dilemma game with a one-round solution of non-cooperation in the form of opportunism from both sides. The dilemma is that *warranted* trust saves money but *misplaced* trust costs money. The solution may be to encourage trust to develop from long term relationships along the lines of Axelrod's (1984) work as discussed in Chapter Two.

A powerful reason for the development of trust is the opportunities it affords for gains from trade to both client and contractor from a flexible approach to the contract. Over the period of a contract, the vicissitudes of uncertainty are likely to throw up situations where the client is in a position to impose high costs on a contractor. For instance, a situation may arise where the contractor may have made an error which would be very expensive for them to rectify. It may also be the case that the benefit of having the particular error rectified is not particularly high for the client, or that an inexpensive compromise solution may be readily acceptable to them. In this situation the client can be in a position to make a 'gift' to the contractor by forbearing to impose the high-cost remedy to which that they are entitled.[13] Indeed, a client is likely to seize the opportunity to make such a gift as it enables them, in effect, to put some 'credit' into a notional account that measures who owes whom a favour.[14] After all, the further play of chance may well place them in a position where the boot is on the other foot, and they will then need to cash in their notional credit to get themselves out of trouble. A notion of fair play may well induce one party to forbear from imposing a high cost on the other even when such forbearance may not be particularly cheap. Mutual forbearance can have clear attractions to both sides and over time the development of trust can allow the 'gifts' to become larger and larger.[15]

The use of this mechanism explains the apparent paradox, observed by Macaulay (1963), of parties bothering to have detailed contracts which they do not stick to. In terms of the above formulation it can be argued that both parties need a clear understanding of what has been agreed upon so that, when deviations arise, adjustments can be made to the notional social capital of both parties. Analogously, when a person buys a round of drinks, their concern may be more that the recipients understand *who* bought the drinks than with making sure that all is square at the end of the evening.

The use of relational contracts and the development of trust incentivised by the possibility of repeat business can thus produce much closer fulfilment of the clients objectives than a rigid 'by the book' approach to contracting. Unfortunately, the current CCT rules do not allow commitment to extensions of contracts (as pointed out by Davis and Walker in Chapter Nine). One reason for this, and the existence of other arm's-length impediments to close working and the development of trust, is that as well as providing scope for efficiency gains in contractual relations, trust provides conditions in which corruption can grow:

> **When social relations are very close, it may be difficult to establish a direct link between an act that could be assumed to reflect corruption and a particular payment for it. An employee who, using his official position does a special favour for an acquaintance – say helps him or her get a valuable licence, a government contract, or a government job – may be compensated with an immediate or explicit payment (clearly a bribe); alternatively he may be compensated at a much later time, with a generous gift to his daughter when she gets married; or with a good job offer for his son when he completes his studies. (Tanzi, 1995)**

Although it has been argued that corruption can be beneficial to social welfare (Leff, 1964), the brief discussion of this chapter assumes that this is not the case. The development of trust can therefore be seen as in *benefit* terms as a powerful aid to the reduction of contractual costs and yet a potential *cost* to the extent that it provides a route for the development of corruption. The danger of corruption is therefore a real barrier to the fullest development of the kind of relational contracting discussed above. There is a dilemma of balancing the costs and benefits of trust. Avoiding the danger of corruption *at all costs* is a simple-minded approach, a point made by Anechiarico and Jacobs (1996) in the title of their book: *The pursuit of absolute integrity: How corruption control makes government ineffective.*

So is it possible to develop high-trust relations and avoid the danger of corruption? One solution that has been proposed to the problem of corruption is to pay very high wages to bureaucrats who could act corruptly so that the possibility of detection and dismissal will weigh heavily in their calculations (Becker and Stigler, 1974, pp 1-19, cited in Ades and Di Tella, 1997, pp 496-515). Interestingly, therefore, robustness against corruption could be an extra benefit of the approach a number of authorities have taken in establishing very small, but very senior and highly-paid client departments intended to match contractor professional expertise.

The control of in-house providers

If contracting for professional services is subject to the contractual hazards of incompleteness, human capital asset specificity, difficulty of specification and monitoring, and opportunities for reneging on trust, the overall result may be very costly for the local authority. This is particularly the case, as argued above, if any corporate control functions are contracted out, as the constraint imposed by the need to please direct service customers is replaced by a rationale of overruling their views. Successful opportunism by external contractors is rewarded by very powerful incentives as it can be converted into pure profit – an attractively malleable form of reward.

The Williamson framework for organisational design suggests that a reduction of the costs of contracting may be achieved by bringing services in-house under hierarchical control. When an activity is carried out in-house, legal redress in disputes is replaced by an internal appeal to hierarchy as one side cannot sue another (Williamson, 1991). Incentives for opportunistic behaviour are attenuated as the rewards of opportunism cannot be taken as pure profit (although they are available in other forms such as on-the-job leisure and scope for empire building). The question now becomes: are white-collar professionals rendered fit to be trusted by being brought in-house? Although the incentives for opportunism may be slightly weaker there are still reasons for caution.

It was recognised as early as the 1920s that bringing activities in-house does not obviate the problems caused by opportunistic behaviour where quality is hard to judge. Replacing contract by hierarchical control leaves similar problems to be solved, as was pointed out long ago by Frank H. Knight:

> **The internal problems of the corporation, the protection of its various types of members and adherents against each other's predatory propensities, are quite as vital as the external problem. (Knight, 1921, p 254, quoted in Klein et al, 1978)**

In fact the problem of internal opportunistic behaviour has been discussed even earlier. As Knight points out, an early description of the problem as found in the private sector is given by Haney (1913), who referred to what he called the 'corporation problem':

> **... the corporate form ... fails to work for the best interest of the stockholders or owners.... The root of the evil is *a lack of reasonable harmony of interests within the corporation*.... Instead of operating harmoniously to produce wealth ...directors and officers too often work for their own gain and against the interests of their constituents, the shareholders. (Haney, 1913, p 355; original emphasis)**

A much more recent analysis of opportunism behaviour leading to dysfunctional behaviour in-house uses the term 'influence activity' to describe problems of internal control:

> **Influence activities arise in organisations when organisational decisions affect the distribution of wealth or other benefits among members or constituent groups of the organisation and, in pursuit of their selfish interests, the affected individuals or groups attempt to influence the decision to their benefit. The costs of these influence activities are influence costs. (Milgrom and Roberts, 1992, p 192)**

Hence, although bringing activities in-house may be seen as an approach to solving the contractual difficulties of outsourcing, it can be argued that it is equally valid to see outsourcing as a sanction against poor in-house performance. Unfortunately, the existence of transactions costs associated with outsourcing as discussed above may mean that internal performance has room to fall well below conceivable standards before outsourcing becomes attractive. Any progress in reducing the cost of contractual arrangements for outsourcing stimulated by the CCT programme may therefore bring dividends in the form of higher minimum standards in in-house white-collar departments.

Although the main purpose of this chapter has been to discuss the question of controlling the activities of white-collar professionals in both in-house and external units, it is worthwhile documenting the actual administrative steps that have been taken in implementing CCT for central services. The last section therefore provides a brief record of the actual practice of white-collar competition.

The white-collar compulsory competitive tendering programme in practice

The origins of white-collar CCT stem from the earlier programme of blue-collar compulsory competitive tendering discussed in detail in Chapter Nine. The overall programme was initiated with legislation in 1980 and 1988, but the extension to white-collar services is comparatively recent and so far the experience of competition in these areas is much less extensive. Although white-collar competition was first proposed by the Government in the 1985 Green Paper on extending CCT (DoE, 1985), and an initial consideration of how it might be implemented was set out in *Competing for quality* (DoE, 1991), there was a comparatively lengthy period of debate before the programme began to be implemented, the earliest dates being set for 1996.

The main legislative basis for white-collar CCT is the 1988 Local Government Act. Section 2(3) gives the Secretary of State for the Environment general powers to 'define' an activity as being subject to competition by regulation rather than primary legislation. Activities made subject to competition in this way are customarily referred to as 'defined activities'.

While in power, the Conservative government issued regulations to compel competition for most of the range of white-collar professional services in local government: legal, construction and property, personnel, finance, IS/IT and housing management. An exception was general administration, which was dropped from the programme.

Generally in CCT regulations, the client side of an activity is excluded from the requirement to subject an activity to competition, though the precise way in which this is done differs between white- and blue-collar competition. In blue-collar CCT the regulations exclude the client side from the definition of the service to be subject to CCT. In white-collar CCT by contrast, it is considered that it is far less easy to take a view on which areas of a service are unsuitable for competition. The approach adopted has been to make the whole of an area of white-collar service (such as the legal service or the finance service) a defined activity and then set a *competition requirement* for each defined activity. This is the percentage of the defined activity to be subject to competition. Each authority could then determine locally for each white-collar service which activities would be subject to CCT in order to meet the relevant competition requirement. Hence, according to the DoE, "work which individual authorities regard as essential to policy making or the client core of the authority need not be subject to competition if they so choose" (DoE, 1996b). In practice, fixing a figure for the competition requirement for each service has involved a long process of commissioning consultants' reports, issuing consultation documents and laying regulations, and the proposed percentages have been changed several times, most recently by the new government in November (DETR, 1997). The latest set of competition requirement percentages is shown in Table 6.

White-collar competition shares with the blue-collar programme minimum de minimis levels of activity below which CCT regulations do not compel competition, as set out in column three of Table 6. The argument for setting a de minimis threshold is that, below a certain size of activity, the costs of subjecting a service to competition are likely to outweigh possible benefits. The regulations for competition allow other 'credits' which reflect areas of work that have already been subject to some form of competition and act to reduce the amount of work that must be subject to competition. The argument is that an authority that had large totals in any of these categories would be likely to find it more difficult to subject the remainder of its services to competition. The credits allowed include credit for work that has already been contracted out in a previous CCT or VCT (voluntary competitive tendering) exercise, credit for bought-in goods and services, credit for work carried out for locally managed schools and 'pre-shrunk allowances', associated with giving credit for white-collar work already voluntarily contracted out.

The original effect of the regulations, including this complicated and wide-ranging set of credits, teamed with ingenuity from local authority finance teams, was that many local authorities, including even many *large* ones were able to report that at least some of their white-collar activities were de minimis (Watt 1996b). In consequence a government review (DoE, 1996c) confirmed that "much less work is in practice to be subject to competition under CCT than had been anticipated" and proposed a significant intensification of the white-collar competition regulations. New regulations were issued after some delay in early 1997, although the new Labour government has in turn introduced some minor relaxations of these regulations (DETR, 1997).

Table 6: Requirements for white-collar CCT in England

Service	Competition requirement	De minimis level of activity	Implementation date: (London and the Metropolitan Areas)
Construction and Property	55%	£450,000	I April 1996
Legal	45%	£300,000	I April 1996
Personnel	40%	£300,000	I October 1996
Finance	40%	£300,000	I April 1997
IS/IT	40%	£300,000	I October 1997
Housing Management	95%	4,000 properties	phased from I April 1996

Source: DETR (1997)

Conclusions

This chapter has argued that the specialised knowledge held by professional white-collar staff makes it difficult to prevent them from opportunistically pursuing their own objectives at the expense of those of the local community. The same problem presents itself in different forms, no matter whether the professional services are provided through contract by a private contractor or by an in-house team. Placing trust in professional self-regulation to take care of the problem has been historically important but is a risky route to take and is being increasingly supplemented by other techniques.

A number of strategies can be used to try to reduce the problem. Constraints on opportunistic behaviour can be placed on in-house teams by a credible threat of outsourcing. Likewise, the threat of moving an activity in-house, or to another contractor, places a constraint on opportunism by external contractors. Outsourcing is increasingly seen as an attractive option, but is particularly risky if the coercive control functions of central services are considered, and this is probably why such functions are usually left in-house. Although in-house provision attenuates incentives to opportunistic behaviour it does not remove them, and the same process of attenuation is likely to extend to incentives to productivity. For support functions, a vigorous internal market, with direct service managers free to use external suppliers, is likely to be a powerful constraint on opportunism by providers. Here, the exercise by direct service managers of the client role in an overall VCT framework conducive to the growth of trust may offer a more powerful route to the development of value for money than the over-regulated framework of CCT. Yet the savings recorded under the early implementation of CCT (Watt, 1996a, p 87) show that all was not well in the absence of compulsion. The way that the new government's policy of 'Best Value' (complete with capital letters) is developing indicates that a lesson has been learnt on the benefits of competition, even if it is not politic to enunciate it clearly.

Author's acknowledgements

The author thanks Andrew Coulson, Simon Delay and John Stewart for helpful comments but retains responsibility for error.

Notes

1   Teachers also provide services direct to the public, but are not considered further in this paper.

2   There are some exceptions such as Housing Benefit administration and Council Tax collection where the relationship is direct to the public.

3   In accountancy, for instance, the support function of providing mechanisms for payment has traditionally been combined with the Treasurer's Section 151 responsibilities.

4   In practice there may be insufficient 'profit-like' incentives to 'internal market entrepreneurs' for this to happen.

5   The use of the terms 'tax' or 'top-slice' indicates that the role of the centre

here is to impose a levy to finance the activities. Voluntary payment would be equivalent to the use of the internal market and invite 'free-riding'.

[6] An outsourced corporate control function would in theory be controlled by the purchasing unit, but this is likely to be difficult in practice. Also, economies of scope between the two functions may make such a split uneconomic.

[7] Such goods are called 'credence goods' (Darby and Karni, 1973; Wolinsky, 1993, p 382).

[8] It may be that it is partly to address this danger that professionals characteristically aver the high standards maintained by their calling.

[9] Sharma (1997, p 785) argues that asset specificity provides protection from agent opportunism by making it costly for the contractor agent if the client breaks off the contract. However, this appears to neglect the fact that the same asset specificity will also make such an act costly for the client.

[10] Milgrom (1981) and Grossman (1981) have shown that under certain somewhat restrictive conditions full disclosure of information occurs in this situation.

[11] One reason that external clients are rare is that the ultimate need for an internal client to direct the external client still remains. Local authorities sometimes use quantity surveyors as external clients to check building work and authorise payments. However, an internal client is still needed to direct their work.

[12] More cynically, another reason for specifying inputs and processes rather than outputs may be to favour the in-house team in a CCT exercise. For a combination of these reasons, the Conservative government felt it necessary to publish detailed guidance on specifications which explicitly discusses how they may be written:

> **Authorities are encouraged to adopt output rather than input based specifications for services. An authority should be prepared to consider proposals from contractors which involve different methods of operation to that of the existing service provider. However, the Secretary of State accepts that for services it may be necessary to specify the nature of the work in terms of the processes to be followed or the type of professional input which a contractor would be expected to offer. Either way authorities should give proper consideration to recognised practice in the services affected, and be prepared to justify any variation from that practice. (DoE, 1996b)**

[13] In a discussion of the motives for gifts, Offer (1997) has argued that their primary purpose is to obtain "regard".

[14] Tanzi (1995, p 166) calls this 'net social capital'.

[15] Breton and Wintrobe (1982, Chapter 4) provide a convincing analysis of the development of trust within bureaucratic organisations.

ELEVEN

Trust and distrust in the arena of regulation and enforcement

Ray Puffitt

Trust bears a price. A price not always exacted but which nevertheless exists. Not the merely trivial price of trust misplaced or even trust betrayed for here the remedies of voice and exit are readily available, but the terrible price of opportunism foregone for which there is neither remedy nor reward this side of the grave. (Ray Puffitt)

Elsewhere in this book trust is portrayed as having the potential to bring positive benefits to all the parties involved in an interdependency: between client and contractor, between purchaser and provider, between citizen and state, and so on. The interdependency upon which this chapter focuses is that of regulator and regulatee. This is not a voluntary relationship but an enforced interdependence. Moreover, it will argue that the adverse results flowing from trust misplaced and also the loss of the possibility for opportunism by the regulator may make trust an inappropriate phenomenon in this particular relationship. Indeed, even Axelrod's strategy (tit-for-tat), much quoted in the literature as a means by which trust can be built and maintained in voluntary interdependencies, when applied to enforced interdependencies implies neither the need or the existence of trust. Instead it calls for sanction where sanction is due, penalty where penalty is due and, in some rare circumstances, persuasion where persuasion backed up by the covert threat of sanctions will achieve the desired level of compliance.

In war, the price of trust misplaced might be vainglorious death, the price of opportunism foregone, the battle lost. In peace, it might be financial ruin or the loss of the possibility of wealth beyond the wildest bounds of avarice. In contract, it could mean the need for redress in the civil courts or the loss of competitive edge. In regulation, it could have adverse results that may imperil the public health of a whole community or deny the opportunity for the regulator to gain even greater influence or control over that which offends society and for which they have been appointed to exercise oversight. It is therefore not surprising that distrust rather than trust might be both the commoner and more prudent characteristic in this particular relationship.

And, as Janet Newman reveals in Chapter Three, trust is culture bound; gender, appearance, ethnicity, class, religion, sexual orientation may all engender the propensity to trust and distrust. Moreover they may have an effect on the regulator's choice of which social influence process to employ when faced with non-compliance. But where trust does not exist, therein lies the possibility of distrust, conflict and disorder, were it not that on this continuum lie also the two phenomena of hope and indifference, which in practice may be much the commoner characteristics. For trust demands *close* interdependence and it is only where this is sought for psychological, economic, social or technical ends (for example, friend with friend, client with contractor, club member with club member, principal with agent) or enforced as with regulator and regulatee, that the existence of either trust or distrust becomes an issue of significance.

If trust were possible in the relationship of regulator with regulatee, then the cost of ensuring compliance with standards might be less, with beneficial results to the public purse. The dilemma is, of course, that the process of regulation is based in part on deterrence, distance and the availability to the regulator of sanctions. And the use of the latter, or even the implied threat of their use, undermines the ability to establish trust were that thought to be a prudent characteristic of the relationship.

Furthermore, trust cannot necessarily be equated with success in any walk of life. When one observes the world outside, be it academia, public service, trade, industry, commerce or indeed anywhere, it is those individuals or agencies that act always to protect and enhance their own interests that ultimately achieve their goals. Indeed, this phenomenon is clearly articulated and recognised in the more recent literature on the regulation of public service and results in a hybrid regulatory mechanism which is a mixture of 'competition' with 'mutuality' (Hood and James, 1996).

More than this, the greatest danger, at least in the view of many regulators, would be that the risk and the adverse results flowing from trust misplaced is so great that only in the rarest regulatory situation would a trusting relationship be deemed to be prudent or feasible. The crucial question then becomes what might be the circumstances where trust, rather then mere hope, indifference or distrust, becomes possible.

To pursue this question further one has to refine and further explore the basic tools of analysis of all regulatory activity: namely, the regulatory cycle, the regulatory situation, the regulatory choice and, even more importantly, the regulatory relationship, with a view to identifying the circumstances in which trust might be a valid strategy.

Defining regulation

Regulation (and here the term is used in Hood's sense, as oversight) can be defined as:

> ... the process of ensuring that standards and legal requirements are met for specific service or public activities, in order to ensure that policies are fulfilled.... (Stewart and Walsh, 1992)

This definition embraces both the role of a regulatory body in regulating the activities of other organisations and individuals, but also the internal regulatory role of public service organisation such as internal audit. Recent proposals have given a new impetus to internal regulation. Increasingly, activities are being undertaken under contract, or service level agreements, or partnership agreements with other agencies, be they private or public. With the development of a 'Best Value' regime at least in local government and probably in the health service, and its ultimate extension to other public service organisations, regulation is becoming a much higher profile and strategically important aspect of public sector life. Moreover, as will be seen later, the regulatory cycle is almost identical to the contractual cycle. The discussion of the place and possibility of trust in the regulatory cycle is thus matched by that regarding its appropriateness and the feasibility of moving from so-called arm's-length contractual processes to relational contracts.

Regulation may be thought to be a relatively straightforward task:

- Standards will be specified as to the desired state to be achieved whether it be in premises, processes, equipment, activities or behaviours.

- Inspection, sampling or other means will be used to verify the actual state.
- Where there is a gap between the actual state and the desired state then one or another or a mixture of the social influence processes will be used to close the gap.

But of course it is not quite as simple as that. Indeed, there is over a century-and-a-half of literature and debate informing us so (see for example, Lambert, 1963; MacDonagh, 1977; Rhodes, 1981; Hawkins, 1984; Hutter, 1988; 1997):

- The specification of standards as to the desired state cannot always be clear and unambiguous.
- The adverse results flowing from non-compliance cannot always be clearly identified.
- Verification mechanisms of inspection, sampling or other means are limited by the availability of resources for this activity.
- There is a critical choice as to how, when and, more important, which of the social influence processes will be used to close the gap.
- The application of sanctions and penalties alone may not necessarily ensure that the specified standards will be met and more importantly, their use by the regulatory body may preclude the principal from achieving other competing policy objectives of equal or greater importance.
- If the regulator gets close enough to the regulatee, so necessary for the establishment of trust, they run the risk of regulatory capture, of cooption, collusion and ultimately corruption of, at least, their values.

It is the issues that arise from these problems that pose the major challenge to all regulatory bodies and expose the four primary dimensions of all regulatory and indeed, contractual activity, namely:

Level of compliance sought: the first decision a regulatory authority has to make is what level of compliance on a scale between 0 and 100% it is seeking to achieve for a particular regulatory or contractual activity. In practice neither end of the continuum is likely to be feasible. In the first instance this is due to the existence of the power of 'mandamus', whereby an aggrieved party can compel a public authority to fulfil its statutory responsibilities. In the second, it is due to limited resource availability in the sense that there is never sufficient regulatory or contract monitoring time to provide continuous information-gathering on compliance.

Social influence process to be used: having explicitly or implicitly chosen a level of compliance to be achieved and by inspection and monitoring ascertained that there is a gap between the desired state to be achieved and the actual state measured or observed, the next question is which, or what mixture, of the basic social influence processes, namely:

- persuasion;
- activation of commitments;
- inducement;
- sanction;
- manipulation of the physical social or informational environment; or
- altering the decision-criteria.

is most likely to bring about the chosen level of compliance. This in turn depends upon the basic characteristics of the regulatory situation and, ultimately, the relationship that is sought with the regulatee.

The regulatory situation: by this is meant whether the regulatory action is (a) oriented on the *past* in the sense that the purpose of it is to check on whether highly specific standards and rules have been complied with, for example, the design specification for a bridge, or (b) oriented to the *future* so as to ensure future safety, quality or whatever, for example, fire prevention, licensing of private hire vehicles, (c) whether the activities to be regulated are highly specific, for example, labelling of foodstuff, or (d) more general, for example, standards of care in residential homes; whether the concern is with (e) behaviour as, for example, care in a nursing home, or (f) with certain physical elements, for example, the presence of equipment to deal with fires, or (g) an outcome, for example, the removal from sale of unfit food or (h) a process, for example, a quality assurance system in a factory. The reality of course is that in many regulatory and contract situations there is a mixture of these elements.

Causes of non-compliance: the fourth dimension is the reasons for or causes of non-compliance. These can be grouped under four general headings:

- *Deficiency in knowledge* on the part of the regulatee as to what is required, due perhaps to unavailability of information, or ambiguity in information as to the standards required, or not knowing what sort of intervention to make to achieve the standards, for example, no clear cause and effect relationship.

- *Deficiency in resources* available to the regulatee, for example, inadequate premises, insufficient time, inappropriate equipment, insufficient staff numbers or skills or insufficient financial resources to meet the standard.
- *Deficiency in support* from the regulator, for example,
    › standards unclear, misleading or uncertainty as to their effect;
    › inadequate control systems to provide appropriate feedback so as to be self-monitoring;
    › attaching a different level of importance to the standards compared with that of the regulator;
    › obstacles, constraints, internally imposed restraints, perverse rules, all of which create additional difficulty in meeting the required standards.
- *Deficiency in intent*, by which is meant that although there is no palpable deficiency in knowledge, resources or support, the regulatee is failing to comply with the required standards because of:
    › different or misaligned values to those of the regulator;
    › a difference in priorities;
    › an imbalance of power, where the power resides with the regulatee rather than the regulator;
    › a desire to act opportunistically to protect and enhance their own interests.

The probing and analysis of these causes of non-compliance will determine whether persuasion-based or sanction-based influence processes will be used to achieve compliance and this in turn will influence the consequent relationship. However, this analysis must be coupled with experience and knowledge of the pre-existing relationship linked with the nature of the regulatory situation and, more particularly, consideration of the adverse results that may flow for all the individuals involved, any groups of which they are a part, the organisations by which they are employed and the community in general.

What then, in more detail, is the process of regulation? For only when a clear understanding of the process has been achieved will there emerge the issues and questions that are pertinent to identifying where trust might be a viable part of the regulatory relationship.

The regulatory cycle

Regulation is a cyclical process that has a number of stages. The cycle begins only when a critical mass of opinion regarding a problem or need is sufficiently weighty for government at national, or sometimes local level to have to take notice and develop a policy response. Policies are broad statements setting out what aims are to be achieved and how to go about their achievement and these will be supplemented by policy instruments. Standards are specifications of quality levels or of constraints to be observed if these policies are to be fulfilled. For example, a standard might be space per employee in an office environment and a constraint might be a time limit within which a certain action must be taken. Such standards and constraints, and sometimes the means by which they will be met, are then expressed in legislation, either statue or regulation, and fleshed out by rules formulated either nationally or locally. Together they define the desired state that is to be achieved.

Inspection, sampling and other means are the mechanisms by which the process of information gathering is undertaken in order to be able to ascertain the actual state – in essence, whether regulation, rules and standards are being attained. The regulator must then make a judgement about whether the regulatee is behaving as required. If not, action must be taken to achieve the desired state. Finally, the knowledge gained during the regulatory process will ideally be used to refine and reformulate policy, standards and often also the remedial legislation. It is a cyclical and iterative process which ultimately brings the initial problems in all their manifestations under legal and administrative control. It may not entirely eliminate the problems, but they will be under control.

Not all the stages identified will necessarily be carried out by the regulatory authority. The development of a critical mass of opinion may proceed independently of the action or involvement of even national government, or policy may have been formulated at national level with only a limited input from the world of regulation. Similarly, standards may have been set not by central government but by the European Union (EU). However, even where involvement is limited in this way, the underlying cycle is taking place and needs to be understood because it determines the nature of the process of regulation. Moreover, each stage in the regulatory cycle needs to be considered in its own right.

Critical mass of concern

Throughout the history of government, individual public authorities have often been involved not merely in responding to but also stimulating concern regarding emerging problems. Sometimes they have acted as a channel of communication between local and national pressure groups, thereby providing information and ideas upon which national government can build policy. Today such activities continue in a variety of ways and through a host of forums and are a means whereby national government becomes aware of local problems and pressures which subsequently may require national attention. On the other hand, there is ample evidence in the historical literature of public authorities, at officer or elected member level, having acted to suppress emerging protest, either because their own individual interests were prejudiced or because such protests might damage the ability to achieve objectives that the public authority considered more important. With the current concern of every public authority to best match the services it provides with the needs of its citizens/consumers, coupled with the increasing ability of citizen groups to gather appropriate information and utilise the media to expose their problems, the opportunity for public authorities to downplay citizens' interests is much reduced. The information revolution will in the long run cause public authorities to be increasingly responsive to the problems in their communities. The central point to be made though is that the development of a critical mass of concern is a necessary condition for the regulatory process to begin.

Formulation of policy

Often lost sight of, but again a necessary condition, is that policy needs to be formulated with a view to its implementation. There is little point in policies that, however laudable, are unattainable or unrealistic. Much of the current debate on EU directives is not about whether or not they are laudable but whether they are attainable or realistic in the context of the United Kingdom. If unattainable policies are formulated, the regulators may find themselves in an untenable position. They may be forced into trying to enforce the unenforceable. With aggrieved citizens having the power to go to the High Court to obtain an Order of *Mandamus* to compel public authority to fulfil its statutory duties, this creates an unwholesome position. For example, if unattainable policies are adopted, say, for the control of markets or Sunday Trading, then regulators may ignore them, but at the risk of *Mandamus*. Nonenforcement is a frequent and typical reaction to legislative requirements that are seen as unrealistic, for example, the requirement under the 1936 Housing Act for local authorities to inspect every dwelling in their area from time to time.

Equally, policy needs to reflect changes in the circumstances confronted. In recent years there has been a growing concern for the environment. Policies that might have been unattainable previously may now be realistic as they gain both public support and feedback from existing regulatory activities on related issues. Furthermore, ideas about what is and what is not acceptable change. Heavily littered streets and fouling dogs have been less acceptable in recent times and local authorities have developed policies to deal with them. In summary, policies need to be:

- clear;
- capable of implementation;
- attainable;
- acceptable;
- durable, but responsive to changing knowledge and circumstances; and
- cost-effective.

If these conditions are met, then at a subsequent stage regulatory action becomes tenable.

Standards

Standards are fundamental to the regulatory process. The standards set will, in part, determine the way that regulation will be carried out. They need to be stated as clearly and unambiguously as possible so that they may be understood both by the regulators and the regulatees. There are three types of standard:

- those that can be measures objectively, for example, the accuracy of a weighting machine or some other recording instrument;
- those that can be observed but cannot be the subject of detailed measurement, for example, standards of cleanliness in a residential home or restaurant;
- qualitative, judgmental standards, for example, the quality of care in a residential home, teaching in a school, employees commitment to food hygiene in a kitchen.

They need to be discrete in the sense that they apply only to that which is controllable. Moreover, it is desirable that those setting the standards state where discretion is possible and where it is not. Failure to do so leads inevitably to the long and costly process of building case law interpretations of ambiguous discretion, for example, it has taken many decades to refine understanding of what the term 'reasonably practicable' might mean in the context of Health and Safety legislation. This leads to confusion both for the regulator and the regulatee.

Statute, regulation and rules

These are at the heart of regulatory activity. Rules are different to standards for they state what has to be done to attain the standard. They are constraints on unfettered action on the part of the regulatee, laying down limits within which they must operate and prescribing the conditions under which the regulator may act. They involve the detailed expression of standards which, if not met by the regulatee, will involve action on the part of the regulator.

Statues, regulations and rules need to be well-drafted. That is to say they must be:

- clear;
- capable of being understood by regulator and regulatee;
- complete;
- practicable;
- acceptable;
- avoid 'creative compliance'; and
- non-discriminatory.

If they are the subject of argument as to their interpretation, disagreement as to their intent and vagueness as to their purpose, hereby encouraging 'creative compliance', then regulation is likely to be ineffectual. Fairness and justice for the regulatee require that they know explicitly the requirements that are laid upon them, burdensome though they may be.

Inspection

The purpose of inspection is fact-finding. This involves gathering information on the matters subject to regulation. A variety of methods can be used:

- observation;
- reviewing policies, records, processes, accounts;
- interviews;
- questionnaires;
- sampling;
- collection of statistics; and
- complaints/incidents data.

Inspection may be open in the sense that an appointment is made to undertake an inspection at some future date. It may be covert as, for example, in the purchase of a product by an inspector to ascertain subsequently that required standards are being maintained or met. Or it may be randomly episodic so that the regulatees cannot have the certainty as to when they may be inspected.

A key input of inspection is the degree to which it involves contact with the person regulated. In some cases, inspectors or contract monitors can gather information without any significant interaction with the regulatee, for example, the sampling of food, air, water, and so on. In other cases, such as an inspection of a residential home, much of the information will be provided by the regulatee, by the servants of the regulatee, or even by the service users. The degree of interaction necessary may well at a future stage determine the social influence process to be used to gain compliance with the required standard, and whether or not trust can be generated or is feasible.

Accurate recording of the information gathered is a crucial part of the process of inspection, for it ensures both that a clear history of a situation can be developed and that objectivity can be demonstrated if a situation is subject to challenge.

Reporting is a further aspect arising from inspection in the simple sense that information needs to be put into a form in which it can be used and understood both by the regulatee and those who may wish to judge the regulator. This is part of the way in which inspectorial staffs and contract monitors are themselves held accountable. Accuracy is again important so that comparability in the approaches of differing inspectors can be ensured.

In some cases reports are likely to take a standard format (this may even be itself statutorily required). In other cases the type of inspection and the nature of the report will vary with circumstances and purpose as, for example in the inspection of a school. In summary, information collection on compliance needs to be:

- accurate;
- consistent across cases;
- equitable;
- relevant;
- focused;
- regular or purposefully random;
- cost-effective; and
- manifestly seen to be objective.

Judgement

The task of judgement is separate from that of inspection and the other means of gathering the information. The information gathered must then be used to reach a decision about whether or not requirements as to the *desired state* are being achieved, even though the information itself may frequently be open to differing interpretation. Care is required because of the need for fairness and the possibility of complaint or appeal and the strength of the evidence will be crucial in determining what intervention to make.

Action

Even in areas that are subject to tight statutory or contractual control, it is rare for there to be only one pattern of action open to the regulatory authority. Having made a judgement based upon the information gathered as to the *actual state*, the regulator must decide what sort of action is appropriate. The first decision the regulator must make is between action and inaction: is the gap between the actual state and the desired state significant enough as to regard it as a problem? It may be so insignificant as to make it perfectly sensible not to take action because, for example, the effort involved in closing the gap would not be worth the gain. This is a critically sensitive decision and requires careful consideration as to what are the *adverse results* (the risks) that might flow for the community in failing to close the gap. These are dependent in large part upon the nature of the omission, but if they are insignificant or trivial then it may be appropriate to take no action on the first occasion of their occurrence.

If the pattern of omission should be repeated on a further occasion, then the regulator may feel that a cumulative situation warrants action on their part.

If intervention is appropriate then, as indicated earlier, a range of 'social influence' processes are available to secure compliance.

Review

The regulatory cycle needs to be a learning cycle. There is little point in securing compliance with standards that are unacceptable to society or out of date, especially when resources are constrained. Public perceptions, tastes and the law itself all change, however slowly. The review process involves assessing how effective a particular regulatory policy has been in meeting community needs.

It may be that a particular set of regulations do not meet changing needs and when, for example, planning regulations were relaxed in enterprise zones. Equally, it may be decided in the light of public concern that certain situations need tighter regulation. For example, regulations on residential establishments have tightened in recent years as they have in many areas of food hygiene and food safety.

The work of those involved in regulation has traditionally been a valuable source of information for they have detailed knowledge derived from practice as to the appropriateness of the actual legislation in achieving policy objectives and on the emergence of new issues which may require remedial action. It is important that the regulatory authority has access to such information and develops a systematic approach to harnessing it to assist in its contribution to the governance of the community. Such information is also critical to central government, for it is an important way in which to evaluate whether policy objectives are being met and whether there is a need for the redrawing of statutes, regulations, rules, notes of guidance, etc.

Trust or distrust?

For the regulatory authority the starting point for discussion of trust is the identification of those regulatory situations in which trust, as opposed to mere hope, indifference or distrust, is an appropriate relationship. The test should be its effectiveness in securing compliance and minimising the adverse results flowing from non-compliance.

An appropriate mechanism for plotting where trust might be appropriate is the MASLIN Multi-dimensional Matrix. This is essentially a device for identifying all the significant dimensions where there is a good match as opposed to a mismatch between the service provided and the significant dimensions of the relationship of the organisation with its environment. In other words, it identifies the 'matching service linkages' (Prince and Puffitt, 1997).

As mentioned earlier, hope and indifference also lie on the continuum between trust and distrust and these intermediate positions need at least explaining if not precisely defining. For the definition of trust, see that given by Andrew Coulson in Chapter Two, but with particular emphasis on the 'willingness to be vulnerable' aspect. However, it is also worth reiterating that this willingness is based on an intuitive cognitive auditing of the gains and losses that might arise in the situation and that only if trust is reciprocated is it likely to develop into the later stages and forms of trust.

By 'distrust' I mean that opportunistic behaviours such as 'self-interest-seeking with guile' are not merely anticipated but expected of the regulatee and moreover that, given the opportunity, they will seek to coopt the regulator, gain their collusion in concealment of their non-compliance or may even attempt to corrupt them.

'Hope' refers to the situation where the zealous regulator, recognising the impossibility of constant surveillance due to the shortage of resources, nevertheless believes that compliance is likely or at least possible.

'Indifference' refers to the situation where the regulator, for a variety of reasons but principally extreme resource restraint, protects themselves and their sanity by manifesting a complete lack of interest in the regulatee until such time as they are able to undertake the appropriate surveillance.

The significant dimensions of the relationship between regulatory authority and the regulatee that have emerged from the earlier discussion are as follows:

- level of compliance sought;
- availability of regulatory resources;
- specificity of standards;
- clarity of cause and effect;
- degree of non-compliance;
- significance of adverse results;
- strength of evidence;

- cause of non-compliance;
- risk of concealment, cooption, collusion or corruption;
- skills of persuasion and influence;
- skills of sanction and enforcement;
- pre-existing relationships; and
- desired future relationships.

Overlaying and then plotting each of these dimensions against the axis 'trust, hope, indifference and distrust' reveals the following pattern of likely and appropriate behaviour. Distrust is appropriate where:

- a high level of compliance is sought but a low level of regulatory resources are available;
- where cause and effect relationships are uncertain and therefore the regulatee can take action to maximise their own interests;
- where standards are non-specific involving behaviour rather than more concrete outcomes;
- where a high degree of non-compliance is a common pattern among those who are to be monitored;
- where the adverse results flowing from non-compliance are highly significant;
- where the strength of evidence is low, thereby allowing latitude to the regulatee to evade or obscure their real intent;
- where the cause of non-compliance arises from a deficiency in intent on the part of the regulatee, occasioned by having different values, priorities or objectives to those of the regulator, rather than a simple deficiency in knowledge, resources or support;
- where the risk of concealment, cooption or corruption is high;
- where the regulator possesses low skills in the techniques of persuasion but has high skills in the use of sanction;
- where there is a poor pre-existing relationship between regulator and regulatee; and
- where the regulator is unconcerned about the quality of any possible future relationship.

Trust, on the other hand, is appropriate only:

- where a low level of compliance is sought and yet where there is a high level of regulatory resources available to monitor non-compliance;

- where there is clarity of cause and effect;
- where there is low specificity in the standards required;
- where there is a low degree of non-compliance among those regulated;
- where there is low significance in the adverse results flowing from non-compliance;
- where there is considerable strength of evidence when non-compliance is found;
- where non-compliance is due to deficiencies in knowledge, resources or support from the regulatee;
- where the risk of concealment, and so on, is low;
- where the regulator possesses substantial skills in persuasion as opposed to the use of sanction;
- where there is a good pre-existing relationship; and
- where the intention is to maintain a good relationship for the future.

There are, of course, many regulators who would suggest that such a combination of characteristics is, in practice, fairly rare. To quote from a long-standing and highly experienced regulator, "fair law enforcement coupled with the extensive use of sanctions is overwhelmingly more effective and, more importantly, cost-effective, than any other approach that is available. When I took office I inherited an excellent team of people who had been giving advice, assistance and support for years and who could 'trust and persuade for England'. The consequences of this was that it was almost impossible to find any regulatee that complied with any of the legislation, let alone all of it. I have no doubt whatsoever that distrust and sanction work and that in the vast majority of cases, trust and persuasion do not" (private letter to author).

With regard to hope and indifference, the principal determinants of which characteristic exists in practice are the level of regulatory resources available compared with the volume of monitoring work to be undertaken, coupled with enthusiasm for and commitment to the values of the regulatory authority. Hope slides into indifference where resources are highly constrained, the volume of work to be undertaken excessively high and commitment to values eroded by the regulatory authority's inability to command sufficient support and resources to function as it was intended. This way leads only to increased non-compliance, volumes of work and desperation on the part of the individual regulator. It is the classic negative, downward, self-fulfilling cycle where distrust becomes the only realistic response. All opportunity for the regulator to act opportunistically so as to gain greater control and influence over that for which they were appointed to exercise oversight is lost. The terrible price becomes due, for had trust been possible then the long-term cost of securing compliance might have been so much the less. On balance, however, the citizen might prefer that those who regulate on their behalf be skilled and practised in the art of distrust rather than trust, for imprudent kinship with the latter may well result in no more than a 'dance with the devil' at the citzen's expense.

Part Five

Trust as the foundation of society

TWELVE

Risk and reciprocity: local governance rooted within civil society

John Benington

Distrust and risk society

The resurgence of talk about trust, in both academic and policy making circles, has come paradoxically at a time when there is also a rising sense of dis-trust, fear and risk in many parts of the wider society. Some of this may be little more than PMT (pre-millennial tension) or fin de siècle angst. However, there is no doubting the evidence from opinion surveys and other research which shows growing feelings of alienation and insecurity within many sections of the population in the West, and a decline in confidence that governments, politicians or public services can be trusted to address such problems. This finds expression both in generalised societal anxieties (about widespread risks like Chernobyl, global warming, AIDS and BSE, for example); in distrust between and within specific groups and sectors within the population (for example, fears about crime and safety, about abuse of children by paedophiles, and about inter-racial violence and inter-generational tension); and in crises of confidence about probity in the business and government sectors (for example, the Barings and Maxwell financial scandals, and sleaze and corruption in governments).

Against this background of risk and uncertainty, the notion of trust is often introduced indiscriminately, like an aerosol haze sprayed lightly over the surface of murky areas to make them smell sweeter. Trust, and the related concept of loyalty, are in danger of being idealised, dematerialised, decontextualised and depoliticised. They are currently discussed in the academic literature, and among practitioners in both public and private sectors, in terms primarily of interpersonal, intergroup or interorganisational relations. However, when considering local governance and public policy, the concept of trust needs to be located within a wider political, economic and social context, which takes account of power relations as well as social relations, contest as well as coalition, conflicts of interest as well as consensual relations, risk as well as reciprocity.

The political, economic and social context in which trust needs to be embedded in relation to local governance can be thought of in terms of the leadership and management of a "risk society" (Beck, 1992). Beck's thesis goes further than just suggesting that 20th-century society faces more widespread risks than previous periods. His argument, and that of several other social theorists (for example, Giddens 1994), is that it is no longer possible to maintain the modernist belief that human beings are able through their knowledge and skill to order or to shape either the physical environment, the economy, the polity or the society, in the ways in which they intend. He argues that Western capitalism has led to such extensive interventions in these spheres that it is not now possible to disentangle their causes and effects, or to predict their outcomes confidently, either in the natural sciences or the social sciences. Far-reaching technological and industrial developments have taken place with so little knowledge of their long-term and ecological consequences, and with so little democratic debate, that we are now faced with a world in which outcomes are often unpredictable and incalculable. In the past, governments and businesses have claimed to be able to predict the possible 'side-effects' of scientific and technological developments, to calculate the 'externality' costs and to mitigate or compensate for these repercussions (for example, industrial pollution, and the polluter pays principle).

Beck argues that the ecological balance has been disturbed to such an extent in so many areas that we live in a world of pervasive and unpredictable risk (for example, of nuclear catastrophes, environmental hazards, genetically engineered disasters), in which the costs and consequences can no longer be treated as side-effects or externalities. He sees risk society as a society in which the production of "bads" has become as central as the production of "goods".

Some writers suggest that similar patterns of risk and unpredictability now affect the economy and the polity. Globalisation of the economy, the growth of transnational corporations and of worldwide financial markets, means that governments can no longer regulate their national economies through traditional macroeconomic measures. Short-term speculation in financial options and money futures has had long term and far-reaching impacts upon the British and Malaysian economies (to name but two) which now lie beyond democratic control (Soros, 1994). As Daniel Bell put it in 1973, in a much quoted remark, the nation-state has become too small to tackle global problems and too large to deal with the local issues. So there is a growing recognition in many quarters that economic management is as much a game of chance as a process of rational choice or planning.

Similarly in the field of social policy, the rise in public reporting of and concern about issues like violent crime, muggings, rapes, child abuse and drug abuse, but the lack of certainty about how best to respond to them, has led to a generalised anxiety about increased risks in society and a loss of confidence in traditional state solutions. Some have turned to private solutions (for example, personal and household security devices), and others to vigilante action outside the democratic process (for example, direct action against drug dealers and anti-social neighbours on housing estates).

Beck and Giddens both interpret this widespread sense of ecological, economic, social and political risks as part of an even more fundamental collapse of confidence in the Enlightenment belief that " the more we get to know about the world, as collective humanity, the more we can control it to our own purposes. Increasing knowledge produced about the social and natural worlds would lead to greater certainty about the conditions under which we lead our lives..." (Beck et al, 1994). In contrast, Giddens sees our lives today as characterised by a generalised fear of the possibility of catastrophe, and by "manufactured uncertainty" – manufactured in the sense that compared with previous sources of uncertainty in the natural world (for example, crop failure because of bad weather), "many of the uncertainties which face us today have been created by the very growth of human knowledge" (Beck et al, pp 184-5).

Active trust

Giddens concludes that a risk society needs to be counterbalanced and matched by a notion of 'active trust'. Active trust in his terms is a " trust that has to be energetically treated and sustained ... active trust is necessarily geared to the integrity of the other. Such integrity cannot be taken for granted on the basis of a person's incumbency of a particular social position. Trust has to be won and actively sustained; and this now ordinarily presumes a process of mutual narrative and emotional disclosure" (Beck et al, 1994, p 187).

Giddens' concept of trust is clearly located in interpersonal and intergroup relations, but it is also set in the context of a structural, political economic analysis of risk at the systemic level. This chapter argues that active trust of this kind is more likely to be cultivated within the collaborative cultures of civil society, than in the command and control traditions of the state or the competitive relationships cultivated by the private market; and that it is within civil society that local government must primarily be grounded, if it is to foster active trust as one of the antidotes to a risk society.

Risk society or civil society?

In the postwar period in the UK we have tended, until fairly recently, to treat private and public sectors as if they were largely watertight compartments, with transfers between them seen as major political choices (for example, privatisation or nationalisation). State and market have been conceptualised as antagonistic rather than interrelated. A major battle of ideas and interests has focused around the question of the boundaries between the state and the market, and how much there should be of each. The model has been that of a zero-sum game in which more of the state implied less of the market and vice versa. For example, in the immediate post-war period the dominant thinking was that the (welfare) state should be extensive and strong (acting as primary provider for a wide range of needs, for example, education, housing, transport, and so on), and that the market should be firmly regulated by the state (both through nationalisation of the commanding heights of industry and Keynesian macroeconomic management). The model for both sectors (public and private) was one of mass production of standardised products and universal services for a population which was treated as largely homogeneous and undifferentiated in its needs. However, the state and the market, public and private, were seen as two compartmentalised sectors, at best in creative tension with each other, at worst in conflict.

In the 1980s the pendulum swung from left to right, with a right-wing challenge to the postwar consensus in support of a strong state. A marked shift in the paradigm took place, with an argument for the market as the primary provider and the state as a safety net of last resort. The model for both sectors (public and private) came to be small batch production rather than mass production, customised goods and services rather than standardised products, and diverse niches rather than homogeneous markets. However, the relationship between the two sectors was still portrayed as one of separation and tension.

During the 1990s thinking has tended to move beyond this polarisation and demarcation between public and private sectors, market and state, to recognise both the interdependencies and the blurring of the boundaries between the two. Private sector organisations are increasingly aware both of their corporate social responsibilities (for example, in relation to the environment and to the local community), and of their dependence upon state policies (for example, not only in relation to taxation but also for education, training, transport, health, and so on). Public sector organisations are similarly increasingly aware of their intersection and interdependence with private sector organisations and with the market (for example, in relation to economic development and regeneration), and are forming new public–private partnerships which give organisational expression to this recognition.

The experience of many policy makers and managers involved in public–private partnerships, and in trying to develop trust-based relationships between these sectors, is that joint ventures of this kind involve not only a crossing of boundaries between different organisations, but that they are profoundly different *kinds* of organisations and that the dynamic whirlpool set in motion in the area of confluence can be extremely complex and volatile. These whirlpool dynamics become even more complex when the partners include not only organisations from the public and private sectors, but also from the voluntary and the informal community sector. Since each of these three sectors, or spheres, is characterised by very different kinds of power relations and processes, their interaction frequently leads to turbulence and churning.

In order to try to understand these sectoral and intersectoral relationships we need to move beyond a model based upon a binary division between state and market as if they are polar opposites. We need to take account of three spheres (the state, the market and civil society), rather than two sectors, and to explore the inter-relationships between them, rather than just the boundaries which separate them. We need to explore the very different organisational structures, cultures, processes and relationships which operate within each of the three spheres and in the whirlpool of cross-cutting currents when and where they intersect and interact.

The rediscovery of civil society

What does civil society mean? Why has it become such an important concept in debates about governance and organisation not only in the USA and Canada, but also in Eastern Europe and in South Africa? Why are policy makers and academics beginning to discuss it again in the UK? What are the relationships of civil society with the state and with the market? What are the implications for theories of risk and trust of a reorientation of state and market towards civil society? What would local governance look like if it was more firmly rooted in civil society?

Civil society is a long-established concept in political science and social theory, having been used in different ways by Aristotle, Locke, Hegel, Marx and Gramsci, to name but a few. In the postwar period in the West it has been overshadowed by thinking about the state and the market. Civil society re-entered public debate in the late 1980s when mass popular movements in Eastern Europe and in South Africa challenged the totalitarianism of their state apparatuses, and reasserted the importance of grassroots movements for change, based upon their neighbourhoods, workplaces, churches and other informal networks.

Definitions of civil society are varied and confusing, too often defined by negatives (for example, the not-for-profit sector, or non-governmental organisations and associations), as if it is little more than what is left over outside the state and the market. Ernest Gellner has defined civil society as "that set of diverse non-governmental institutions which is strong enough to counterbalance the state and, while not preventing the state from fulfilling its role of keeper of the peace and arbitrator between major interests, can nevertheless prevent it from dominating and atomising the rest of society" (Gellner, 1994).

Cohen and Arato have a broader working definition of civil society as "a sphere of social interaction between economy and state, composed of all of the intimate sphere (especially the family), the sphere of associations (especially voluntary associations), social movements, and forms of public communication" (Cohen and Arato, 1992).

Ralf Dahrendorf (1996) offers perhaps the clearest practical definition:

The term civil society is more suggestive than precise. It

suggests for example that people behave towards each other in a civilised manner; the suggestion is fully intended. It also suggests that its members enjoy the status of citizens, which is again intended. However the core meaning of the concept is quite precise. Civil society describes the associations in which we conduct our lives, and which owe their existence to our needs and initiatives rather than to the state. Some of these associations are highly deliberate and sometimes short-lived, like sports clubs or political parties. Others are founded in history and have a very long life, like churches or universities. Still others are the places in which we work and live – enterprises, local communities. The family is an element of civil society. The criss-crossing network of such associations – their creative chaos as one might be tempted to say – make up the reality of civil society. It is a precious reality, far from universal, itself the result of a long civilising process; yet it is often threatened, by authoritarian rulers or by forces of globalisation. (Dahrendorf, 1996)

This definition reveals the normative, value-laden dimension of the concept, and also indicates its implicit reliance on notions of trust, the key issue to which we will return in the next section.

John Keane, in his book *Civil society and the state* (1988), argues that three types of development have brought the concept of civil society back into prominence in the last few years:

- Global restructuring of the capitalist economy, which has decreased the ability of states to anticipate and control their economies, or to guarantee full employment. This has exposed the deep dependence of the current welfare state upon both the labour market and the household (which is seen as one of the key institutions of civil society).
- The controversies surrounding the Keynesian welfare state, and the recognition, on both the left and the right, that certain forms of statist intervention in some circumstances can lead to the withering away of the bonds of social solidarity within the informal community, and of trust between the informal community and the organisations of the state.

- The growth of new social movements, particularly in Eastern Europe and Africa and Latin America, but also in the West (black and civil rights campaigns, women's organisations, tenants and residents associations, environmental and peace groups, animal rights groups, and so on). These have either challenged or (increasingly) bypassed the traditional channels of political and state representation, and the values of the private capitalist market.

Taken together, factors like these are seen as leading to a growing disenchantment with the postwar settlement, and a recognition that neither the Keynesian welfare state nor the private competitive market have adequately met basic human needs for employment, housing, health, education, safety, security, and above all the human need for a sense of meaning, purpose, trust and belonging within a wider community.

Attention is therefore being turned once again to civil society, and to the ways in which the state and the market relate to this third sector. Civil society can be pictured as differing from both the private market and the public state in several dimensions – in its forms of governance, forms of coordination, types of relationships and modes of regulation. It must be emphasised that the distinctions outlined below are based upon ideal types rather than actual practices and are therefore oversimplifications of reality. In practice, there is much overlap and interpenetration between the three sectors, and this will be explored below. However, it is analytically useful to begin from the theoretical differences.

The forms of governance for the three spheres (see Figure 5) can be pictured as differing in the following ways:

- The state is governed through democratically elected representatives and the law.
- The market is governed by the discipline of competition.
- Civil society is pictured as being self-governed and regulated through participation and involvement.

Figure 5: Governance of the interrelationships between three intersecting spheres

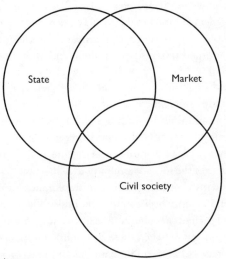

Source; John Benington

The forms of coordination for each sphere can be pictured, in terms of ideal types, in the following ways:

- the state is regulated traditionally through bureaucratic hierarchies;
- the market is managed primarily through competitive markets;
- civil society is coordinated mainly through relational networks.

The types of organisational relationships within each sphere can be construed as follows:

- the state traditionally has been organised through command and control relationships;
- the private market is primarily organised around competitive relationships;
- civil society is organised mainly through collaboration, coalition and consensus.

The modes of regulation within each sphere also differ (following Hirschman, 1970):

- the state is governed primarily through the mechanism of voice (the right of citizens to elect their representatives and to vote them in or out);
- private markets are regulated primarily by the mechanism of exit (the customers choice to take their business elsewhere);
- civil society is orchestrated primarily through loyalty (the bonds which are forged through involvement and association).

In practice the distinctions between the three spheres are more complex as they overlap and inter-penetrate, and as each becomes subject to cross-cutting pressures and pulls towards the characteristics of the other two spheres. For example, as councillors and officers increasingly try to move beyond simply managing the local authority bureaucracy and into a more active governance of the local community, they increasingly have to work across the boundaries between public, private, voluntary and community organisations, and to move between the very different styles of organisation which prevail in each of the spheres. Local government actors are moving increasingly across and between these three different spheres which each have very different cultures, rules, traditions and lines of accountability. An increasing amount of organisational activity is taking place in the areas of overlap and intersection between the three spheres, where there is a whirlpool of different organisational and cultural cross-currents.

There are two main phenomena to analyse here. The first is what happens when organisations from different sectors come together in partnerships and joint ventures which cut across the boundaries between public, private, voluntary and community sectors. The second is the implication for local governance of the fact that organisations in each of the three spheres are subject to contradictory pulls and pressures towards the other two. For example, many public sector organisations are being required to adopt more commercial and market-like behaviour in some areas of their activity, while at the same time being encouraged to develop more active relationships with voluntary organisations and community associations within civil society. Private sector organisations are being pressured to establish norms of corporate social responsibility and public accountability (the four-fold bottom line of accountability to shareholders, employees, customers and the community) that have until recently been more associated with the public sector. Voluntary organisations are being invited, in some cases, to act as dedicated sub-contractors to the public services, while in other cases to operate within a climate of competitive tendering within the market.

In normative terms, social relations within civil society and its informal associations are regulated through trust and loyalty. This contrasts with the state where, in ideal typical terms, regulation is primarily through voice (for example, voting and pressure group activity to change unsatisfactory policies), and with the market where regulation is primarily through exit (for example, the customers' capacity to take their business to another supplier if dissatisfied) (Hirschman, 1970). The current fascination with the concepts of trust and loyalty in both the public and the private sectors may be because voice and exit are increasingly recognised to be forms of regulation which are too crude and inflexible to respond adequately to the continuous fluctuations in the political, economic, social and technological context, and particularly to the uncertainties of "risk society". The public bureaucratic state and the private competitive market are both being found to be inadequate instruments for responding to many of the complex changes in patterns of need within society. The law of requisite variety would suggest that more complex and variegated forms of organisation are needed, and that these may be found, in ideal type terms at least, in the trust-based networks and loyalty-based associations supposedly characteristic of civil society.

Local governance within civil society

The previous section has outlined the concept of civil society as an ideal type, just as the market and the state are often conceptualised in their idealised forms. However, in reality and in practice of course, civil society is just as likely to be characterised by competition, bureaucracy, division, distrust, betrayal and risk, as by collaboration, solidarity, trust and reciprocity. It is important to start from these realities if local government is to be able to root governance in civil society, and to regenerate confidence in the political and democratic process, and to develop citizen-centred public services.

The radical restructuring of European and British society over the past 15 years has led to sharp increases in inequality in relation to wealth, income, employment, housing, health and education, and to a deepening gap between private affluence for some and public squalor for the many. This has caused, or at least been accompanied by, increases in crime, violence and disorder, and cultural brutalisation (Hoggart, 1995; Donnison, 1998).

Dahrendorf does not see all inequalities as incompatible with a decent civil society, but regards the new inequality as of a different kind "better described as inequalisation, the opposite of levelling, building paths to the top for some and digging holes for others, creating cleavages, splitting" (Dahrendorf, 1996, p 28).

How can local authorities contribute to the building of trust and reciprocity within a fragmenting and risk-filled society like this?

In times of major disasters (for example, Lockerbie, Hillsborough, the Dunblane massacre, the Manchester bombing and, earlier, Coventry after the blitz) people have often turned to their local council, not only to coordinate the emergency services, but also for support in their grief, fears and uncertainties, to express their latent desire to belong to a community governed by trust rather than by distrust, and to mobilise their own capacities for caring and reciprocity.

(It would be interesting to analyse the relative roles played by the church and by the local authority in these situations.)

The reason why local authorities seem to carry and to embody these latent hopes on behalf of people at risk is partly because of their unique role as the only organisation with a democratic mandate to represent the interests of the whole local community rather than any of its separate parts. It can also represent future generations as well as current customers or voters, regardless of personal or political beliefs.

The official report of the local authority's role in the aftermath of the Lockerbie disaster gives a glimpse of a local government fully embedded in civil society, albeit at a moment of extreme crisis. Immediately after he was notified of the crash the chief executive visited the disaster area, and quickly moved his whole office there to personally operate this as a 24-hour point of coordination both for the emergency services (for example, fire, police, ambulance), the direct services (engineers, refuse and cleansing), and the personal support services (for example, social work, bereavement and counselling services) and as a focal point for the local community and the families of those who had died in the crash. In a similar way, Stirling Council became a focal point for both the local and the worldwide community in the wake of the Dunblane massacre, not only in the immediate period of shock, anger and grieving, but also in the longer-term process of coming to terms with trauma and loss, and in the ensuing campaign to ban handguns.

Similarly close relationships between the local authority and its people can also be established at times of celebration (for example, when Coventry won the FA Cup in 1987). Disasters, emergencies and celebrations are of course situations in which people are likely to be less aware of their divisions and more united with each other and with the authorities. The much bigger challenge for local authorities in more everyday situations is first how to rebuild trust *within* communities which are disunited, divided and demoralised (how to build a sense of common purpose and hope out of diverse and sometimes conflicting interests) and, second, how to (re-)establish confidence and trust *between* the people and the local authority (how to generate a sense that the local council reflects and represents the real concerns of the people as they experience them, whether or not they fit into the authority's departmental or service delivery categories).

The first principle for the local authority in this kind of situation is to start by listening to the differences, the diversities and the conflicts of interest within the community, rather than to begin by asserting the common purpose or the communal interest. Local councillors are of course used to responding to, and trying to reconcile, representations from a range of local pressure groups, associations and different interest groups, and having to balance their competing claims and demands. However, councillors are often reduced to being little more than a conduit for channelling the diverse views of these factional interests to the local authority, and for selling the local authority's policies back to the people.

Councillors concerned to build 'active trust' within their wards and communities are increasingly trying to develop more proactive ways of identifying and then weaving the threads of common interest between apparently diverse and conflicting groups. This is often not at all easy, and requires great skills and time. It might involve, for example, inter-generational work to resolve tensions between pensioners' groups and unemployed young people about rowdyism on a housing estate, and a search for ways in which the young people could get involved in paid or voluntary work to care for the older people in practical ways and thus gain an appreciation of their needs. It might involve inter-racial work to try to overcome conflicts between black and white and ethnic minority communities within the area. This kind of proactive capacity-building work to promote communal solidarity, support and trust is familiar within many traditions of community development and community action in the UK and the USA (Marris and Rein, 1982), and also in South Africa.

(for example, in the township committees and civic associations (Fitzgerald et al, 1995).

However, much of this experience is oppositional – it is perhaps easier to build coalitions of interest and of solidarity when there is a common enemy to fight, or a common problem to unite around. The current context of risk and uncertainty is much more complex. Community development therefore has to be propositional as well as oppositional. It has to help local groups to decide what they are for, not just what they are against. It has to try to identify and to develop the common interests within diverse and sometimes divided communities. For example, it has to generate joint action on practical issues like environmental improvements, play schemes, childcare support networks, pensioners luncheon clubs, street festivals and other forms of neighbourhood activity.

The second task is even more difficult – how to link local government in to these complex grassroots communities. Part of the problem is that local government has traditionally been organised around departments, professions and services (for example, education, housing, social services, trading standards), rather than around the needs of individuals, households or groups of citizens (for example, older people, young people, the residents of a particular estate), or the cross-cutting problems and issues which they face (for example, poverty, unemployment, ageing). The two main models for local authority organisation in the UK are still the state-bureaucracy (based on vertical hierarchical structures which rise like separate skyscrapers with little connection between them at the ground level), and the competitive market (based on a splitting of the organisation into semi-autonomous trading units, purchasers and providers, clients and contractors).

In order to respond adequately to the complex cross-cutting problems which face households and neighbourhoods, however, we now need to develop new more flexible forms of local authority organisation, based less upon state bureaucracy or competitive market models than upon forms derived from civil society. This would mean developing networked forms of organisation capable of responding and interacting in a holistic way to changing and fluctuating patterns of need in the community. The aim must be to assist citizens to receive a seamless integrated service across all departments and agencies and tiers of government, rather than leaving them with the responsibility for finding their way through the bureaucratic maze. One-stop shops, single call centres, integrated neighbourhood offices and forums will all be a necessary part of the new citizen-centered governance.

Conclusion

A local authority committed to the development of an active civil society would therefore imply a different kind of local governance, going beyond the representation and reflection of diversity and plurality. Rooted in civil society, it would aim to regenerate the bonds of trust and the networks of reciprocity that have been undermined by the risk society. A local authority which wants to foster such relationships of trust with, and within, its community, will need to reorient itself towards new kinds of developmental capacity-building relationships which strengthen the confidence and the 'authority' (authorship) of its people. This implies a more proactive developmental role for both councillors and officers, in a concerted attempt to foster reciprocity even under conditions of risk, to cultivate loyalty in the midst of fragmentation and alienation, and to build trust even under conditions of distrust.

THIRTEEN

Citizenship in the public domain for trust in civil society

Stewart Ranson and John Stewart

Not long ago we were asked to believe that 'there was no such thing as society' – only individuals, their rights, interests and the contracts which bind them together. Now, as the turn of the 21st century approaches and the need grows to grasp the conditions for cooperative action so as to enhance economic regeneration, let alone social, environmental and cultural renewal, the significance of 'society' and its institutions presses in upon us. The transitions of our time are causing leaders of public institutions, as well as governments, to relearn the virtues of 'civil society', of the arts of association which grow out of shared moral values, and mutual responsibilities as well as rights. Such civic virtues enable the 'social capital' for mutual trust which, as Fukuyama argues, provides the foundation for all economic and social cooperation: "a nation's well-being, as well as its ability to compete is conditioned by a single, pervasive cultural characteristic: the level of trust inherent in the society" (Fukuyama, 1995, p 7). Yet, modern capitalist democracy, he proposes, depends upon pre-modern cultural conditions of reciprocity, moral obligation and social duty that provide the grounds for people to trust one another – without which economic or civic association crumbles.

Fukuyama's work is part of a growing literature (Luhmann, 1979; Dunn, 1985; 1988; 1996; Douglas, 1987; Gambetta, 1988) which argues the significance of trust for contemporary social, political and economic institutions. For Dunn, trust is the central issue in the understanding of politics:

> In so far as politics is conceived in terms of agency, the cooperative and strategic interaction of individuals and groups, the issue of the rationality of trust is ineliminable from it. (Dunn, 1988, p 82).

> **Trustworthiness, the capacity to commit oneself to fulfilling
> the legitimate expectations of others is both the constitutive
> virtue of, and the key causal precondition for, the existence
> of, any society. It is what makes human society possible.**
> **(Dunn, 1985, p 42)**

The concept of trust was central also to Kieron Walsh's (1994; 1995)
major contribution to our understanding of the role of contracts in the
new management of public services that unfolded during the 1980s: "A
contractual system will not be fully grounded in itself and will need
supporting social conventions and institutions amongst which will be a
degree of trust" (Walsh, 1995b, p 50).

The predicament of our time, nevertheless, is that these values of trust,
which society needs to secure its regeneration in the face of structural
economic and social changes, are systematically eroded by the very
institutions which have been created to sustain society through these
changes. Walsh, like Hirsch (1977) before him, was aware of these deep
paradoxes of contemporary (market/contract) institutions that require a
basis in values which they at the same time systematically undermine:
"the danger is that the more commercial market based approaches to
service management can undermine the traditional bases of trust" (Walsh,
1995, p 51) rooted in professional commitments and cultures.

While reinforcing the urgent need for social renewal and
acknowledging the importance of trust in realising such ends, this chapter
will argue that there is a need for a more complex analysis of trust. Trust
is not the foundational quality in society and polity which is being claimed
for it. Trust in the agreements formed within relationships presupposes
that those relationships and agreements are already flourishing. Trust is
rather an intermediary social virtue, itself dependent upon the social and
political processes which created those relationships and agreements.
Moral and social forms depend upon structures of public rationality and
action.

Thus the central argument of this chapter is that trust in civil society
depends upon the capacity of the public domain to generate the
communicative rationality (Habermas, 1984) that is the foundation of
trust and *civitas* (cooperative action). The argument that modernity's
economic and political problems lie in the erosion of trust mistakes their
true source. In fact, they lie in the institutional failures of the public
domain over the postwar period to generate the purposes and conditions

for civil society. Such an historical analysis reveals, moreover, the changing role which trust has played over time in the polity.

The chapter begins by clarifying the meaning of trust. It then proceeds to theorise its location within the public domain by analysing those public purposes and institutional forms which create the conditions for sustaining agreements and trust in civil society. What holds society together and provides some sense of direction, however, is less trust as such than shared understandings, purposes and agreements.

The chapter continues by tracing the significant but varying role which trust has played in the public domain during two distinct periods since the Second World War: the period of social democracy (with its apogee in the late 1960s) and the period of neo-liberalism (from the 1980s). The challenge of the time is now to remake the public domain so as to enable a democratic citizenship that will provide the purposes and conditions for a learning civil society into the 21st century (Ranson and Stewart, 1994). Finally, the chapter ends by suggesting new ways in which citizens can be actively involved.

Understanding trust

Trust, it is argued, is the foundation that secures cooperation within personal and institutional relations. For Gambetta, "when we say we trust someone or that someone is trustworthy, we implicitly mean that the probability that he will perform an action that is beneficial or at least not detrimental to us is high enough for us to consider engaging in some form of cooperation with him" (Gambetta, 1988, p 217). For Dunn, the significance of trust lies in the freedom of action which must be accorded those who assume responsibility within the polity:

> ... what politics consists in ... is a huge array of free agents coping with each others' freedom over time. In politics so understood the rationality of trust will always be the most fundamental question. (Dunn, 1996, p 98)

> ... politics, at its best is an intricate field of cooperative agency, linking a multiplicity of free agents, none of whom can know each other's future actions but all of whom must in some measure rely upon each other's future actions. (Dunn, 1988, p 83)

The essence of trust for Dunn, therefore, "... is the confident expectation of benign intentions in another free agent" (Dunn, 1988, p 74). In the realm of institutions as well as the personal, relationships describe patterns of expected belief and behaviour. Yet it is not just, all other things being equal, that consistency is expected, but also reliability and commitment: that one can depend upon another to remain true to the meanings, purposes and promises as well as the interests which were invested in creating the relationship. Trust is therefore the belief that these expectations and commitments form a tie which must hold firm, and the relationship is sustained as long as this trust remains credible. Thus the quality of trust depends upon the integrity and honesty which the relationship can engender. Such human qualities can, however, be vulnerable against the winds of contingent pressures. Depending upon the strength of emotional as well as rational disposition, trust is intrinsically uncertain. While it can be tested, in the end it rests, beyond the eye of scrutiny, on an element of faith that expectations will be loyally observed. Confidence lasts as long as the fidelity.

The emphasis, in Gambetta and Dunn, upon trust as benign benefit, fails to grasp sufficiently what is at stake in making and breaking trust: what holds relationships together. Trust is more than belief in benign expectations in others: these grow out of shared understanding and agreements, often formalised.

The more of ourselves we immerse in a relationship the higher the emotional and material stakes. Our ideals (beliefs) and material interests are comprehensively committed in the most significant institutional as well as personal relationships. Our individual and collective identity – who we are – is at risk, as well as the capacity for cooperative action that holds personal and institutional relations together.

The stakes are revealed in the steps taken to secure the expectations embodied in the relationship. It is the juxtaposition of intensive commitments and human frailty which draw the parties to formalise their bonds of trust by grounding them in agreements, covenants and promises of commitment in public oaths and ceremonies. The public word is believed to be the securest bond. To break the bond is to betray and threaten the integrity of the relationship.

Luhmann (1979) has argued that although trust has become increasingly important in complex modern societies, the transition to modernity has changed the nature of trust. The functional working of all modern social, economic and political institutions depends upon trust, upon confidence in the commitment of others to deliver expectations over time in the face of contingency, uncertainty and the inevitability of partial disappointment. Thus trust, he argues, comes to depend less, as it did in pre-modern eras, upon direct experience of emotional ties in known and familiar relationships. Instead it becomes a more indirect cognitive and rational grasp of the indispensable dependence of modern systems upon public confidence in institutions and their role holders. Trust, increasingly reflexive about itself, grows out of a rational, causal analysis of the conditions for the working of modern society and the centrality of trust for securing any form of cooperative action.

Trust depends upon 'causal' conditions. Dunn, following Locke, believes that the problems of political communities "were always problems of how best to construct, reproduce or repair structures of well-founded mutual trust" (Dunn, 1988, p 88). According to our analysis, however, the task is rather to develop the structures which provide the foundation for trust. Yet the nature of these causal structures that promote trust is not well analysed by either Luhmann or Dunn. What is needed, but only alluded to in their work, is a theory of communicative rationality as providing the conditions for trust in the public domain.

Theorising trust in the public domain

Luhmann distinguishes between the grounding of trust in the personal and emotional in the pre-modern era as against its basis in the forms of rationality that characterise the modern world. Yet, arguably because of the intrinsic qualities of uncertainty in trust, its practice must always remain, to some degree, an expression of faith. In this sense, Fukuyama (1995) is correct to characterise trust as a pre-modern quality. The paradox of trust for the modern world is, however, that these pre-modern aspects of faith which it expresses will still have to rest, if they are to be sustained, increasingly upon post-modern structures of interpersonal communicative rationality – as robust as the public domain can generate.

Whether a 'civil' society which expresses social relations of trust and cooperative action can be created out of the 'life world' of contemporary social relations will depend upon the capacity of the public domain to generate qualities of shared understanding and agreement. The life world, following Habermas (1984), describes the sphere of social relations, cultural traditions and identities which characterise groups and communities in society. This life world can take many forms: it could be harmonious, competitive, or divided ˜ in the words of Hobbes, "nasty brutish and short". The post-modern life world is typically believed to be characterised by clashes of cultural traditions whose values are chronically agonistic and thus incommensurable, compounded by a poverty of recognition and mutual understanding (Gray, 1995a; 1995b; Rorty, 1989; Owen, 1995).

Others argue that the predicament of reconciling the post-modern value of difference with the Enlightenment's narratives of justice and equality provides the inescapable challenge for our fin de siècle world. The resolution lies, argues Taylor (1995), not in denying the reality of moral conflicts but in recognising the possibility of a 'transvaluation' of moral demands "which could open the way to a mode of life, individual and social, in which these demands could be reconciled". An understanding of these processes which can secure social trust and cohesion can be developed through an analysis of communicative rationality (Habermas, 1990; Gadamer, 1975; Taylor, 1995) as secured by a democratic public domain sustained by discourse (Ranson and Stewart, 1994).

Communicative rationality

Contemporary societies have been typically characterised by an instrumental, calculative rationality oriented to gaining competitive advantage. Yet an alternative conception of reason is oriented to communication with others, developing shared understanding and agreement. This communicative rationality unfolds through stages of openness, dialogue, shared understanding and judgement.

Openness to understanding: learning to widen horizons: Taylor (1985) has argued that the forms of knowing and understanding, as much as or at least as part of, a shared moral order, are the necessary basis of civic virtue and trust. Historically conditioned prejudices about capacity, reinforced by institutions of discrimination, set the present context. The possibility of mutuality in support of personal and collective development will depend upon generating interpretative understanding, that is on hermeneutic skills which can create the conditions for learning in society: in relationships within the family, in the community and at work. In society we are confronted by different perspectives, alternative life forms and views of the world. The presupposition of such understanding is *openness* to mutual recognition: we have to learn to be open to difference, to allow our pre-judgements to be challenged; in so doing we learn how to amend our assumptions and develop an enriched understanding of others.

Discourse: the key to the transformation of prejudice lies in what Gadamer (1975) calls "the dialogic character of understanding": through genuine conversation the participants are led beyond their initial positions, to take account of others and move towards a richer, more comprehensive view, a "fusion of horizons", a shared understanding of what is true or valid. Conversation lies at the heart of learning: learners are listeners as well as speakers. It is precisely in confronting other beliefs and presuppositions that we are led to see the inadequacies of our own and transcend them. Rationality, in this perspective, is the willingness to admit the existence of better options, to be aware that one's knowledge is always open to refutation or modification from the vantage point of a different perspective.

Reason emerges through dialogue with others: through which we learn not necessarily 'facts' but rather a capacity for learning, for new ways of thinking, speaking and acting. It is Habermas (1984) who articulates the conditions for such communicative rationality as being "ideal speech contexts" in which the participants feel able to speak freely, truly, sincerely.

Shared understanding: for Habermas (1984; 1990), the processes of argumentation which characterise discourse are oriented towards reaching shared understanding that grows out of developing relations of mutual recognition. The search for mutual understanding is intrinsic to all intersubjective relations in the life world and drives the actors to share their interpretation of the situation. The concept of "*bildung*" describes for Gadamer this process through which individuals and communities enter a more and more widely defined community of shared understanding – they learn through dialogue to take a wider, more differentiated view, and thus acquire sensitivity, subtlety and capacity for judgement.

Judgement growing out of understanding: the deliberative processes lead to judgement about what is to grow out of the understanding – what is to be done (Ranson and Stewart, 1994, pp 272-3). A faculty is required which avoids the illusion of determining objective decisions, while at the same time avoiding the immanent possibility of arbitrary subjectivism. Judgement, argues Beiner (1983), offers the precious, indispensable faculty which requires individuals through deliberation to reach detached reasons for decisions and action. The issues that we face in everyday public life are then made amenable to reflective reason, public discourse, dialogue and common deliberation.

Citizenship and the making of selves and communities

A civil society of trust and cooperative action grows out of the capacity of the public domain to generate an orientation to communicative rationality. The motivation of members of society to acknowledge mutuality, to deliberate with others and to search for shared understanding is more likely to succeed if they regard each other as citizens with shared responsibility for making the communities in which they are to live. This makes the *agency* of citizens central to personal and social development. Our active participation in creating the projects which are to shape our selves as well as the communities in which we live provides the sense of purpose to work together with others and to secure trusting relations with them.

There is no solitary development or learning: we can only create our worlds together. The unfolding agency of the self always grows out of the interaction with others. It is *inescapably a social and creative making.* We can only develop as persons with and through others. The conception of the self presupposes an understanding of what we are to become and this always unfolds through our relationship with others; the conditions in which the self develops and flourishes are social and political. The self can only find its identity in and through others and membership of communities. The possibility of shared understanding requires individuals not only to value others but to create the communities in which mutuality and thus the conditions for learning can flourish. The telos of citizenship is to learn to make the communities without which individuals and others cannot grow and develop.

Institutional spheres of communicative action

The conditions for communicative rationality, citizenship and the mutual trust they generate lie in the appropriate institutional forms of the public domain. The connection between individual well-being and the vitality of the moral community is made in the public domain of the polity: the good (learning) person is a good citizen. Without political structures which bring together communities of discourse, the conditions for communicative rationality, mutual understanding and therefore trust will not exist: it is not possible to create the virtues of a learning civil society without the forms of life and institutions which sustain them. This is the moral purpose of the polity as articulated by Aristotle (Nussbaum, 1990; 1993; Sen, 1992; Nussbaum and Sen, 1993). A robust, accountable and more legitimate political order is needed to empower the public. The institutional preconditions for such a public domain suggest the need for: the arts of association in intermediary institutions, forums for participatory democracy, and structures of justice which establish what Rawls calls "the basic structure of society" in its fair distribution of fundamental rights, duties, opportunities and "advantages from cooperation" (Rawls, 1971, p 7).

Practice of mediation through the art of association: we regard intermediary institutions not only as an essential prerequisite for a participatory democracy (Gellner, 1994) but also as an inclusive network in which all citizens may voluntarily associate. Our definition concurs with that of Bryant (1995) that the key component for a civil society is the universal principle of inclusion. This presupposes a moral idea of the public and the sovereign authority of a community (Seligman, 1995). By community, however, we do not mean the bounded community reliant upon cultural homogeneity of which Gellner speaks (and which Tester [1992] mistakenly takes as the failure of society), but rather an inclusive community or rather inclusive communities in an associative democracy. Indeed, the plurality of spheres with permeable boundaries is a necessary condition for the free association essential for the public domain. In the same way as de Tocqueville highlighted the importance of the art of association in the civil society, Shils describes the hallmark of a civil society as the autonomy of private associations and institutions characterised by a pluralism which:

> ... comprises the partially autonomous spheres of economy, religion, culture, intellectual activity and political activity ... these spheres are never wholly autonomous in their relations with each other; their boundaries are not impermeable. (Shils, 1991, p 9)

Such a network of intermediary institutions creates the domain in which private meets public; a public sphere where private interests are reconciled in the context of the public good. As such the civil society will not be just a space to be colonised (Kumar, 1993) but a process of mediation:

"The 'concrete person' of civil society differs from the isolated subject of the sphere of morality in that he gradually comes to recognise himself as a member of society and realises that to attain his ends he must work with and through others." Institutional arrangements which recognise different interests and accommodate cultural diversity will strengthen the public sphere through an active democracy.

Participative democracy: we can only make ourselves and our communities when empowered by a public domain which recognises the distinctive contributions each have to give. Such a discourse will depend upon the existence of a strong, participatory democracy which legitimates and values politics, because it is only through politics that people can constitute the conditions for making a life that: acknowledges their values, recognises their differences, accords them identity and sustains the material conditions of their existence. Such a participative democracy complements and gives meaning to the purposes of representative democracy.

Basing the new order upon the presupposition of agency leads to the principle of the equal rights of citizens both to participate in determining what conditions the expansion of their powers and to share responsibility for the common good. The ancient Athenians believed, moreover, that every citizen could take part in the democratic process because the art of political judgement (without which there could be no civilised society) was a capacity which all ordinary people were capable of. Politics could not be for specialists alone. The political task of our time is to develop the polity as a vehicle for the active involvement of its citizens, enabling them to make their contribution to the development of the learning and caring civil society. There is a need, in this age of transition, to fashion a stronger, more active democracy than the postwar period has allowed. The postwar polity specialised politics and held the public at bay except periodically and passively.

The principle which constituted classical democracy – of "proper discussions", of free and unrestricted discourse, with all guaranteed a right to contribute – needs to be restored in a form appropriate to the modern world. The aim would be to enable all to contribute to public discourse, the purpose of which is to ground decisions in the force of the better argument. The challenge is to restore a culture which values the practice of public discussion and the open giving and taking of reasons as grounds for conclusions (Dunn, 1992).

The constitutive conditions for citizenship within a more active democracy is a polity that enables the public to participate and express their voice about the issues of the transition, but also a polity that will permit public choice and government (Ranson and Stewart, 1989; 1994). The politics of public expression, but also the government of choice and action, is the challenge for the new polity. Within such a polity the procedures for involving the public and for negotiating decisions will be important. Yet it is through the prerequisites of procedural justice (Habermas, 1984; Hayden, 1987; Gould, 1988; Hampshire, 1989) that an educated public of citizens can emerge. Citizens need to acquire the dispositions of listening and taking into account as well as asserting their view:

> **The deliberative process of democratic decision-making requires that each participant not only permit the others to express their views and offer their judgements but take others' views seriously into account in arriving at his or her own judgement. Clearly this does not require agreement with the views of others, but rather serious attention to, and respect for, their views. Such reciprocal respect also presupposes that disagreements be tolerated and not suppressed. (Gould, 1988)**

By providing forums for participation, the new polity can create the conditions for public discourse and for mutual accountability, so that citizens can take each other's needs and claims into account and learn to create the conditions for each other's development (Ranson, 1994; 1998).

Justice: a contract for the basic structure: the conditions for agency of self and society depend upon agreement about its value as well as about allocating the means for private and public self-determination. Freedom rests upon justice (Rawls, 1971; 1993; Barry, 1989; Nagel, 1991; Sen, 1990; 1992). But this makes the most rigorous demands upon the polity which has to determine the very conditions on which life can be lived at all: membership, the distribution of rights and duties, the allocation of scarce resources, the ends to be pursued. The good polity must strive to establish the conditions for virtue in all its citizens: the conditions – material (for example, clean public water); institutional (for example, education); and moral (a civic ethic). These issues are intrinsically political and will be intensely contested, especially in a period of transformation that disturbs traditions and conventions.

If decisions about such fundamental issues are to acquire the consent of the public, then the procedures for arriving at those decisions will be considered of the greatest significance for legitimate authority of the polity. The process of making the decisions – who is to be involved and how the disagreements that will inexorably arise are to be resolved – will be as important as the content of decisions themselves.

This section has argued that trust in civil society depends upon establishing the appropriate institutional forms. Cooperative action which provides the basis for trust needs to grow out of institutional arrangements which support and reinforce mutual understanding and agreement. The institutional preconditions argued for here – intermediary associations, participative democracy and just distribution – have not characterised the modern political order, although some initiatives within the public domain allow us to glimpse them and thus the possibility of creating trust within a civil society.

The changing role of trust in the public domain

Though the public domain is the condition for trust, public institutions have typically not been organised to enable the necessary qualities of cooperative and discursive action. The institutional arrangements which have characterised the public domain since the Second World War have defined very different and attenuated forms of trust. To understand how the present is to be reconstructed we need to grasp the limitations of the political orders – of social democracy and neo liberalism – which have dominated the postwar era.

Trust as passive dependency in the age of professionalism

During the era of social democracy from the 1950s to the early 1970s, public organisations were typically shaped by 'the mantle of professionalism' (Burns, 1977). Such was the dominance of professionals and their values that Perkin (1989) has called it the high point in an 'age of professionalism'. The postwar world placed its faith in specialist knowledge to modernise society: the skills of doctors and nurses, teachers and social workers, together with many other professionals, would provide the condition for improved public services.

The professional 'mantle' offered distinctive benefits for society. Professionals bring to complex tasks of health, education or community development a specialist expertise that has grown out of extensive training rounded out by supervised experience. This unique knowledge enabled professionals to interpret the needs of their clients whose interests were protected by the professionals' sense of 'vocation' reinforced by a 'code of ethics' monitored by the peer group. Professionals claimed the right to autonomy in their practice and in interpreting the needs of their clients to carry it out. Clients were expected to place their trust in professional expertise and the 'segmented bureaucracies' of highly differentiated specialist services upon which the public domain was founded.

The age of professionalism achieved a great deal in its project of modernising society, improving health and education and the quality of life opportunities. But the public began to lose faith in the omnipotence of the specialist. Recognition grew that many of the problems which professionals faced were resilient to specialist expertise alone, and that the belief in its code was misplaced: that the good society could be *provided* and, as it were, 'handed down' to the public, *delivered* by knowledgeable specialists; that a passive public in awe of the knowledge and universal rules of the professional bureaucracy would receive the conditions for a new and better world. This suggested an intrinsic flaw. Trust founded upon passivity and dependence was mistaken, for the good society can only be lived and created by an active public with the support of professionals.

Trust as the limits of contract in the neo-liberal marketplace

The need to renew trust by actively involving the public in the development of public institutions and policies began to gain wider consent. Yet for more than a decade until the mid-1990s the strategy for empowerment emphasised the public as consumer of services in the marketplace. The polity sought to erode the distinctive purposes of public organisation and make the purposes of the private sector the organising principles for all organisations. Public choice as customer choice would enhance the effectiveness of public services by making them responsive and accountable to the customer. Trust would be secured by contractual obligations – professionals would have to do what they were contracted for. But if that benefit was achieved, what was lost was the commitment to give much more in an ideal of public service.

The market has not been ideally suited to the needs of public services. Markets cannot by themselves provide what is needed for society. The unintended consequences which follow from individuals acting in isolation ensure that self-interest is often self-defeating. More importantly, markets are formally neutral but substantively biased. Under the guise of neutrality, the market actively confirms and reinforces the pre-existing social order of wealth and privilege. Markets are, therefore, the supreme institution of winners and losers, with the winners imposing their power on the losers without redress, because of the structure of social selection: they produce survivals and extinctions in a Darwinian zero-sum game. Markets, therefore, are political – that is, a way of making decisions about power in society – and they ensure that the already powerful win decisively. Whereas the postwar state sought to construct a public domain which diminished the effects of class advantage, the neo-liberal state constructed a public domain which released and reinforced class division and advantage through the market mechanism.

The problems we face derive from the transformations of the time: the restructuring of work, environmental erosion and the fragmentation of society. These transformations raise questions about what it is to be a person, what is the nature of the community, what kind of polity we need to secure the future well being of all. They in turn present issues of identity, well-being, rights, liberty, opportunity and justice. The predicaments that confront us cannot be resolved by individuals acting in isolation nor by 'exit', because we cannot stand outside them. Markets by themselves can only exacerbate these problems.

The predicaments we face are collective or public in nature and require public action to resolve them. As Dunn (1992) argues "In the face of the obscure and extravagantly complicated challenges of the human future, our most urgent common need at present is to learn how to act together more effectively". The predicament we face, however, is that although the problems confronting society are public and require a public solution, our society is denigrating and dismantling the very conditions necessary to sustain its future welfare. We live in a society whose institutions are not constituted for, yet require, public participation and cooperation.

Only in the public domain can the physical problems of the environment or the moral and social problems facing our society – the conditions for which lie in collective action – be solved. Yet if such issues are to be confronted, it will imply not only public action, but a reconstituting of the organising principles of the public domain in the context of the emerging polity.

Towards trust secured by a democratic public sphere

The principle here is to create a public domain of active citizens. The challenge for our time is to renew the purposes and institutions of democracy which allow citizens to participate in the creation of a society, enabling each to develop as a person but also to contribute to the good of the community as a whole. Civic responsibility and individual development are perceived as mutually reinforcing creating the conditions in which "anyone might do best and live a flourishing life" (Aristotle). Change depends upon new institutional reforms which renew the public domain. The task is to recreate, or create more effectively than ever before, an educated public which has the capacity to participate actively as citizens in the shaping of a learning society and polity.

Such an active citizenship requires the necessary conditions for participation: a constitutive condition for any citizenship is to provide arenas for active public participation. By providing such forums, the new polity can create the conditions for public discourse and for mutual accountability, so that citizens can take each other's needs and claims into account and learn to create the conditions for each other's development. *Learning as discourse* must underpin the learning society as the defining condition of the public domain, building a habit of citizenship.

A model in the recent past has been the creation of local youth councils which have enabled young people to debate and make decisions about youth policy and provision. Some schools have developed community councils, which involve a broader representation than formal governing bodies, in order to make the life of the school wherever possible serve the needs of the community as a whole as well as parents.

Public services which seek actively to involve citizens in policy making and become accountable to the community as a whole need to constitute local community forums or councils. These would enable several interests – including women's groups, the black and ethnic minorities and the disabled – within a community to participate, articulate needs and contribute to decision making. Where an authority has formed a pool of resources – perhaps from urban aid funds, EEC or local grants – to support community groups, decision making about distribution could be delegated to these forums. In this way citizens within the community are enfranchised to influence and further to take responsibility for the remaking of their communities.

Forums allow a wider public debate about the purpose and process of public services in areas such as the learning needs of individuals and groups; the rights and entitlements of the disadvantaged; complaints and injustice; ideas for improving the quality of service delivery. But forums, however important, are only one aspect within a much wider panoply of initiatives to extend active public involvement.

Recent experiments to strengthen democratic participation have included: extensive consultation, the use of surveys as well as using the authority's outreach staff to listen to the views of the public; deliberative opinion polls; citizens' juries; teledemocracy; and issue forums as well as neighbourhood forums (Fishkin, 1991; Gyford, 1991; Burns et al, 1994). Innovations are possible in democratic practice to enhance citizen participation (Stewart, 1995; 1996; 1997). Public bodies should recognise the need to develop citizen participation and develop a repertoire of approaches meeting different purposes and relating to different conditions.

The informed citizen

This chapter takes as its main illustration of the possibilities, a family of approaches that are designed to find the informed views of a representative group of citizens. They are not the only approaches, and a wider range of possibilities will be touched on.

There are three main defining characteristics of these approaches. Firstly, they all involve groups of citizens deliberately chosen as representative samples of citizens generally, that is, the modern equivalent of the Athenian principle of selection by lot. In that way people from all sections of the population are involved, avoiding the danger that only the articulate and the joiners take part. Although the numbers involved are small, they are a microcosm of the citizenry at large. Secondly, they also ask from citizens not a continuing involvement, impossible to sustain, but a particular commitment over a limited period of time. Thirdly, the approaches ensure that citizens only give their views after hearing about the issue in depth, with an opportunity to question and challenge.

There is a fundamental difference between these approaches and those of opinion polls, which can be merely a device for obtaining the uninformed and often unconsidered views of citizens. Recently the Local Government Commission for England sought citizens' views on local government reorganisation in most counties. Generally they showed opinions were divided, although there was a tendency to favour 'no change' in many areas. However, on one issue there was general agreement;

about 80% on average said they knew nothing or very little about the issues on which they were giving their views. One might consider that this robbed their views of some of their value.

These approaches also ensure that the citizens involved have discussed the issues amongst themselves. Democracy, if it is to be meaningful, must be more than a recording system for individual views. It should involve discourse in which citizens explore views together, test ideas, seek agreement, yet become aware of difference. These approaches bring deliberation by citizens into the process of government.

The distinction between the inclinations of the moment and public opinions that are refined by 'sedate reflection' is an essential part of any adequate theory of democracy. Political equality without deliberation is not of much use, for it amounts to nothing more than the power without the opportunity to think about how that power could be exercised.

Citizens' juries

Citizens' juries are an example of these approaches. These bring together a representative group of citizens to consider an issue in depth over three to five days. During that period they receive evidence, hear and cross-question witnesses and discuss the issue among themselves, before forming their conclusion. A report is prepared setting out the conclusions, recording both agreement and disagreement.

This is the model that has been developed by Ned Crosby in America where they are called citizens' juries and by Professor Peter Dienel in Germany where they are called planning cells. The approaches used are similar, but there are differences:

> **Citizens' Juries [in America] are much more focused than Planning Cells. Typically Citizens' Juries are asked to express a preference among three or four pre-selected policy options. Planning Cells [in Germany] are more engaged in designing policy options, as well as making recommendations about what additional criteria might lead to policy acceptance. (Renn et al, 1995, p 344)**

In Germany, where the use of citizens' juries is more developed, Professor Peter Dienel and the Research Institute for Public Participation and Planning Procedures at the University of Wuppertal, accept commissions from local authorities, the Länder federal government. The authority commissioning the citizens' jury does not undertake to accept its views but will, however, undertake to consider the opinions expressed and to respond to them. This emphasises that the role of the citizens' juries is not decision making, but to inform decision making, in the same way as participatory democracy generally can inform, where it does not replace, representative democracy.

Citizens' juries were used to consider designs for development in and around Cologne City Square, and led to reconsideration of the proposals of the council's professional advisers. (One wonders whether some town centre developments in Britain would have survived appraisal by citizens' juries.) In Grevelsburg, a citizens' jury examined alternative approaches to traffic problems in a historic town centre. They have also been used to explore broader policy issues on which they may well produce guidelines rather than specific recommendations. In Germany they have considered the social consequences of new technology and, in Greater New Haven in the United States they have explored the problems of 'at-risk' children.

The phrase 'citizens' juries' as used in America commands attention and connects the approach with an established tradition involving citizens in the process of government. It can mislead, however, because the process differs from the formality of courts of law (the phrase is not used in Germany). There is no judge, but rather a moderator whose role is to facilitate discussion and certainly not to maintain quasi-legal procedures. The procedure celebrates discourse rather than legality. The jury does not have to reach agreement, but only record its different views if agreement is not reached. Importance is attached to discussion which can take place throughout the process. In Germany, with juries of 25, some of the discussion takes place in groups of five, before coming back to the wider group. The emphasis is on informality in easing discussion.

A number of citizens' juries have been held in this country. The Local Government Management Board sponsored six pilot projects, and an evaluation report was prepared (Hall and Stewart, 1997). The authorities and subjects involved were as follows:

- Norwich on the impact of new technology;
- Lewisham on drugs in the community;
- South Somerset on regeneration of an area in Yeovil;
- North Kesteven on the requirements of flourishing villages;
- Hertfordshire on waste disposal;
- Islington on policies governing libraries.

Since then citizens' juries have been held in other local authority areas and a number have been held by health authorities. For instance, Buckinghamshire Health Authorities used a citizens' jury to look at the purchase of services from osteopaths and chiropractors and the Sunderland Health Authority did the same to consider alternative providers of GP services.

The authorities concerned would all be prepared to hold further juries on suitable subjects. They were especially impressed with the way in which the juries worked. Over the three to four day period, jurors developed considerable understanding of the issue being discussed, were ready to modify their views and came up with recommendations which have been seen as valuable by the authorities and will be acted on. Above all, the exercise has shown there are innovative approaches to most issues likely to be supported by citizens who have the chance to consider the matter in depth.

What these juries demonstrate is the ability of ordinary citizens to contribute to the consideration of policy issues and so highlight the potential that is generally unrealised in the practice of government. The jurors themselves generally considered the juries to be a valuable process and a satisfying experience. They felt they were making a real contribution to the business of government and welcomed the readiness of the authority to involve citizens. It extended their interest in public affairs and may, for admittedly small numbers, have helped to build up a habit of citizenship.

Deliberative opinion polls

Deliberative opinion polls also seek the informed views of citizens. However, while citizens' juries take as their starting point the jury system and then modify it, deliberative opinion polls take the opinion poll and seek to overcome its weaknesses. Fishkin, their main advocate, has argued: "An ordinary opinion poll models what the public thinks, given how little it knows. A deliberative opinion poll models what the public would think, if it had a more adequate chance to think about the questions at issue" (Fishkin, 1991).

Deliberative opinion polls differ from citizens' juries in that they involve larger numbers and can involve less time and less intense discussion. They differ from normal opinion polls in that opinions will be tested after the participants have had an opportunity to hear witnesses, ask questions and discuss the issue, although for the purpose of comparison views may also have been tested at the outset of the process.

Fishkin piloted a deliberative opinion poll on issues of law and order in Britain through Channel Four Television and the *Independent* newspaper (Fishkin, 1991). In January 1996 a National Issues convention was held in the United States which included a deliberative opinion poll based on 600 voters selected as a representative sample of the American population. They discussed key issues facing America, including the economy, America's role in the world and the state of the family.

Citizens' panels

Citizens' panels are representative panels of citizens called together as sounding boards. In 1993 eight health panels, each consisting of 12 people selected to be a representative sample of the population, were set up by the Somerset Health Commission to discuss the values that should guide health resource allocation decisions. The panels held four meetings over the following year. At the first, panel members were asked to bring their own health issues. At the succeeding meetings they discussed issues raised by the health authorities, chosen because they were being actively considered at the time. These included whether the health authority should pay for coronary artery by-pass operations for people who smoke, and whether certain treatments should be given at all.

There is an emphasis on deliberation: "An important rationale of our approach to consultation was that those involved should have the opportunity to explore issues in some depth. Most people need a period of listening to the views of others and talking about issues themselves in order to clarify their thoughts on any complex questions" (Richardson and Sykes, 1995). After discussion, panel members complete a series of decision sheets, in effect voting on the issue. The research team organising the project prepared reports for the health authority on the panels, using the discussion to convey the flavour of the panel meeting as well as the results from the decision sheets. The panels are continuing with four members of the panels replaced at each meeting.

The same principle has been suggested for a local authority, but with a panel of 200 to 300 to meet once a month as a sounding board, again with a number changing each month. The panel would again be representative to ensure the inclusion of sections of the public from whom the authority rarely heard.

Consensus conferences

Consensus conferences are another variant. They were designed to incorporate public interests and concerns into processes of science policy making – often seen as a matter for experts but increasingly raising ethical or environmental issues. The approach was developed in Denmark and a consensus conference was organised in Britain by the Science Museum in London on plant biotechnology in 1994.

Simon Joss and John Durant define consensus conferences as "a forum in which a group of lay people put questions about a scientific or technological subject of controversial political and social interest to experts, listen to the experts' answers, then reach a consensus about this subject and finally report their findings at a press conference" (Joss and Durant, 1994).

In Denmark, subjects have included air pollution, childlessness, food irradiation and electronic identity cards. The procedure is well-established in that country, and differs from citizens' juries in having a less representative method of selection, based on written applications. More time is spent in giving necessary scientific information and the emphasis on consensus is an important difference. Consensus conferences are a variation on the theme of the informed citizen.

A range of innovation

These are not the only possible innovations. Other examples include:

- Mediation groups which bring together groups which are in conflict over, for example, environmental issues, to see if differences can be reconciled or at least reduced through discussion.
- New forms of public meetings designed to enable discussion in groups, rather than the more traditional structure of platform and audience.
- Community forums in which authorities can reach out to diverse communities, remembering that as well as communities of place there are communities of interest.
- Stakeholder conferences in which all those interested in an issue can be brought together in forms of discussion designed to identify areas for action.
- Teledemocracy which, as time passes, could have an increasing role in providing access for and involving the public.

- Involvement of citizens in scrutiny panels, village appraisal, environmental assessments, and so on.

All of these can enhance participatory democracy and strengthen representative democracy. Direct democracy can also be valuable for specific issues. For instance, there is more of a tradition of referenda at local level than is often appreciated on such matters as libraries, local licensing options, Sunday opening of cinemas and private bills. Although most of these are in the past, the right of electors to call parish polls remains. Indeed, what are, in effect, referenda were instituted by the Conservative government for parents on options for grant maintained status and for tenants on the transfer of local authority housing stock. Similarly, some local authorities have recently held referenda on local issues such as the Sunday opening of leisure centres. The use of such referenda on issues of community concern that lie outside the main framework of party political divides can be an exercise in citizenship, encouraging public discussion.

Each of these approaches has a value in itself as an aid to or a means of decision making. What is important, however, is not their impact on decisions, but their role in transforming the institutions of government by building a habit of citizenship through arenas of discourse. We envisage the possibility of all citizens having opportunities to participate in such arenas at some stage in their lives. The development of active citizenship will reconstitute the polity or the basis of discourse, enabling thereby the development of communication rationality.

Towards community governance

Strengthening democracy and public learning requires a learning government. The capacity of central government to constitute the basis for this is limited, with many tiers in the organisational hierarchy separating ministers from action and impact. Central government cannot easily encompass diversity of circumstance and achieve diversity in response. Yet learning comes from a recognition of diversity of need, diversity of aspiration and diversity of response. From uniformity one may learn little except the scale of one's failure. From diversity, one may learn about relative success and relative failure. A central government can achieve learning if it uses the diversity of local government as its base.

Participation is built more easily at local than at national level and the evidence is that citizens are more ready to participate at this local level. A commitment to the strengthening of participatory democracy is a commitment to decentralisation within the system of government, both to local authorities and within local authorities. Within local government, too, decentralisation and more effective local democracy involves a commitment to strengthen participatory democracy, through innovation in democratic practice for which a repertoire of approaches is being and can be developed.

This final section has discussed a family of approaches for reconstituting the public domain for public learning and active citizenship. Participation is needed to complement representation if the evolution of a more elaborate system of community governance is to be developed. Such a system would encourage public choices which were more responsive to the community as a whole and thus based upon consent while, at the same time, holding services more accountable to the public (Bogdanor, 1994). The basis for trust can only be established through such transformations.

Bibliography

Ackoff, R.L. (1993) 'Corporate perestroika', in W.H. Halal, A. Gernmayeh and Pourdehnad (eds) *Internal markets*, New York: Wiley.

Ades, A. and Di Tella, R. (1997) 'The new economics of corruption: a survey and some new results', *Political Studies*, vol XLV, pp 496-515.

Akerlof, G.A. (1970) 'The market for "lemons", qualitative uncertainty and the market mechanism', *Quarterly Journal of Economics*, vol 84, pp 488-500.

Anechiarico, F. and Jacobs, J.B. (1996) *The pursuit of absolute integrity: How corruption control makes government ineffective*, Chicago: University of Chicago Press.

Arrow, K.J. (1973) *Information and economic behaviour*, Stockholm: Federation of Swedish Industries.

Ashrif, H. (1993) 'Total quality management implementation within high union density organisations', unpublished dissertation, Masters in Management Development and Social Responsibility, University of Bristol.

Atkinson, A.B. and Stiglitz, J.E. (1980) *Lectures on public economics*, New York: McGraw-Hill.

Audit Commission (1986) *Improving council house maintenance*, London: HMSO.

Audit Commission (1994) *Behind closed doors: The revolution in central support services*, London: HMSO.

Audit Commission (1997) *A learning experience: Service delivery planning in local government*, Occasional Paper, May, London: Audit Commission for Local Authorities and the NHS in England and Wales.

Axelrod, R. (1984) *The evolution of cooperation*, New York: Basic Books.

Baddeley, S. (1989) 'Political sensitivity in public managers', *Local Government Studies*, March/April, vol 15, no 2, pp 47-66.

Baddeley, S. (1992) 'Integrity in a political environment', Proceedings of the 1st Annual Leadership Academy, Canadian Association of School Administrators, 12-17 July, Chateau Montebello, Quebec.

Baddeley, S. (1997) 'Constructing trust: conversations in political-management space', Public Dimensions of Public Services: Issues of Equity, Accountability and the Role of Professions, Public Services Research Unit Conference Proceedings, Cardiff Business School, University of Wales, 27 March.

Baddeley, S. and James, K. (1987a) 'Owl, fox, donkey, sheep: political skills for managers', *Management Education and Development*, vol 18, part 1, Spring.

Baddeley, S. and James, K. (1987b) 'From political neutrality to political wisdom', *Politics*, vol 7, no 2.

Baddeley, S. and James, K. (1991) 'The power of innocence: from politeness to politics', *Management Education and Development*, vol 22, part 2.

Baker, N. (ed) (1996) *Building a relational society: New priorities for public policy*, Aldershot: Ashgate Publishing.

Bakunin, M. (1916) *God and the state* (reprinted 1970), New York: Dover.

Barnard. C.I. (1938) *The functions of the executive*, Cambridge, MA: Harvard University Press.

Barnes, M. (1997) *Care, communities and citizens*, Harlow: Addison Wesley Longman.

Barnes, M. and Prior, D. (1995) 'Spoilt for choice? How consumerism can disempower public service users', *Public Money and Management*, vol 15, no 3.

Barnes, M. and Prior, D. (1996) 'From private choice to public trust: alternatives to consumerism in welfare', *Public Money and Management*, vol 16, no 4.

Barnes, M. and Shardlow, P. (1997) 'From passive recipient to active citizen: participation in mental health user groups', *Journal of Mental Health*, vol 6, no 3, pp 275-86.

Barrow, J. (1989) *The Mutiny of the Bounty*, Oxford: Oxford University Press.

Barry, B. (1989) *Theories of justice: Vol 1: A treatise on social justice*, London: Harvester Wheatsheaf.

Bass, B.M. (ed) (1981) *Stogdill's handbook of leadership*, New York: Free Press.

Batley, R. and Campbell, A. (1992) *The political executive: Politicians and management in European local government*, London: Frank Cass.

Beck, U. (1992) *Risk society: Towards a new modernity*, London: Sage.

Beck, U., Giddens, A. and Lash, S. (1994) *Reflexive modernization*, Cambridge: Polity Press.

Becker, G. and Stigler, G. (1974) 'Law enforcement, malfeasance and the compensation of enforcers', *Journal of Legal Studies*, vol 3, no 1, pp 1-19.

Beiner, R. (1983) *Political judgement*, London: Methuen.

Bell, D. (1973) *The coming of post-industrialisation society*, New York: Basic Books.

Bennis, W.G. (1959) 'Leadership theory and administrative behavior: the problems of authority', *Administrative Science Quarterly*, vol 4, pp 259-301.

Berger, P. and Luckmann, T. (1976) *The social construction of reality*, Harmondsworth: Penguin.

Bernard, L.L. (1927) 'Leadership and propaganda', in J. Davis and H.E. Barnes, *An introduction to sociology*, New York: Heath.

Bingham, W.V. (1927) 'Leadership', in H.C. Metcalf, *The psychological foundations of management*, New York: Shaw.

Blake, R.R. and Mouton, J.S. (1964) *The managerial grid*, Houston: Gulf.

Bogdanor, V. (1994) 'Rejuvenate our democratic practice', in S. Ranson and J. Tomlinson (eds) *School cooperation: New forms of local governance*, Harlow: Longman.

Boswell, J. (1976) *Life of Johnson* (1st pub 1791), Oxford: Oxford Paperbacks, p 849.

Bowlby, J. (1973) *Separation, anxiety and anger*, New York: Basic Books.

Bowlby, J. (1982) *Attachment* (2nd edn), London: Hogarth Press.

Braverman, H. (1974) *Labor and monopoly capital*, New York: Monthly Review Press.

Breton, A. and Wintrobe, R. (1982) *The logic of bureaucratic conduct*, Cambridge: Cambridge University Press.

Brown, M.H. and Hosking, D.-M. (1984) 'Distributed leadership and skilled performance as successful organisation in social movements', *Human Relations*, vol 39, pp 65-79.

Bryant, C. (1995) 'Civic nation, civil society, civil religion', in J. Hall (ed) *Civil society*, Cambridge: Polity Press.

Buchanan, D.A. and Huczynski, A.A. (1985) *Organisational behaviour*, Hemel Hempstead: Prentice-Hall International.

Burchell, G., Gordon, C. and Miller, P. (eds) (1991) *The Foucault effect: Studies in governmentality*, London: Harvester Wheatsheaf, pp 87-104.

Burns, D., Hambleton, R. and Hoggett, P. (1994) *The politics of decentralisation: Revitalising local democracy*, London: Macmillan.

Burns, T. (1977) *The BBC: Public institution and private world*, London: Tavistock.

Burrell, G. and Hearn, J. (1989) 'The sexuality of organization', in J.Hearn, D.L.Sheppard, P.Tancred-Sheriff and G.Burrell, *Sexuality of organization*, London: Sage, pp 1-28.

Burton, M. (1992) 'The secret services', *Municipal Journal,* January, pp 10-11.

Cadbury, Sir Adrian (1992) *Report on the financial aspects of corporate governance*, London: Gee Publishing.

Calnan, M. and Williams, S. (1992) 'Images of scientific medicine', *Sociology of Health and Illness*, vol 14, no 2, pp 233-54.

Carnaghan, R. and Bracewell-Milnes, B. (1993) *Testing the market*, London: Institute for Economic Affairs.

Carter, L.F. (1953) 'Leadership and small group behavior', in M. Sherif and M.O.Wilson (eds) *Group relations at the crossroads*, New York: Harper.

Cartwright, D. (1959) 'A field theoretical conception of power', in D. Cartwright (ed) *Studies in social power*, Ann Arbor, Michigan: University of Michigan.

Cartwright, D. and Zander, A. (1968, 1st edn 1953) 'Leadership: introduction', in D. Cartwright and A. Zander (eds) *Group dynamics: Research and theory* (3rd edn), London: Tavistock.

Chamberlayne, P. and King, A. (1996) 'Method as genre: case reconstruction of carer accounts' (draft received from the authors, Department of Sociology, University of East London, Longbridge Road, Dagenham RM8 2AS).

Child, J. (1984) *Organisation*, London: Harper and Row.

Clapham, D., Kemp, P. and Smith, S.J. (1990) *Housing and social policy*, London: Macmillan.

Clarke, J. and Newman, J. (1997) *The managerial state: Power, politics and ideology in the remaking of social welfare*, London: Sage.

Clarke, M. and Stewart, J. (1987) 'The public service orientation and the citizen', *Local Government Policy Making*, vol 14, no 1, pp 34-40.

Clarke, M. and Stewart, M. (1988) *The enabling council*, Luton: Local Government Training Board.

Clinard, M.B. (1990) *Corporate corruption: The abuse of power*, New York: Praeger.

Coase, R. (1937) 'The nature of the firm', *Economica*, New Series vol IV (16), November, pp 386-405.

Coase, R. (1964) 'The regulated industries: discussion', *American Economic Review*, vol 54, May, pp 194-7.

Cohen, J. and Arato, A. (1992) *Civil society and political theory*, Cambridge, MA: MIT Press.

Commission on Social Justice (1994) *Social justice: Strategies for national renewal*, London: Vintage.

Committee of Public Accounts (1994) 'The proper conduct of public business', 8th report, 17 January, House of Commons, London: HMSO.

Committee on Standards in Public Life (the Nolan Committee) (1995) 1st report, Cm 2850-I, London: HMSO.

The Co-operative Bank (1997) *Strength in numbers: Our partnership approach*, Manchester: The Co-operative Bank.

Cooley, C.H. (1902) *Human nature and the social order*, New York: Scribners.

Copeland, N. (1942) *Psychology and the soldier*, Harrisburg, PA: Military Service Publishing.

Corfield, P.J. (1995) *Power and the professions in Britain 1700-1850*, London: Routledge.

Corrigan, P. (1996) 'Recreating the public: A responsibility for local government', Inaugural lecture, University of North London, 11 March.

Coulson, A. (1997) *Trust and contract in public sector management*, Occasional Paper 10, Birmingham: University of Birmingham.

Cronin, V. (1990) *Napoleon*, London: Fontana Collins.

Dahrendorf, R. (1996) 'Economic opportunity, civil society and political liberty', in C. Hewitt de Alcántara (ed) *Social futures, global visions*, Oxford: Blackwell.

Dallas, G. and Gill, D. (1985) *The unknown army: Mutinies in the British Army in World War I*, London: Verso.

Darby, M.R. and Karni, E. (1973) 'Free competition and the optimal amount of fraud', *Journal of Law and Economics*, vol 16, pp 67-88.

Dasgupta, P. (1988) 'Trust as a commodity', in D. Gambetta (ed) *Trust: Making and breaking cooperative relations*, Oxford: Basil Blackwell, pp 49-72.

Davis, H. and Walker, B. (1997) 'Trust based relationships in local government contracting', *Public Money and Management*, vol 7, no 4, pp 47-54.

Deakin, N. (1987) *The politics of welfare*, London: Methuen.

Deakin, N. (1991) 'The new managerialism and the new state', in C. Navari (ed) *British politics and the spirit of the age*, Staffordshire: Keele University Press, Chapter 12.

Deakin, N. (1994) 'Accountability: the superstructure', *Policy Studies*, vol 15, no 3, pp 1-15.

Deakin, N. and Walsh, K. (1996) 'The enabling state: the role of markets and contracts', *Public Administration*, vol 74, no 1, pp 33-48.

Deakin, N., Davis, A. and Thomas, N. (1995) *Public welfare services and social exclusion: The development of consumer-oriented initiatives in the European Union*, Dublin: European Foundation for the Improvement of Living and Working Conditions.

Deakin, S. and Wilkinson, F. (1996) 'Contracts, cooperation and trust: the role of institutional frameworks', in D. Campbell and P. Vincent-Jones (eds) *Contract and economic organisation: Socio-legal initiatives*, Aldershot: Dartmouth Publishing Company.

DETR (Department of the Environment, Transport and the Regions/ Welsh Office) (1997) *Guidance on the CCT framework for professional services*, November.

Deutsch, M. (1968) 'Field theory in social psychology', in G. Lindzey and E. Aronson (eds) *Handbook of social psychology*, vol 1, 478, Reading, MA: Addison-Wesley.

Deutsch, M. (1973) *The resolution of conflict*, New Haven: Yale University Press.

Dixon, N. (1979) *On the psychology of military incompetence*, London: Futura.

DoE (Department of the Environment) (1985) *Competition in the provision of local authority services*, Consultation Paper, February.

DoE (1991) *Competing for quality: Competition in the provision of local services*, London: HMSO.

DoE (1992) *The scope for the competitive tendering of housing management*, London: HMSO.

DoE (1996a) *CCT and local government in England*, Annual Report for 1995, March.

DoE (1996b) *Guidance on the conduct of compulsory competitive tendering*, Circular 5/96 2 April.

DoE (1996c) *Changes to CCT framework for professional services and housing management*, Consultation Paper, 21 May.

DoE (1997) 'Better value for local authority services', News Release, No 197, June.

Dolgoff, S. (1971) *Bakunin on anarchy*, London: George Allen and Unwin.

Domberger, S., Hall, C. and Ah Li, E. (1995) 'The determinants of price and quality in competitively tendered contracts', *Economic Journal*, vol 105, no 433, pp 1454-70.

Domberger, S., Meadowcroft, S.A. and Thompson, D.J. (1986) 'Competitive tendering and efficiency: the case of refuse collection', *Fiscal Studies*, vol 7, part 4, pp 69-87.

Donnison, D. (1998) Policies for a just society, London: Macmillan.

Douglas, M. (1987) *How institutions think*, London: Routledge.

Dowding, K. (1996) *Power*, Milton Keynes: Open University Press.

Duck, S. (1977) *The study of acquaintance*, Farnborough: Saxon House.

Duck, S. (1994) *Dynamics of relationships: Understanding relationship processes series*, vol 4, London: Sage.

Dunbar, R. (1996) *Grooming, gossip and the evolution of language*, London: Faber.

Dunleavy, P. (1991) *Democracy, bureaucracy and public choice*, London: Harvester Wheatsheaf.

Dunn, J. (1985) *Rethinking modern political theory*, Cambridge: Cambridge University Press.

Dunn, J. (1988) 'Trust and political agency', in D. Gambetta (ed) Trust: *Making and breaking cooperative relations*, Oxford: Basil Blackwell.

Dunn, J. (1992) *Democracy*, Oxford: Oxford University Press.

Dunn, J. (1996) *Interpreting political responsibility*, Oxford: Polity Press.

Eisenstadt, S.N. and Roniger, L. (1984) *Patrons, clients and friends: Interpersonal relations and the structure of trust in society*, Cambridge: Cambridge University Press.

Emons, W. (1997) 'Credence goods and fraudulent experts', *Rand Journal of Economics,* vol 28, no 1, Spring, pp 107-19.

Ereira, A. (1981) *The Invergordon Mutiny*, London: Routledge & Kegan Paul.

Etzioni, A. (1961) *The comparative analysis of complex organisations*, Glencoe, IL: Free Press.

Evans, D.S. and Grossman, S.J. (1983) 'Integration', in D.S. Evans (ed) *Breaking up Bell: Essays on industrial organisation and regulation,* New York: North Holland.

Fayol, H. (1949) *General and industrial management*, London: Pitman.

Festinger, L. and Aronson, E. (1968) 'Arousal and reduction of dissonance in social contexts', in D. Cartwright and A. Zander (eds) *Group dynamics: Research and theory* (3rd edn), London: Tavistock, pp 125-36.

Fiedler, F.E. (1964) 'A contingency model of leadership effectiveness', *Advances in Experimental Social Psychology*, vol 1, pp 149-90.

Fiedler, F.E. (1967) *A theory of leadership effectiveness*, New York: McGraw-Hill.

Fiedler, F.E. (1978) 'Recent developments in research on the contingency model', in L. Berkowitz (ed) *Group processes*, New York: Academic Press, pp 209-25.

Fishkin, J. (1991) *Democracy and deliberation*, New Haven: Yale University Press.

Fitzgerald, P., McLennan, A. and Munslow, B. (1995) *Managing sustainable growth in South Africa*, Cape Town: Oxford University Press.

Foote, S. (1992) *The Civil War: A narrative*, London: Pimlico.

Foucault, M. (1978) *Discipline and punish*, Harmondsworth: Penguin.

Frankel, S.H. (1977) *Money: Two philosophies: The conflict of trust and authority*, Oxford: Basil Blackwell.

Fraser, A. (1973) *Cromwell our chief of men*, St Albans: Granada.

Freeman, J. (1970) *The tyranny of structurelessness*, Hull: Anarchist Workers Association.

French, J.R.P. (1956) 'A formal theory of social power', *Psychological Review*, vol 63, pp 181-94.

French, J.R.P. and Raven, B. (1959) 'The bases of social power', in D. Cartwright (ed) *Studies in social power*, Ann Arbor, Michigan: University of Michigan.

Friedman, M. (1962) *Capitalism and freedom*, Chicago: University of Chicago Press.

Friedman, M. and Kuznets, S. (1945) *Income from independent professional practice*, New York: National Bureau of Economic Research.

Fukuyama, F. (1995) *Trust: The social virtues and the creation of prosperity*, London: Hamish Hamilton.

Gadamer, H.G. (1975) *Truth and method*, London: Sheed & Ward.

Gambetta, D. (ed) (1988) *Trust: Making and breaking cooperative relations*, Oxford: Basil Blackwell.

Gaster, L. (1995) *Quality in public services: Managers' choices*, Buckingham: Open University Press.

Gaster, L. (1996) 'The "citizen question" – re-thinking service design', in L. Gaster and S. McIver, *Consumerism and citizenship: Improving the quality of public services*, Discussion Paper in Public Management 3, School of Public Policy, University of Birmingham.

Gaster, L. (1997) *Quality in local government: Next steps*, London: Local Government Management Board.

Gaster, L. and Hoggett, P. (1993) 'Neighbourhood decentralisation and local management', in N. Thomas et al (eds) *Learning from innovation*, Birmingham: Birmingham Academic Press.

Gaster, L. and Taylor, M. (1993) *Learning from consumers and citizens*, Luton: Local Government Management Board.

Gellner, E. (1994) *Conditions of Liberty: Civil society and its rivals*, London: Hamish Hamilton.

Gerth, H. and Mills, C.W. (1953) *Character and social structure*, New York: Harcourt-Brace.

Gibb, C.A. (ed) (1969a) *Leadership* (1st edn 1958), Harmondsworth: Penguin.

Gibb, C.A. (1969b) 'Leadership', in G. Lindzey and E. Aronson (eds) *Handbook of social psychology* (2nd edn), vol 4, Reading, MA: Addison-Wesley, pp 205–82.

Giddens, A. (1972) *Politics and sociology in the thought of Max Weber*, London: Macmillan.

Giddens, A. (1990) *The consequences of modernity*, Cambridge: Polity Press.

Giddens, A. (1994) 'Living in a post-traditional society', in U. Beck, A. Giddens and S. Lash (eds) *Reflexive modernization*, Cambridge: Polity Press, pp 56–109.

Gilbert, M. (1994) *First World War*, London: Harper Collins.

Goldberg, V.P. (1976) 'Regulation and administered contracts', *Bell Journal of Economics*, vol 7, pp 426–48.

Good, D. (1988) 'Individuals, inerpersonal relations, and trust', in D. Gambetta (ed) *Trust: Making and breaking cooperative relations*, Oxford: Basil Blackwell, pp 31–48.

Goold, M., Campbell, A. and Alexander, M. (1994) *Corporate-level strategy*, New York: Wiley.

Gordon, J.R. (1987) *Organizational behavior* (2nd edn), Boston: Allyn & Bacon.

Gould, C. (1988) *Rethinking democracy: Freedom and social cooperation in politics, economy and society*, Cambridge: Cambridge University Press.

Granovetter, M. (1988) 'Economic action and social structure: a theory of embeddedness', *American Journal of Sociology*, vol 91, pp 481–510.

Graumann, C.F. and Moscovici, S. (eds) (1986) *Changing conceptions of leadership*, New York: Springer-Verlag.

Gray, J. (1995a) *Enlightenment's wake: Politics and culture at the close of the modern age*, London: Routledge.

Gray, J. (1995b) *Berlin*, London: Fontana.

Grayson, L., Hobson, M. and Walsh, K. (1990) *INLOGOV informs on competition*, INLOGOV, The University of Birmingham.

Grossman, S.J. (1981) 'The informational role of warranties and private disclosure about product quality', *Journal of Law and Economics*, vol 24, pp 461-83.

Guardian, The (1995) 'Depressed – or just decent?' [by I. Katz], 30 May, G2, pp 4-5.

Guttridge, L.F. (1992) *Mutiny: A history of naval insurrection*, Shepperton: Ian Allan.

Gyford, J. (1991) *Citizens, consumers and councils*, London: Macmillan.

Habermas, J. (1984) *The theory of communicative action: Vol 1: Reason and the rationalization of society*, London: Heinemann Educational Books.

Habermas, J. (1990) *Moral consciousness and communicative action*, Oxford: Polity Press.

Hall, D. and Stewart, J. (1997) *Citizens' juries*, London: Local Government Management Board.

Halmos, P. (1973) 'Introduction', in *Professionalisation and social change*, Sociological Review Monographs (20).

Hambleton, R. and Hoggett, P. (1990) *Beyond excellence: Quality local government in the 1990s*, Working Paper 85, Bristol: SAUS Publications.

Hampshire, S. (1989) *Innocence and experience*, London: Allen & Unwin.

Handy, C. (1993) *Understanding organizations*, Harmondsworth: Penguin.

Handy, C. (1995) 'Trust and the virtual organisation', *Harvard Business Review*, May-June, pp 40-50.

Haney, L.H. (1913) *Business organisation and combination*, New York: Macmillan.

Harrison, L. (1993) 'Newcastle's mental health consumer group: a case study of user involvement', in R. Smith et al, *Working together for better community care,* Bristol: SAUS Publications, Chapter 5.

Harrow, J. and Shaw, M. (1992) 'The manager faces the consumer', in L. Willcocks and J. Harrow (eds) *Rediscovering public services management*, London: McGraw-Hill.

Hastings, M. (1984) *Overlord: D-Day and the Battle for Normandy 1944*, London: Macmillan.

Hawkey, P. (1997) 'Rising above the competitive mire', in R.V. Smith (ed) *Public sector PLC*, London: LGC Communications.

Hawkins, K. (1984) *Environment and enforcement*, Oxford: Clarendon Press.

Hayden, G. (ed) (1987) *Education for a pluralist society*, Bedford Way Papers 30, University of London, Institute of Education.

Hemphill, J.K. (1949) *Situational factors in leadership*, Columbus, Ohio: Ohio State University.

Hicks, M.J. (1991) *Problem-solving in business and management: Hard, soft and creative approaches*, London: Chapman and Hall.

Hirsch, F. (1977) *The social limits to growth*, London: Routledge.

Hirschman, A. (1970) *Exit, voice and loyalty: Responses to decline in firms, organizations and states*, Cambridge, MA: Harvard University Press.

Hofstede, G. (1991) *Cultures and organizations: Software of the mind*, London: McGraw-Hill.

Hofstede, G. (1994) *Cultures and organizations: Intercultural cooperation and its importance for survival*, London: Harper Collins.

Hoggart, R. (1995) *The way we live now*, London: Pimlico.

Hollander, E.P. (1964) *Leaders, groups and influence*, New York and London: Oxford University Press.

Hollander, E.P. and Webb, W.B. (1955) 'Leadership, followership, and friendship: an analysis of peer nominations', in E.E. Maccoby, T.M. Newcomb and E.L. Hartley (eds) *Readings in social psychology* (3rd edn), London: Methuen.

Holmström, B. (1982) 'Moral hazard in teams', *Bell Journal of Economics*, vol 13, pp 324-40.

Holmström, B. and Milgrom, P. (1991) 'Multitask principal agent analysis: incentive contracts, asset ownership and job design', *Journal of Law, Economics and Organisation*, vol 7, special issue, pp 24-51.

Homa, P. and Bevan, H. (1996) 'If your hospital did not exist, how would you create it?', in *The healthcare management handbook*, London: Kogan Page, Chapter 2.4.

Hood, C. and James, O. (1996) 'Reconfiguring the UK executive: from public bureaucracy state to re-regulated public service', Paper presented to ESRC Conference, 'Understanding central government: theory into practice', University of Birmingham.

Hosking, D.-M. and Morley, I.E. (1991) *A social psychology of organizing*, New York: Harvester Wheatsheaf.

Hungenberg, H. (1993) 'How to ensure that headquarters add value', *Long Range Planning*, vol 26, no 6, pp 62-73.

Hunt, J.G. (1991) *Leadership: A new synthesis*, London: Sage.

Hunt, J.G., Hosking, D.-M., Shriesheim, C.A. and Stewart, R. (1984) *Leaders and managers: International perspectives on managerial behavior and leadership*, New York: Pergamon.

Hutter, B (198 8) *The reasonable arm of the law? The law enforcement paradies of environmental health officers*, Oxford: Clarendon Press.

Hutter, B. (1997) *Compliance, regulation and the environment*, Oxford: Clarendon Press.

James, L. (1987) *Mutiny in the British and Commonwealth Forces, 1797-1956*, London: Buchan & Enright.

Joss, S. and Durant, J. (1994) *Consensus conferences*, London: Science Museum.

Kanter, R.M. (1977) *Men and women of the corporation*, New York: Basic Books.

Katcher, P.R.N. (1994) *The army of Robert E. Lee*, London: Arms and Armour Press.

Katcher, P.R.N. and Youens, M. (1975) *The army of North Virginia*, Reading: Osprey.

Keane, J. (1988) *Civil society and the state*, London: Verso.

Keat, R., Whiteley, N. and Abercrombie, N. (eds) (1994) *The authority of the consumer*, London: Routledge.

Keegan, J. (1987) *The mask of command*, Harmondsworth: Penguin.

Keegan, J. (1990) *The Second World War*, London: Arrow.

Keegan, J. (1992) *Six armies in Normandy: From D-Day to the liberation of Paris*, London: Pimlico.

Keegan, J. (1995) *Who's Who in World War II*, London: Routledge.

Kelvin, P. (1970) *The bases of social behaviour*, London: Holt, Rhinehart & Winston.

Kessel, R.A. (1958) 'Price discrimination in medicine', *Journal of Law and Economics*, vol 1, pp 20-53.

Kilbourne, C.E. (1935) 'The elements of leadership', *Journal of Coast Artillery*, vol 78, pp 437-39.

Kipnis, D. (1996) 'Trust and technology', in R.M. Kramer and T.R. Tyler (eds) *Trust in organisations: Frontiers of theory and research*, London: Sage, pp 39-50.

Klein, B. (1992) 'Contracts and incentives: the role of contract terms in assuring performance', in L. Werin and H. Wijkander (eds) *Contract economics*, Oxford: Basil Blackwell.

Klein, B., Crawford, R. and Alchian, A. (1978) 'Vertical integration, appropriable rents and the competitive contracting process', *Journal of Law and Economics*, vol 21, pp 297-326.

Knight, F.H. (1921) *Risk, uncertainty and profit* (reprint 1933), Boston and New York: Houghton Mifflin.

Kraemer, S. and Roberts, J. (1996) *The politics of attachment: Towards a secure society*, London: Free Association Books.

Kramer, R.M. and Tyler, T.R. (1996) (eds) *Trust in organisations: Frontiers of theory and research*, London: Sage.

Kreps, D.M. (1990) 'Corporate culture and economic theory', in J. Alt and K. Shepsle (eds) *Perspectives on positive political economy*, Cambridge: Cambridge University Press.

Kumar, K. (1993) 'Civil society: an inquiry into the usefulness of an historical term', *British Journal of Sociology*, vol 44, no 3.

Laffin, M. and Young, K. (1990) *Professionalism in local government*, London: Longman.

Laffont, J.-J. and Tirole, J. (1993) *A theory of incentives in procurement and regulation*, Cambridge, MA: The MIT Press.

Lambert, R. (1963) *Sir John Simon, 1816-1904, and English social administration*, London: MacGibbon and Kee.

Leach, S., Stewart, J. and Walsh, K. (1994) *The changing organisation and management of local government*, London: Macmillan.

Lee, R. and Lawrence, P. (1991) *Politics at work*, Cheltenham: Stanley Thornes.

Leff, N. (1964) 'Economic development through bureaucratic corruption', *American Behavioural Scientist*, pp 8-14.

Le Grand, J. and Bartlett, W. (1993) *Quasi-markets and social policy*, London: Macmillan.

Leland, H. (1979) 'Quacks, lemons and licensing: a theory of minimum quality standards', *Journal of Political Economy*, vol 87, pp 1328-46.

Levine, C. (1974) 'Tyranny of tyranny', *Black Rose*, vol 1.

Lewis, J. (1994) 'Choice, needs and enabling: the new community care', in A. Oakley and A. Susan Williams (eds) *The politics of the welfare state*, London: UCL Press.

Lewis, J. and Weigert, A. (1985) 'Trust as social reality', *Social Forces*, vol 63, pp 967-85.

Leyton, E. (ed) (1974) *The compact: Selected dimensions of friendship*, Newfoundland Social and Economic Papers No 3, Institute of Social and Economic Research, Memorial University of Newfoundland, University of Toronto.

Lewicki, R.J. and Bunker, B. (1996) 'Developing and maintaining trust in work relationships', in R.M. Kramer and T.R. Tyler (eds) *Trust in organisations: Frontiers of theory and research*, London: Sage, pp 114-39.

Ling, T. (1994) 'The new managerialism and social security', in J. Clarke, A. Cochrane and E. McLaughlin (eds) *Managing social policy*, London: Sage.

Lorenzoni, G. and Baden-Fuller, C. (1995) 'Creating a strategic center to manage a web of partners', *California Management Review*, vol 37, no 3, pp 146-63.

Lowndes, V. and Stoker, G. (1992) 'An evaluation of neighbourhood decentralisation, Part I: customer and citizen perspectives', *Policy and Politics*, vol 20, no 1, pp 47-61.

Luhmann, N. (1979) *Trust and power* (ed) T. Burns and G. Poggi, New York: Wiley.

Lupton, D. (1996) 'Your life in their hands: trust in the medical encounter', in V. James and J. Gabe (eds) *Health and the sociology of emotions*, Oxford: Blackwell.

Lukes, S. (1974) *Power: A radical view*, London: Macmillan.

Lukes, S. (ed) (1986) *Power*, Oxford: Basil Blackwell.

Macaulay, S. (1963) 'Non-contractual relations in business: a preliminary study', *American Sociological Review*, vol 28, February, pp 55-67.

MacDonagh, O. (1977) *Early Victorian government, 1830-1870*, London: Weidenfeld and Nicolson.

MacGregor-Burns, J. (1978) *Leadership*, New York: Harper & Row.

Mackintosh, M. (1995) *Putting words into people's mouths? Economic culture and its implications for local governance*, Open Discussion Paper in Economics, No 9, Faculty of Social Sciences, Open University.

Macksey, K. (1988) *Military errors of World War Two*, London: Arms and Armour Press.

Macneil, I.R. (1974) 'The many futures of contracts', *South California Law Review*, vol 47, pp 691-816.

Macneil, I.R. (1980) *The new social contract: An inquiry into modern contractual relations*, New Haven and London: Yale University Press.

Macneil, I.R. (1981) 'Economic analysis of contract relations', in P. Burrows and C.G. Veljanovski (eds) *The economic approach to law*, London: Butterworth.

Mainwaring, G.E. and Dobrée, B. (1935) *Mutiny: The floating republic*, London: The Crescent Library.

Marris, P. (1996) *The politics of uncertainty: Attachment in private and public life*, London : Routledge.

Marris, P. and Rein, M. (1982) *Dilemmas of social reform*, 2nd edn, Chicago: Chicago University Press.

Martin, B. (1993) *In the public interest? Privatisation and public sector reform*, London: Zed Books.

Martin, L. and Gaster, L. (1993) 'Community care planning in Wolverhampton: involving the voluntary sector and black and ethnic minority groups', in R. Smith et al, *Working together for better community care*, Bristol: SAUS Publications.

Masten, S.E. (ed) (1996) *Case studies in contracting and organisation*, Oxford: Oxford University Press.

McEwan, I. (1988) *The child in time*, London: Picador.

McIntosh, I. and Broderick, J. (1996) 'Neither one thing nor the other: compulsory competitive tendering and Southburgh Cleansing Services', *Work, Employment and Society*, vol 10, no 3, pp 413-30.

Meredith, P. (1993) 'Patient participation in decision making and consent to treatment: the case of general surgery', *Sociology of Health and Illness*, vol 15, no 5, pp 315-36.

Merton, R.K. (1969) 'The social nature of leadership', *The American Journal of Nursing*, vol 69, pp 2614-18.

Milgrom, P. (1981) 'Good news and bad news', *Bell Journal of Economics*, vol 12, no 2, Autumn, pp 380-91.

Milgrom, P. and Roberts, J. (1992) *Economics, organisation and management*, New Jersey: Prentice-Hall.

Mintzberg, H. (1983) *Structures in fives: Designing organisational effectiveness*, London: Prentice-Hall.

Mishra, A. (1996) 'Organisational responses to crisis: the centrality of trust', in R.M. Kramer and T.R. Tyler (eds) *Trust in organisations: Frontiers of theory and research*, London: Sage, pp 261-87.

Misztal, B. (1996) *Trust in modern societies*, Cambridge: Polity Press.

Morgan, G. (1997) *Images of organization*, London: Sage.

Morley, I.E. and Stephenson, G. (1977) *The social psychology of bargaining*, London: George Allen & Unwin.

Munson, E.L. (1921) *The management of men*, New York: Holt.

Musgrave, R.A. (1959) *The theory of public finance*, New York: McGraw-Hill.

Nagel, T. (1991) *Equality and partiality*, Oxford: Oxford University Press.

Nash, J.B. (1929) 'Leadership', *Phi Beta Kappan*, vol 12, pp 24-5.

Newman, J. (1996) *In search of the public in the new public management*, School of Public Policy Discussion Paper, University of Birmingham.

Newman, J. and Clarke, J. (1994) 'Going about our business? The managerialization of public services', in J. Clarke, A. Cochrane and E. McLaughlin (eds) *Managing social policy*, London: Sage.

New Statesman (1996) 'The public expects, even demands, that our politicians provide answers where there are none. In short we all need to grow up' [by A. Coote], 9 August, pp 32-3.

Newton, K. (1976) *Second city politics: Democratic processes and decision-making in Birmingham*, Oxford: Clarendon, pp 145-64.

Niskanen, W.A. Jr (1971) *Bureacuaracy and representative government*, Chicago: Aldine Atherton.

Norton, A. (1992) *The role of the chief executive in British local government: Its origins and development, present reality and future*, Birmingham: Institute of Local Government Studies.

Nussbaum, M. (1990) 'Aristotelian social democracy', in R. Douglas, G. Mara and H. Richardson (eds) *Liberalism and the good*, London: Routledge.

Nussbaum, M. (1993) 'Non-relative values: an Aristotelian approach', in M. Nussbaum and A. Sen (eds) *The quality of life*, Oxford: Oxford University Press.

Nussbaum, M. and Sen, A. (eds) (1993) *The quality of life*, Oxford: Oxford University Press.

Oakeshott, M. (1962) 'Political education', in *Rationalism in politics and other essays*, London: Methuen.

Offer, A. (1997) 'The economy of regard', *Economic History Review*, L, vol 3, pp 450-76.

Owen, D. (1995) *Nietzsche, politics and modernity*, London: Sage.

Perkin, H. (1989) *The rise of professional society*, London: Routledge.

Petersen, T. (1995) 'The principal-agent relationship in organisations', in P. Foss (ed) *Economic approaches to organisations and institutions: An introduction*, Brookfield, Vermont: Dartmouth Publishing Company.

Pollitt, C. (1993) *Managerialism and the public services* (2nd edn, 1st edn 1990), Oxford: Basil Blackwell.

Pollitt, C. and Bouckaert, G. (1995) *Quality improvement in European public services: Concepts, cases and commentary*, London: Sage.

Powell, W. (1996) 'Trust-based forms of governance', in R.M. Kramer and T.R. Tyler (eds) *Trust in organisations: Frontiers of theory and research*, London: Sage, pp 51-67.

Prime Minister (1991) *The citizen's charter*, London: HMSO.

Prince, L. (1988) 'Leadership and the negotiation of order in small groups', unpublished PhD thesis, Birmingham: University of Aston.

Prince, L. and Puffitt, R. (1997) 'MASLIN: matching service linkages – a multi-dimensional matrix for clarifying service relationships', work in progress, University of Birmingham.

Prior, D., Stewart, J. and Walsh, K. (1993) *Is the citizen's charter a charter for citizens?*, The Belgrave Papers No 7, Luton: Local Government Management Board.

Prior, D., Stewart, J. and Walsh, K. (1995) *Citizenship: Rights, community and participation*, London: Pitman.

Punch, M. (1996) *Dirty business: Exploring corporate misconduct*, London: Sage.

Quinn, R.E. (1984) 'Applying the competing values approach to leadership: towards an integrative framework', in J.G. Hunt, D.-M. Hosking, C.A. Shriesheim and R. Stewart (eds) *Leaders and managers: International perspectives on managerial behaviour and leadership*, New York: Pergamon, pp 10-27.

Ranson, S. (1994) *Towards the Learninig Society*, London: Cassell

Ranson, S. (ed) (1998) *Inside the Learning Society*, London: Cassell.

Ranson, S. and Stewart, J. (1989) 'Citizenship and government: the challenge for management in the public domain', *Political Studies*, vol 37, no 1, pp 5-24.

Ranson, S. and Stewart, J. (1994) *Management for the public domain: Enabling the learning society*, London: Macmillan.

Ranson, S. and Thomas, H. (1989) 'Education reform: consumer democracy or social democracy?', in J. Stewart and G. Stoker (eds) *The future of local government*, London: Macmillan.

Rawls, J. (1971) *A theory of justice*, Oxford: Clarendon.

Rawls, J. (1993) *Political liberation*, Columbia, Ohio: Columbia University Press.

Reason, P. and Rowan, J. (eds) (1981) *Human inquiry: A sourcebook of new paradigm research*, Chichester: John Wiley.

Regan, G. (1991) *The Guinness book of military blunders*, London: Guinness.

Renn, O., Webler, T. and Weidemann, P. (1995) *Fairness and competence in citizen participation*, Kluwer Academic Publishers.

Rhodes, G. (1981) *Inspectorates in British government*, London: George Allen and Unwin.

Richardson, A. and Sykes, W. (1995) *Eliciting public values on health*, London: Social Research and Consultation.

Ricketts, M. (1987) *The economics of business enterprise: New approaches to the firm*, Brighton: Wheatsheaf Books.

Ridley, N. (1988) *The local right: Enabling not providing*, London: Centre for Policy Studies.

Rolla, G. (1992) 'The relationship between the political and the executive structure in Italian local government', in R. Batley and A. Campbell, *The political executive: Politicians and management in European local government*, London: Frank Cass.

Rorty, R. (1989) *Contingency, irony and solidarity*, Cambridge: Cambridge University Press.

Rothstein, A. (1985) *The soldiers' strikes of 1919*, London: Journeyman, in association with Macmillan.

Rueschemeyer, D. (1983) 'Professional autonomy and the social control of expertise', in R. Dingwall and P. Lewis (eds) *The sociology of the professions*, London: Macmillan.

Sappington, D.E.M. (1991) 'Incentives in principal agent relationships', *Journal of Economic Perspectives*, vol 5, no 2, pp 45-66.

Schein, E.E. (1970) *Organizational psychology* (2nd edn), Englewood Cliffs: Prentice-Hall.

Schenk, C. (1928) 'Leadership', *Infantry Journal*, vol 33, pp 111-22.

Schwartz, A. (1992) 'Legal theories and incomplete contracts', in L. Werin and H.H. Wijkander (eds) *Contract economics*, Oxford: Blackwell.

Seal, W. and Vincent-Jones, P. (1997) 'Accounting and trust in the enabling of long-term relations', forthcoming in *Journal of Accounting, Auditing and Accountability*.

Selby, J. and Roffe, M. (1971) *The Stonewall Brigade*, Reading: Osprey.

Seligman, A. (1995) 'Animadversions upon civil society and civic virtue in the last decade of the 20th century', in J. Hall (ed) *Civil society*, Cambridge: Polity Press.

Sen, A. (1990) 'Individual freedom as social commitment', *New York Review of Books*, 14 June.

Sen, A. (1992) 'On the Darwinian view of progress', *London Review of Books*, 5 November.

Shapiro, D., Sheppard, B.H. and Cheraskin, L. (1992) 'Business on a handshake', *Negotiation Journal*, vol 8, pp 365-77.

Sharma, A. (1997) 'Professional as agent: knowledge asymmetry in agency exchange', *Academy of Management Review*, vol 22, no 3, pp 758-98.

Shaw, G.B. (1906) *The doctor's dilemma* (reprinted in 1930), London: Constable.

Sherif, M. (1967) *Group conflict and cooperation*, London: Routledge & Kegan Paul.

Shils, E. (1991) 'The virtue of civil society', *Government and Opposition*, vol 26, no 1.

Sidgwick, H. (1887) *Principles of political economy*, London: Macmillan.

Simon, H. (1982) *The sciences of the artificial*, Cambridge, MA: MIT Press.

Sonnet, K. and Wakefield, H. (1997) 'The UNISON view', in R. V. Smith (ed) *Public sector PLC*, London: LGC Communications.

Soros, G. (1994) *The alchemy of finance: Reading the mind of the market*, New York: John Wiley and Sons.

Stewart, J. (1994) *Councillor–officer relations*, T254 Local Government Management Board.

Stewart, J. (1995) *Innovation in democratic practice*, Occasional Paper, University of Birmingham, School of Public Policy.

Stewart, J. (1996a) *Further innovation in democratic practice*, Occasional Paper, University of Birmingham, School of Public Policy.

Stewart, J. (1996b) 'Democracy and local government', in P. Hirst and S. Khilnani (eds) *Reinventing democracy*, Political Quarterly special publication, Oxford: Blackwell.

Stewart, J. (1997) Thinking collectively in the public domain, *Soundings*, Issue 4, Autumn 96, pp 213-19.

Stewart, J. and Walsh, K. (1989) *The search for quality*, Luton: Local Government Management Board.

Stewart, J. and Walsh, K. (1992) *Influence or enforcement: the nature and management of inspection and regulation in local government*, London: Local Government Management Board.

Stogdill, R.M. (1950) 'Leadership, membership and organization', *Psychological Bulletin*, vol 47, pp 1-14.

Stogdill, R.M. (1974) *Handbook of leadership: A survey of research and theory*, New York: Free Press.

Stoker, G. (1997) 'Local political participation', in *New perspectives in local governance*, York: Joseph Rowntree Foundation, Chapter 5.

Syrett, M. and Hogg, C. (1992) *Frontiers of leadership*, Oxford: Basil Blackwell.

Tannen, D. (1984) *Conversational style: Analysing talk among friends*, New Jersey: Ablex Publishing.

Tannen, D. (1992) *You just don't understand: Women and men in conversation*, London: Virago.

Tanzi, V. (1995) 'Corruption: arm's length relationships and markets', in G. Fiorentini and S. Peltzman (eds) *The economics of organised crime*, Cambridge: Cambridge University Press.

Taylor, C. (1985) *Philosophy and the human sciences*, Philosophical papers 2, Cambridge: Cambridge University Press.

Taylor, C. (1995) *Philosophical arguments*, Cambridge, MA: Harvard University Press.

Taylor, M., Hoyes, L., Lart, R. and Means, R. (1992) *User empowerment in community care: Unravelling the issues*, Studies in Decentralisation and Quasi-Markets, No 11, Bristol: SAUS Publications.

Tead, O. (1935) *The art of leadership*, New York: McGraw-Hill.

Tester, K. (1992) *Civil society*, London: Routledge.

Thompson, P. and McHugh, D. (1990) *Work organisation: A critical introduction*, London: Macmillan.

Trompenaars, F. (1993) *Riding the waves of culture: Understanding cultural diversity in business*, London: Nicholas Brealey.

Udehn, L. (1996) *The limits of public choice: A soiological critique of the economic theory of politics*, London: Routledge.

Vincent-Jones, P. and Harries, A. (1996) 'Conflict and cooperation in local authority quasi-markets: the hybrid organisation of internal contracting under CCT', *Local Government Studies*, vol 22, no 4, pp 187-209.

Wainwright, H. (1994) *Arguments for a new left*, Oxford: Blackwell.

Walker, B. (1993) *Competing for building maintenance*, London: HMSO.

Wall, A. (1995) 'Every manager's nightmare', *The Health Service Journal*, 30 November.

Walsh, K. (1991a) *Competition for local government services: A research report to the Department of the Environment*, University of Birmingham: Institute of Local Studies.

Walsh, K. (1991b) *Competitive tendering for local authority services: Initial experiences*, London: HMSO.

Walsh, K. (1994) 'Citizens, charters and contracts', in R. Keat, N. Whiteley and N. Abercrombie (eds) *The authority of the consumer*, London: Routledge.

Walsh, K. (1995a) *Public services and market mechanisms: Competition, contracting and the new public management*, London: Macmillan.

Walsh, K. (1995b) *Contracts and specifications in housing management*, Birmingham: INLOGOV, University of Birmingham.

Walsh, K. and Davis, H. (1993) *Competition and service: The impact of the Local Government Act 1988*, London: HMSO.

Walsh, K., Deakin, N., Smith, P., Spurgeon, P. and Thomas, N. (1997) *Contracting for change: Contracts in health, social care and other local government services*, Oxford: Oxford University Press.

Watson, P. (1980) *War on the mind: Military uses and abuses of psychology*, Harmondsworth: Penguin.

Watt, P.A. (1996a) *Local government principles and practice*, London: Witherby.

Watt, P.A. (1996b) 'Compulsory competitive tendering for the finance service in local government', *Local Government Policymaking*, vol 23, no 3, December, pp 15-21.

Webb, E.J. (1996) 'Trust and crisis', in R.M. Kramer and T.R. Tyler (eds) *Trust in organisations: Frontiers of theory and research*, London: Sage, pp 288-301.

Welsh, I. (1995) *The acid house*, London: Vantage.

Widdicombe, D. (Chairman) (1986) 'The conduct of local authority business', Cmnd 9797, London: HMSO.

Williams, B. (1988) 'Formal structures and social reality', in D. Gambetta (ed) *Trust: Making and breaking cooperative relations*, Oxford: Basil Blackwell, pp 2-13.

Williamson, O.E. (1975) *Markets and hierarchies: Analysis and anti-trust implications*, New York: Free Press.

Williamson, O.E. (1979) 'Transaction cost economics: the governance of contractual relations', *Journal of Law and Economics*, vol XXII, no 2, October, pp 233-61.

Williamson, O.E. (1983) 'Credible commitments: using hostages to support exchange', *American Economic Review*, vol 73, pp 519-40.

Williamson, O.E. (1985) *The economic institutions of capitalism*, New York: Free Press.

Williamson, O.E. (1991) 'Comparative economic organisation: the analysis of discrete structural alternatives', *Administrative Science Quarterly*, June, pp 269-96.

Williamson, O.E. (1993) 'Calculativeness, trust, and economic organization', *Journal of Law and Economics*, vol 36 (reprinted as Chapter 12 of O.Williamson [1996] *The mechanisms of governance*, Oxford: Oxford University Press).

Williamson, O.E. (1996a) *The mechanisms of governance*, Oxford and New York: Oxford University Press.

Williamson, O.E. (1996b) 'Economics and organisation: a primer', *California Management Review*, vol 38, no 2, Winter, pp 131-46.

Wilson, D. and Rosenfeld, R. (1990) *Managing organizations: Text, readings and cases*, London: McGraw-Hill.

Wolinsky, A. (1993) 'Competition in a market for informed experts' services', *Rand Journal of Economics*, vol 24, no 3, Autumn, pp 380-98.

Woodcock, G. (1977) *The anarchist reader*, London: Fontana Collins.

Wrong, D.H. (1979) *Power: Its forms, bases and uses*, Oxford: Basil Blackwell.

Yetton, P. (1984) 'Leadership and supervision', in M. Gruneberg and T. Wall (eds) *Social psychology and organizational behaviour*, Chichester: Wiley, pp 9-35.

Zucker, L.G. (1986) 'Production of trust: institutional sources of economic structure, 1840-1920', *Research in Organizational Behaviour*, vol 8, pp 53-109.

Index

[Page numbers in italics refer to tables and figures]